ROLANDO HIN

ROLANDO

HINOJOSA

A Reader's Guide

Klaus Zilles

University of
New Mexico Press
Albuquerque

© 2001 by the University of New Mexico Press
All rights reserved.
FIRST EDITION

Library of Congress Cataloging-in-Publication Data:
Zilles, Klaus, 1963–
Rolando Hinojosa : a reader's guide / Klaus Zilles.—
1st ed.
   p. cm.
Includes bibliographical references and index.
ISBN 0-8263-2275-1
1. Hinojosa, Rolando—Criticism and interpretation.
2. Mexican Americans in literature.
3. Texas—In literature. I. Title.
PS3558.I545 Z94 2001
813'.54—dc21
                                    2001002287

Ich widme diese Arbeit meiner
Familie Eva-Maria, Alfred und Jörg
Y a María José

Me gustas cuando callas porque estás como ausente.
Distante y dolorosa como si hubieras muerto.
Una palabra entonces, una sonrisa bastan.
Y estoy alegre, alegre de que no sea cierto.

Pablo Neruda

CONTENTS

Acknowledgments	IX
Introduction	XI

PART ONE: The *Klail City Death Trip Series*: Beyond the Formula Novel   1

1 Estampas del Valle	7
2 The Valley	9
3 El condado de Belken: Klail City	11
4 Klail City	15
5 Korean Love Songs: Korea Liebes Lieder	23
6 Claros Varones de Belken: Fair Gentlemen of Belken County	25
7 Mi querido Rafa	29
8 Dear Rafe	33
9 Rites and Witnesses	37
10 Partners in Crime: A Rafe Buenrostro Mystery	39
11 Becky and Her Friends	43
12 Los amigos de Becky	51
13 The Useless Servants	57

14 *Ask a Policeman: A Rafe Buenrostro Mystery*   65

15 *A Concluding Note*   73

Part Two: Rethinking the Postmodern: Gender, Ethnicity, and Language in Belken County   75

16 *The Critics and the Question of the Postmodern*   77

17 *Postmodernism Revisited: Initiatory Debates and Recent Criticism*   81

Part Three: "Fooling Around with Time and Space"   91

18 *The Death Trip: A Quest for Life*   93

19 *The Charting of Chicano Literature*   95

20 *A Faulknerian Legacy*   101

Part Four: The Four Sections of the Klail City Death Trip Series   103

21 *Jehú Malacara: A Moral Delinquent*   107

22 *Esteban Echevarría: Memories of Arcadia*   137

23 *Rafa Buenrostro: The Making of Texas*   145

24 *P. Galindo and the Literary Quest: A Conclusion*   195

Notes   203

Bibliography   213

Index   221

ACKNOWLEDGMENTS

I would never have set out on this project without the encouragement of Enno Ruge; he gave me his support from beginning to end and I cannot thank him enough. I am indebted to my English teacher Hartmut Schemionek and to my teacher and friend Michael Shiels. Very special thanks go to Maria Teresa Márquez from the Zimmerman Library at the University of New Mexico for her tireless assistance and overwhelming hospitality and for stepping in when I was in a tight spot in Granada. I am indebted to Marina Tristán from Arte Público Press in Houston for the galley proofs that she was kind enough to make available to me before the official publication of *Ask a Policeman*. I am grateful to Matthew Ray and Michelle Courtright for their unflagging support and editorial scrutiny. My heart goes out to Ellen Wiemann, Ralf Gerhard, Hajo Zenzen, Glenn Levine, Rodrigo Andrés, Ellen Simmons, Cat Otey, and to "the Burk." Their friendship has contributed in many different ways to the completion of this project. I also thank my editors at the University of New Mexico Press, Barbara Guth, David Holtby, and Dawn Hall, and the copyeditor, Nancy C. Ford, who did an excellent job transforming the manuscript into an actual book. Finally, there is Dr. Rolando Hinojosa whom I wish to thank for his gracious and patient correspondence, his hospitality, and the homemade *tortillas de maíz*.

This book was made possible thanks to the support of Dr. Dieter Schulz, Dr. Frauke Gewecke, and Dr. Beat Glauser who helped me obtain a grant from the Friedrich-Naumann Foundation in association with the German *Ministerium für Bildung, Forschung und Technologie*.

I resolved to seek a refuge amongst my enemies, braving all dangers. But before taking this step, I sent in my resignation to the Corporation of San Antonio, as Mayor of the city, stating to them, that, unable any longer to suffer the persecutions of some ungrateful Americans, who strove to murder me, I had determined to free my family and friends from their continual misery on my account, and go and live peaceably in Mexico. That for these reasons I resigned my office, with all my privileges and honors as a Texan.

Juan Nepomuceno Seguín, 1858
(mayor of San Antonio, 1836–1842)

What will it mean to be an American in the 21st Century? Who indeed are the Americans? What are the core beliefs and social bonds to which one must adhere in order to be American? What are the essential elements of a social accord that would allow people who are characterized by profound differences to function as a society and to prosper and share leadership in a global setting?

For the better part of American history one could predict the race, gender and educational background of America's leadership group. Visible manifestations helped sort out who would decide and who would lead. Skin color, ethnic origin, country of birth, gender, accent and last name were the common bonds, the glue of prestige and power that held the leadership structure and the country together. As those external characteristics become a less-accepted means of deciding, of leading us to consensus, I wonder what will take their place.

Henry Cisneros, 1992
(mayor of San Antonio, 1981–1989)

INTRODUCTION

THE fourteen books of Rolando Hinojosa's[1] *Klail City Death Trip Series* (*KCDTS*) attest to 250 years of Spanish-Mexican presence in the Lower Río Grande Valley in the southernmost region of the present state of Texas. The arrival of Anglo-American settlers in the early nineteenth century initiated a period of gradually intensifying racial disharmony that reached a first climax with the settlers' rebellion against the Mexican government, resulting in the independence of Texas in 1836. The subsequent incorporation of Texas into the United States of America gave rise to the Mexican American War, after which the victorious United States annexed about half the original Mexican territory that today is known as the American Southwest. The signing of the Treaty of Guadalupe Hidalgo in 1848, which converted the descendants of the early Spanish colonists into U.S. citizens, marked the birth of a minority and the beginning of its subjugated existence.

Aside from documenting the 150-year duration of this consequential period, the two epigraphs preceding this introduction also make explicit commentary on the protracted predicament of Texas Mexicans in the Valley and ethnic Americans in the United States at large. In 1986, Henry Gabriel Cisneros, the first Texas Mexican mayor of San Antonio since Juan Seguín, hosted the sesquicentennial celebration of the Battle of the Alamo, the cradle of Texas independence. In his public address before the Alamo, he emphasized the Texan identity of Texas Mexicans, "for Cisneros himself represents the reconciliation that has taken place between Anglo and Mexican in Texas" (Montejano 1987:306). For the Hispanic American community, which still lags far behind in education, health, income, and political influence, Cisneros was the leading Hispanic spokesperson in America. After becoming mayor of San Antonio in 1981, being re-elected with 94.2 percent of the vote in 1983, and earning two more terms, Cisneros ascended in the party hierarchy and became secretary of Housing and Urban Development in the Clinton administration in 1992.[2]

This goes to show that Texas-Mexican career expectations have come a long way since Juan Nepomuceno Seguín had to run for his life in 1842, simply for being a Texan of Mexican descent. Lieutenant Colonel Seguín had fought for the independence of Texas, had distinguished himself in the battle of San Jacinto against the Mexican troops, and would have died in the Alamo if he had not been sent for help on a dangerous mission through enemy lines. In his memoirs, he expressed his bitterness about the treatment he received at the hands of Anglo Texans, stating that they made him feel like "[a] foreigner in my native land" (quoted in Weber 1973:177). Perhaps it was fortunate for him that he had to leave the Valley for Mexico, considering that those Texas Mexicans who stayed saw the beginning of a 150-year-long period during which they were second-class citizens in their native land.

Rolando Hinojosa's *KCDTS*, while documenting the Hispanic presence in the Valley as early as 1749, centers around the troubled period that took such an ill-boding beginning with Juan Seguín's resignation as mayor of San Antonio in 1842 and reaches into the early 1990s. The Series is set on the U.S.-Mexico border in the fictitious Belken County, which we have to imagine about halfway between Río Grande City and Brownsville on the Gulf Coast. The county seat is Klail City, a small rural town (pop. 9,624), named after cattle baron Rufus T. Klail whose ancestors, the Klail-Blanchard-Cooke (KBC) clan, have controlled the county politically and economically since the turn of the century. Besieged by the greedy Anglo bosses, the Buenrostro family is among the few original landowners who successfully defended their patrimony against the lawyers, Texas Rangers, and hired killers. After their father's death in 1947, Rafael, Israel, and Aaron Buenrostro own and farm the *Rancho del Carmen*, which has been the family's homestead since the King of Spain awarded the land grant to the first Buenrostro who had come to the Valley (then Nuevo Santander) in 1749 with the Escandón expedition. The Buenrostros' archenemies are the Leguizamóns, sellout Mexicanos who arrived late by Valley standards (after 1865) and immediately started to side with the KBC against the old families.

Against this historical backdrop, Hinojosa charts the lives of his two protagonists, Rafa Buenrostro and his orphaned cousin Jehú Malacara, who are born into the rigidly segregated world of a South Texas farming community during the 1930s and 1940s. With each new serial text, the lives of Jehú and Rafa come to represent a new stage in the constantly changing racial order of South Texas, until they eventually reach the still conflictive, but largely integrated world of Belken County in the 1990s. Besides Jehú and Rafa and their families, friends and enemies, Hinojosa populates his Belken County with a cast of over a thousand characters that appear, disappear, and reappear in disjointed episodes that may or may not have a bearing on the central plots.[3]

The *KCDTS* constitutes a truly novel approach to novel writing since almost every new installment differs from the previous ones, generically (i.e., it implements a different genre or mixes various styles of narration) or linguistically (i.e., original Spanish-language installments may later be rendered in English by Hinojosa himself). Most critics emphasize that while the serial texts form one continuous novel-in-progress, with consistent plots, characters and settings, each individual book constitutes an independent generic entity. The form seems to reflect the author's literary agenda, suggesting that all textual fragments are parts of a greater design, with elements being drawn in and drifting apart at once, thus mirroring the disintegrating America of today, where groups and minorities circle in their very own orbit while forming an integral part of the larger cosmos "America."

Several compelling theoretical constructs have been suggested to explain the peculiar effect achieved by Hinojosa through the creation of books that contribute to the Series while at the same time detaching themselves from it. José David Saldívar (1984a:48) calls the *KCDTS* "both integrated and disintegrated" while Rosaura Sánchez (1984:76) identifies a "unitary text with a macrostructure within which are articulated the microstructures." Yolanda Julia Broyles (1984:123) evokes the metaphor of "interlocking circles," and Héctor Calderón (1984:133) applies the image of "a mosaic in which the reader fits each piece or sketch within a linear narrative."

With these constructs in mind, this study aims to capture the double notion of an integrated and disintegrated *KCDTS* with the purpose of demonstrating that while each installment is in itself an intriguing object for study, it acquires an additional dimension of significance when read in the context of the entire Series. Such an approach calls for an in-depth knowledge of the individual serial texts, how the Series has evolved, and how each new installment contributes to the generic profusion that makes the Series unique among literature of its kind. Bearing in mind the paradoxical necessity to capture the disintegrated character of the text in order to describe its integration, I organize my discussion in four parts:

Part one emphasizes the disintegrated perspective by providing a comprehensive overview of the entire Series by exploring the fourteen installments individually, summarizing their generic originality and purposeful architectural construction, as well as linguistic features, literary influences, publishing history, noteworthy criticism, and narrative techniques. The fourteen installment expositions of this first chapter were especially designed to serve as a quick reference guide for readers who seek a concise briefing on a particular installment.

In accordance with the purpose of laying the groundwork for my subsequent exploration of the integrated text, it was essential to provide commentary on the evolution and composition of the Series as a whole. Thus, I foreground passages, themes, and motifs that serve to illustrate how the various installments are interconnected.

Part two is a theoretical follow-up on the discussion of the disintegrated character of Hinojosa's work, which urgently calls for a positioning in the modern-postmodern continuum of literary styles. Hinojosa's unmistakable renunciation of chronological plots, static narrative perspectives, moral positions, and clear-cut generic boundaries has prompted a number of critics to apply the terms "postmodern" and "postmodernist" to Hinojosa's work. Still, I believe the question of the true postmodern nature of Hinojosa's work remains controversial, and in view of the dearth of scholarship on the subject, I submit an examination of the author's agenda against the backdrop of the most prominent postmodernist theories along with more recent contributions to the postmodern debate.

Part three prepares the theoretical groundwork for reading the *KCDTS* as an integrated unitary text. The theoretical approach covers two areas of investigation. The first examines the subject of the Valley's oral memory as a vehicle to expose certain thematic deep structures that can be traced across several volumes of the Series. The critic Juan Bruce-Novoa has developed a diagrammatic representation in the form of a topological paradigm that reflects the dynamic function of oral rituals in literary texts (Bruce-Novoa 1990b:153). I found that these charts also serve to illustrate how the text invites the reader's active collaboration in the completion of traditional oral rituals that remain incomplete in the text. In this first segment of part three, I summarize Bruce-Novoa's theory and demonstrate the application of the charted paradigm. The device will then be put to use in critical passages of the text in part four, whenever the charting is conducive to a deeper comprehension of the oral ritual.

The second area of investigation in part three is concerned with the transparency in the discussion of the *KCDTS* as one extensive, continuing novel that grows and expands with the publication of each new installment. In order to accomplish a coherent presentation, I propose to consider the *KCDTS* as a novel consisting of four sections. Much like the four sections of William Faulkner's *The Sound and the Fury* (1987), each of these sections centers around one narrator/protagonist (i.e., Jehú Malacara, Rafa Buenrostro, Esteban Echevarría, and P. Galindo). However, the sections in *The Sound and the Fury* are four successive, uninterrupted blocks of narration, each with one consistent point of view (albeit fragmented in space and time). In contrast, the four sections of the *KCDTS* are scattered across the volumes of the entire Series. Plot and characters are presented in a seemingly arbitrary succession of fragments with a deliberate absence of transitions and rapidly shifting points of view. Together, these features create the extremely disintegrated narrative typical of the *KCDTS*.

As a possible strategy to achieve a certain degree of transparency, I suggest a reconstruction, or a reassembling, of the four "scattered sections" on the basis of the characters' biographies, in this case, the protagonists Jehú Malacara and Rafa Buenrostro. Esteban Echevarría and P. Galindo, while of little importance to the unfolding of the plot, are principal organizing forces in the *telling* of the *KCDTS*. Therefore, distilling an Echevarría section and a Galindo section from the multitudinous fragments (and analyzing their roles as narrators, with their particular narrative agenda) will lend further coherence and unity to the discussion.

Part four undertakes the reconstruction of the four scattered sections of the *KCDTS* by showing that Hinojosa ostensibly instrumentalizes his narrators as structural guides in the narrative. Each of these guides acts according to a specific agenda. The first section, which has Jehú Malacara at its center, specifies his agenda as one of moral delinquency. I have chosen the label of moral delinquent for him because he is a synthesis of a classical Spanish *pícaro* and a contemporary Huckleberry Finn with a keen sense of justice, fairness, and loyalty. Thus, the reconstruction of the Jehú plot will acquire an additional dimension by incorporating it in an exploration of the genre of the picaresque.

The Echevarría section and the subsequent Rafa section function in tandem as they collaborate in a sociohistorical account of the Valley's past and present. But while I highlight Echevarría's perspective as one of nostalgia, harking back to the isolation, simplicity, and prosperity of Nuevo Santander, I portray Rafa Buenrostro as the revisionist chronicler of a Texas history that counters the Anglo-centric historiography that has managed to exclude and belittle the contributions of Texas Mexicans in the making of Texas.

Finally, I examine P. Galindo as a mediator between the Belken County community, the reader, and the nonfictional academic community. This space between fiction and the real is classical Galindo territory. His existence epitomizes Hinojosa's authorial program. Galindo's impartial gathering of data, voices, and notes typifies the heteroglossic nature of the Series; his death stands for the continual renewal of the aesthetic design of the Series, and his strategy of making only partial disclosures invites the reader to share in the experience of the discovery.

The principal objective of this book is to push the boundaries of the growing body of scholarship on Rolando Hinojosa's work a little further. At the same time, large parts were written with the avowed purpose of making Hinojosa's admittedly complex work more accessible to readers who are infrequent visitors to Belken County. I have heard it said by university professors, who include works by Chicano authors on their syllabi, that their students complain about the inaccessibility of Hinojosa's books. With that in mind, I have tried to achieve a synthesis between maintaining an acceptable academic standard and making my work informative and transparent for both casual and expert readers of Chicano literature. Thus, readers may find expositions of individual serial texts in part one. Those who seek to familiarize themselves with the evolution of story lines across the entire Series should proceed to the Jehú or the Rafa section in part four. The chapter on Rafa is particularly helpful to readers who require a briefing on the historical backdrop of Hinojosa's novels. The reconstruction of the Buenrostro family history is interspersed with clearly demarcated passages that provide extensive facts and data on the history of Spanish-Mexican presence and Anglo-Mexican race relations in the Lower Río Grande Valley over the past 250 years.

Hinojosa's artistic ambition resides in the desire to make his readers experience the suppressed oral history of Mexican Texas. He wants to take us along on his passionate quest for this elusive, alternate history; as with William Faulkner's books, this requires an inordinate, yet rewarding, effort on the part of the reader. The secret of Hinojosa's serial texts lies in their intertextuality and the detective work it takes to find the clues. Each installment of the Series will acquire an additional dimension when read in the context of the entirety of the Series. The individual expositions that comprise the first part of this study strive to give readers a glimpse of this dimension without having to read *all* the installments in *all* their various editions and language versions. I am confident, though, that Belken County regulars will find numerous completely new angles, approaches, and conclusions that widen the scope of the scholarship on Hinojosa.

The *KCDTS* is a mega-novel, a saga of the South Texas Río Grande border that treats of heroes and villains, fools and sages, intrigue, adultery, romance, perversion, obsession . . . the *KCDTS* has it all.

PART ONE

The *Klail City Death Trip Series:* Beyond the Formula Novel

IN his 1984 essay "The Sense of Place," Rolando Hinojosa takes stock of his career as a writer, trying to pinpoint the juncture at which he discovered that the complexity and heterogeneous nature of his *sujet* would preclude the applicability of conventional practices in novel writing. Indeed, his literary project called for an approach that must forgo the showcasing of the unfolding plot in favor of centering on the setting and the characters. "And so much so" he writes, "that my stories are not held together by the *peripeteia* or the plot as much as by *what* the people who populate the stories say and *how* they say it" (Hinojosa 1984a:22, original italics). Evidently, in view of the heteroglossic, multigeneric quality of Hinojosa's oeuvre, it seems easier, at times, to say what the *KCDTS* is not, rather than defining it in affirmative terms. Thus, the author himself, for lack of a better term, falls back on the idea of the formula novel as an antithetical point of departure: "It's clear, then, that I am not speaking of the formula novel. . . . I consider the formula novel as a fine art, if done well, and many of us know that they do exist. I speak of something else— neither nobler nor better, no—merely different from that genre."

He goes on to explain how his treatment of Spanish and English and their blending merely reflected the linguistic practice on the border where he grew up, though it took him "many years of hesitancy, and fits and spurts, and false starts" until he realized that he was indeed free to use them at his discretion. Henceforth, everything fell into place:

The freedom to do this also led me to use the folklore and the anthropology of the Valley and to use whatever literary form I desired and saw fit to use to tell my stories: dialogs, duologs, monologs, imaginary newspaper clippings, and whatever else I felt would be of use. (Hinojosa 1984a:23)

The principal aim of this chapter, then, is to show how Rolando Hinojosa uses this freedom purposefully and creatively with every new installment of his South Texas chronicle. Each of the fourteen books is a carefully composed unit in its own right that can be read separately and independently. At the same time, I intend to demonstrate that the *KCDTS*, in its entirety, is really greater than the sum of its parts. Below I present expositions of each book that touch upon such points as the publishing history, Hinojosa's linguistic choices, and literary influences, as well as aspects of genre and narrative devices. While I strive to abstain from retelling the books, I do concern myself with the intricate structural organization of the books and the sometimes oblique plot developments. Thus, it will be indispensable to furnish brief synopses of salient passages whenever this is conducive to a better understanding of a book's composition.

Similarly, observations on *dénouement* and recurrent motifs will be offered in cases that expressly illustrate how the works are intertwined and where a particular installment is situated in the context of the whole of the *KCDTS* (see for example the discussion of nontraditional women characters as an introduction to *Becky and Her Friends*).

Other major concerns that will be foregrounded in the present chapter are the complex linguistic nature of Hinojosa's texts and the significance of the process of self-translation. The portrayal of cultures in contact through true-to-life representation of the community's linguistic behavior is undoubtedly one of the most intriguing features of Hinojosa's work. The faithfulness of the author's representation of the linguistic realities in the American Southwest is underscored by the fact that even in his Spanish-language books, the English language invariably intrudes in some oblique fashion. Observe, for instance, the legal depositions in *Estampas del Valle* (68–82), Jehú's conversation with Harmon Gillette in *Claros Varones de Belken* (161), or Jehú's ad lib translations of Bible passages and Teodoro Riva's exchange with the Anglo pharmacist in *El Condado de Belken* (122–23 and 92–93) to name only a few. These passages and particularly the code-switching technique employed in the epistolary novel *Mi querido Rafa* have only very recently begun to attract the scholarly attention they deserve.

Problems arise when an attempt is made to adequately label the diverse linguistic strategies used by Hinojosa to depict his characters communicating in both Spanish and English. To group these different forms of verbal and written interactions under the term "bilingual" would be misleading since sociolinguists use "bilingualism" as a clearly defined term and in opposition to "diglossia." Fernando Peñalosa clarifies the concepts in his book *Chicano Sociolinguistics:*

> Diglossia refers to the recognition and acceptance of different forms of speech within a given society, whereas *bilingualism* refers to the linguistic characteristics of individuals within that society. (Peñalosa 1980:42, original italics)

He goes on to further break down the term "diglossia" into in-diglossia (i.e., the relationship between varieties/dialects of the same language family) and out-diglossia (the relationship between languages that are not closely related such as English and Spanish). Since in most circumstances more than two varieties are in use, Peñalosa favors the term "polyglossia."[1]

Clearly, in the bicultural world of Belken County, there are manifestations of both bilingualism and polyglossia. However, conceptualizing the various phenomena found on the printed pages of the *KCDTS* would require a kind of in-depth linguistic analysis that goes beyond the scope of the present literary study. Even the term "code-switching," which is frequently used to describe the language used by Jehú in his letters to his cousin Rafa, is problematic because in sociolinguistics code-switching is manifested in verbal behavior, not in writing. In order to obviate the need to employ controversial linguistic terminology, I therefore propose coining a new term "mixed-code" and denominate all texts and passages that reflect the Chicanos' spoken or written usages of Spanish and English as "mixed-code" texts.

While scholars found the linguistic peculiarities of Hinojosa's work fascinating objects of study, the author himself recognized the restrictions his mixed-code texts placed on his readership and concluded that he needed to transfer all texts into English for the benefit of readers not literate in Spanish. Thus, Hinojosa's work includes a series of "duo texts" consisting of a source text and the author's own English-language rendition, thereby making his narrative accessible to monolingual English readers while at the same time offering bilingual readers both the chance to experience Chicano polyglossia and bilingualism on the printed page and explore Hinojosa's method of self-translation.

In this study, the English-language translations of the source texts will predominantly be scrutinized with respect to the particular strategies Hinojosa employs in the process of self-translation, taking liberties that are completely out of bounds for the translator of fiction. The author himself favors the terms "rendition" or "recast" rather than "translation." Indeed, Hinojosa did not take up the practice of self-translation until ten years after the inception of the Series, when he decided to transfer the stories narrated in the predominantly Spanish-language *Estampas del Valle y otras obras* (1973) into English in a book entitled *The Valley* (1983a). During the decade that elapsed between the publication of the source text and its rendition, the Series had grown to a total of five books, and the plots and story lines of the *KCDTS* had evolved in ways that eventually came to bear on the text of *The Valley*. This practice of departing from the source text in the process of translation is a particular feature in all of Hinojosa's renditions. In fact, aside from adding new contextual elements to the translated text, the author incorporates changes in diction, puns, and points of view. He alters, adds, or suppresses individual fragments and adapts his overall usage of idiosyncratic cultural repertoire to the needs of his new book.[2] Hinojosa's recasts must thus be considered essentially new texts in their own right and are therefore counted among the fourteen installments of the *KCDTS*.

In terms of logistics, I was faced with the question of how to sequence the discussions of original books and their renditions. Seeing that the renditions have undergone significant contextual and structural changes, it seemed logical, at first, to generally follow the chronological order of publication, thereby highlighting the evolution of the Series as a work-in-progress.

On the other hand, the phenomenon of the duo texts is a unique feature of the *KCDTS* and an intriguing object of study for scholars and readers who are genuinely interested in the linguistic singularity of Hinojosa's work. Placing the discussions of the duos at separate and distant points would obstruct readers who wish to compare them more closely, and it would inevitably create redundancies in the expository passages of my text.

With no ideal solution at hand, I opted for dealing with the duo texts in consecutive chapters. Thus, the first two books discussed are *Estampas del Valle* and *The Valley*, even though the English-language rendition was published ten years after its source text. In order to avoid confusion over the actual sequence of composition and the perplexing publishing history of the *KCDTS* with its varying editions, duo versions, bilingual printings, and changed titles, I have furnished a schematic overview of all fourteen

5 : *The Klail City Death Trip Series*

books containing information on publication dates, editions, changed titles, languages, and the abbreviations I will use for the individual titles as well as a few—hopefully enlightening—comments.

The Klail City Death Trip Series (KCDTS)

Year	Title	Title (abbreviated)	Comments
1973	*Estampas del Valle y otras obras*	ESTAMPAS	First *KCDTS* installment. Came out of Hinojosa's first publication "Por esas cosas que pasan." Won the Premio Quinto Sol. I cite from the 1994 edition *Estampas del Valle*.
1976	*Klail City y sus alrededores*	CONDADO	Second installment. These two are actually the same book published at different times. I cite from the 1994 edition *El condado de Belken: Klail City*, also the same book with a different title.
1977	*Generaciones y semblanzas*		
1978*	*Korean Love Songs*	SONGS	Third installment. A short novel in verse, written in English.
1981	*Mi querido Rafa*	RAFA	Fifth installment. Epistolary novel blending Spanish and English. Beginning of a new phase. Marks shift away from Spanish as genuine Chicano idiom.
1982*	*Rites and Witnesses*	RITES	Sixth installment. First prose book entirely in English.
1983*	*The Valley*	VALLEY	Seventh installment. English recast of **ESTAMPAS**.
1985*	*Dear Rafe*	RAFE	Eighth installment. English recast of **RAFA**.
1985*	*Partners in Crime: A Rafe Buenrostro Mystery*	PARTNERS	Ninth installment. Murder mystery featuring Lt. Rafe Buenrostro.
1986	*Claros Varones de Belken: Fair Gentlemen of Belken County*	VARONES	Fourth installment. (Publication was delayed). No English rendition has been provided by the author, yet. English subtitle refers to translator's English version in the same volume.

* English-language titles   *Continued overleaf*

The Klail City Death Trip Series (KCDTS)—continued

Year	Title	Title (abbreviated)	Comments
1987*	Klail City	KLAIL	Tenth installment. English recast of CONDADO (i.e., Klail City y sus alrededores, and its different editions)
1990*	Becky and Her Friends	FRIENDS	Eleventh installment. English-language version of AMIGOS. Reportage style.
1991	Korea Liebes Lieder/ Korean Love Songs	SONGS	German/English edition. Translated by Wolfgang Karrer.
1991	Los amigos de Becky	AMIGOS	Twelfth installment. Spanish-language version of FRIENDS.
1993*	The Useless Servants	SERVANTS	Thirteenth installment. Rafa Buenrostro's journal from the Korean War
1994	Estampas del Valle	ESTAMPAS	New critical edition of the 1973 Estampas del Valle y otras obras. Volume 7 in the Clásicos Chicanos/Chicano Classics series.
1994	El condado de Belken: Klail City	CONDADO	New critical edition of the 1976 Klail City y sus alrededores and the 1977 Generaciones y semblanzas. Volume 8 in the Clásicos Chicanos/Chicano Classics series.
1998*	Ask a Policeman: A Rafe Buenrostro Mystery	POLICEMAN	Fourteenth installment. Sequel to PARTNERS. Rafe is now chief inspector.

* English-language titles

1
ESTAMPAS DEL VALLE (1994)

IN 1972, the Chicano periodical *El Grito* published Hinojosa's short story "Por esas cosas que pasan," ["Sometimes It Just Happens That Way; That's All," **VALLEY**:56] an innovative piece of writing dealing with the stabbing and killing of Ernesto Tamez by another Chicano, Baldemar Cordero, in a bar. It consists of a series of legal documents, most of which are transcripts of recorded testimonies made in both Spanish and English by the defendant and various witnesses. Newspaper clippings from the local Anglo newspaper precede and conclude the story. The slapdash Anglo journalism, indifferent to Mexican bar room brawls, is starkly offset against the deeply personal statements of those involved and thus vividly documents the kind of justice Chicanos are bound to expect from an Anglo public and its judicial system.

Soon after publishing "Por esas cosas que pasan," Hinojosa submitted it as part of a larger work to the Chicano publishing house Quinto Sol in Berkeley. It was published in 1973 as a novel entitled *Estampas del Valle y otras obras*.[1] That same year, it won the Third Annual Premio Quinto Sol national Chicano literary award.

After the release of a second edition in 1977 and a third one in 1980, the book stayed out of print for over a decade, owing largely to the publication of the author's own English-language version *The Valley* in 1983. In 1994, a new critical edition, now simply entitled *Estampas del Valle*, appeared in the excellent Clásicos Chicanos/Chicano Classics series.

The original, longer title (*Estampas del Valle y otras obras*) seemed more appropriate, because the first of the book's four chapters is actually entitled "Estampas del Valle." It is a pastiche of twenty-two fragmented narrative pieces, many of which are character portraits of individual members of the Belken County Chicano community. These *estampas,* or sketches, are modeled—albeit in a humorous fashion—on the literary character portraits of the fifteenth century Spanish writer Fernán Pérez de Guzmán.[2]

The first eleven fragments are commonly described as a *pícaro's* journey. Much in the vein of the classical Spanish rogue *Lazarillo de Tormes* (1554), the orphaned Jehú Malacara holds jobs with various masters all over Belken County.

The second chapter, the aforementioned "Por esas cosas que pasan," features an unfamiliar cast of characters, a different mode of narration, and no apparent connection to the Jehú story. It is not until later installments that additional and contradictory information links Jehú Malacara to the killing of Ernesto Tamez.[3]

The third chapter, "Vidas y milagros," consisting of another seven *estampas,* opens with an introductory dedication in which the narrator reflects on writing and his concept of fiction. Each of the following sketches focuses either on one individual character or a group of persons whose portrait will serve the writer's purpose of elucidating a certain aspect of Belken County life and history: Chicanos who side with Anglo land grabbers ("Los Leguizamón"), Texas Mexicans who fight in the Mexican Revolution ("Los revolucionarios"), or Chicano con men who take advantage of gullible Chicanos struggling with the Anglo bureaucracy ("Coyotes").

The final section "Una vida de Rafa Buenrostro" is dedicated—rather late it would seem—to the other hero of the *KCDTS*.[4] It consists of thirty very succinct miniatures, offering short glimpses of Valley life as well as crucial episodes from Rafa's childhood and adolescence until his departure from the Valley.

These episodes should be considered against the backdrop of the single most mentioned incident in all of the *KCDTS*: the killing of Rafa's father, Don Jesús Buenrostro. This incident lies at the center of the longtime feud between the sellout Leguizamón clan and the upright Buenrostro family (e.g., "Los Leguizamón," **ESTAMPAS**: 99–101).

As early as 1973, Hinojosa began to exploit new resources of Chicano expression, couching the themes of dispossession, loss, and orphaning of his people in a new discourse that seeks to inscribe and recuperate that which is at risk of being lost. **ESTAMPAS**, then, already contains the seminal ingredients through which Hinojosa's work has evolved into a multifaceted history of the Chicano community in the southern Río Grande Valley.

2

THE VALLEY (1983)

WHEN Rolando Hinojosa wrote this English recast of his first novel *Estampas del Valle y otras obras* and entitled it *The Valley*, he must have been aware of relinquishing to some degree the novel's relationship with Spanish literary history. Naturally, any scholar, literary aficionado, or inquisitive reader is free to investigate the circumstances of the novel's creation with its original title, and the literary form of the *estampa*. And even though the title *The Valley* itself divulges no such information, there is evidence of how Hinojosa salvaged the theme of portraiture and synthesized it with his English recast.

In a 1993 interview with Manuel M. Martín Rodríguez (1993a:73), Hinojosa describes the grim impressions that took hold of him while looking at photographs that the members of a Scandinavian colony in Wisconsin took of their dead and that were used by Michael Lesy to illustrate his book *Wisconsin Death Trip* (2000). Aside from prompting Hinojosa to look at his own stories as another death trip, Lesy's use of "aspectos gráficos," as Martín Rodríguez (1993a:73) calls them, provided Hinojosa with the perfect vehicle with which to translate the features of the Spanish *estampa* into the context of his English book *The Valley*.

Unlike the reader of **ESTAMPAS**, who can draw upon the metatext of the entire genre of character portraits, the reader of **VALLEY** is given a different set of parameters to consider upon opening the book with this lengthy subtitle:

10 : Chapter Two

> A re-creation in narrative prose of a portfolio of etchings, engravings, sketches, and silhouettes by various artists in various styles, plus a set of photographs from a family album.

Thus the author calls on his audience to contemplate the texts as if they were visual arts like photography, drawing, or painting. Thereby, he achieves in his narrative portraits the same objectivity and impartiality that one would associate with today's powerful documents in photojournalism or with literary portraits in the Spanish medieval tradition.

Under this new title, the four original sections of **ESTAMPAS** are regrouped under new subheadings, opening with "AN OLIO. One Daguerreotype Plus Photographs," followed by "RAFE BUENROSTRO. Delineations for a first portrait with sketches and photographs (individually and severally)," and closing with "LIVES AND MIRACLES. Final Entry in the Photographic Variorum."

Upon close observation, it becomes obvious that in 1983 the author separated the first block of sketches according to whether they belonged directly to Jehú's picaresque journey or not. Then, he moved the autobiographical sketches of his second protagonist, Rafa Buenrostro, from the end of **ESTAMPAS** into second position of his new book, thereby achieving an almost classical exposition of his main characters.

At this juncture, I would like to bring to mind that part four of this study proposes a close reading of Hinojosa's texts based on reassembling the four scattered sections of the *KCDTS*. Surely, the author's own reassembling and repositioning of fragments and episodes greatly corroborates the feasibility and utility of such an approach. Looking back at the steady expansion of his narrative project over the period of ten years, Hinojosa not only decided to recast his first Spanish-language novel in English but to seize the occasion to radically rearrange the interior and exterior structure of the book. Evidently, Hinojosa's ongoing concern with the overall aesthetic design of his creation feeds on the tension between an underlying, yet clearly visible, unraveling of the plot on the one hand and textual disintegration and fragmentation on the other. His notion of the precise equilibrium, however, seems to have become more acute over the years and has come to bear on the English recast of **ESTAMPAS**. Says Hinojosa, "Few writers have the chance to rewrite their own work. I was lucky because I went from one language to the other" (my interview with Rolando Hinojosa on September 17, 1996).

3

EL CONDADO DE BELKEN

Klail City (1994)

AS if the already existing confusion over the different linguistic versions of the *KCDTS* were not enough, the second Spanish-language installment alone has appeared under three different titles.[1] The first edition was published by Casa de las Américas (La Habana) in 1976, after it had won the highly coveted Latin American literary prize Premio Casa de las Américas.[2]

In 1977, the book was published in the United States as *Generaciones y semblanzas* with an accompanying translation by Rosaura Sánchez. The new title was taken from the first of the novel's three chapters, which pays homage to Fernán Pérez de Guzmán's medieval collection of character and family portraits.[3]

In 1987, Hinojosa provided his own English-language version entitled *Klail City*. During the following years, the Spanish original stayed out of print, until it was included in the Clásicos Chicanos/Chicano Classics series in 1994. The editors, with the author's consent, opted for yet another title: *El condado de Belken: Klail City* (**CONDADO**).[4]

In many ways, the book is a sequel to **ESTAMPAS** because it extends its time frame into the future, portraying Jehú and Rafa as adolescents and young adults. **CONDADO** furthermore concedes extra space to the other two narrative voices, namely those of the *anciano* Esteban Echevarría and P. Galindo, a distant relative of the Buenrostros. The former serves as the voice of the Valley's collective memory, which he notoriously imparts in the form of cantina monologues after having had a few drinks. Galindo, on the other hand, is a conscientious collector of data on the Valleyites, his zeal owing largely to his desire to restore a lost sense of place to the Chicano's confusing bicultural existence.

Similar to **ESTAMPAS** in its architecture, **CONDADO** is divided into three chapters with headings and subheadings. Mention has already been made regarding the origins of *Generaciones y semblanzas,* which is also the title of **CONDADO**'s first chapter. After a prologue and a few rather laconic paragraphs on the author's concept of heroism *(Marcando tiempo),* ["Time Marked and Time Bided," **KLAIL**:9] we are treated to an assortment of loosely related pieces that include a shotgun wedding, the nostalgic jeremiads of Esteban Echevarría, and four episodes that pick up Jehú's picaresque journey where it left off in **ESTAMPAS**.

The second chapter, entitled "Notas de Klail City y sus alrededores, II" is a collection of ten miscellaneous fragments that seem to be shuffled together arbitrarily with no particular theme to hold them together. Although they may be considered from any number of angles, three common categories seem to stand out more than others: race relations, humorous character portraits, and migrant harvest workers.

Race relations, for instance, are at the center of episodes "1. Casa de putas," "2. 3. North Ward/Corea," and "5. Una carta." The by now well-established humorous character portraits are here represented by sketches 4 ("Don Efraim") and 10 ("Don Orfalindo Buitureyra").

The remaining sketches 6, 7, 8, and 9 revolve around the theme of the migrant harvest workers, portraying the Valleyites as they prepare for their annual trip north ("Pa Indiana"), the misfortunes that may befall them on the road ("Un accidente"), or simply reminiscing about Valley folks in the cab of the *contratista's* truck ("El Rápido de Oklahoma"). The effect created by these talks about home while being away from home is twofold: First, for the reader, they put some of the disjointed narrative and isolated character sketches into one and the same context. Second, for Galindo, the chronicler, writer, compiler etc. it results in a salvaging of his "sense of place in the world"—"el recuerdo de ser quién, qué y de dónde es" (**CONDADO**:99) ["the memory of who he is, what he is, and where he's from"].

The third and final chapter of **CONDADO** carries the title "Brechas nuevas y viejas" ["Old and New Wounds"]. It presents a rather motley collection of nine pieces of narrative and dialogue (lettered a–j). The common denominator here seems to be that of the character sketch/short biography, which either serves to elucidate the humorous side of Valley customs and mores or to evoke a typical Faulknerian element in Hinojosa's writing. Faulkner's characters endure. Their perseverance is matched by

Hinojosa's *"aguante"*—a character's ability to patiently wait and hope that justice prevails, as portrayed in the sketches "Don Marcial de Anda" (a), "Aureliano Mora" (e), or "Echevarría/Los Tamez" (h). In "Una conversación" (d), Rafa Buenrostro overhears two couples in two simultaneous conversations represented on the page in two side-by-side columns. The women exchange gossip and discuss household remedies while frowning on outlandish Anglo ideas like removing a child's tonsils. At the same time, the men nearby talk about the drought, farming, and bizarre Anglo inventions like smash-car derbies.

Both endurance and an unusual biography are at the center of the fragment entitled "Viola Barragán"(g). Viola, who is featured in many of the installments of the *KCDTS*, has been married and widowed several times and has mourned various lovers. Her travels have taken her from the Valley to Mexico, from there to India and South Africa, and then to Germany and back to the Valley.

Humorous character sketches portray philosophical Chicano undertaker "Damián Lucero" (b), radio broadcaster "Enedino Broca Lopez" (f),[5] and Protestant preacher Tomás Imás in the fragment "Texto sagrado" (c) ["Holy Scripture"], which includes the final leg of Jehú Malacara's picaresque journey through Belken County.

In the book's closing sketch "A Class Reunion"(i–j), Jehú cuts ahead to the time when he himself is an English teacher at his old high school. In this piece, Jehú reveals an awareness of his being an active part in the writing of the *KCDTS*. He offhandedly states that he is filling in for Rafe, who was supposed to take care of this particular fragment of "este cronicón del condado de Belken y su gente" (**CONDADO**:144) ["the Belken County Chronicles," (**KLAIL**:138)]. Jehú provides a laconic, sometimes facetious rundown of his fellow students, Mexicans and Anglos; how they did or did not stand out in class; and what will become of them after their graduation. The sketch is presented as a series of recollections triggered by a children's rhyme in English, playing on the name Elsinore ("Apple core!/Baltimore!/Who's your friend?/Elsinore!"). Jehú particularly remembers her name, because she was the Anglo student who guarded the library, from which he was banned for "loud talk in Spanish." The underlying ethnic implications prompt Jehú to give his account a rather segregated flavor, indicative of the atmosphere in a racially mixed high school in the 1940s in South Texas. Jehú concludes the sketch, and the book, with the same rhyme, this time, however, leaving the question unanswered and the reader to wonder whether Jehú has buried his grudge.

4

KLAIL CITY (1987)

ELEVEN years went by between the publication of *Klail City y sus alrededores* (here referred to as **CONDADO**) and the printing of its English rendition *Klail City*. During that period, readers not literate in Spanish had to make do with a translation of Hinojosa's most cited, award-winning keystone work. When **KLAIL**, at last, did come out in 1987, it materialized as the same story, and yet it seemed quite a different book.

By now, we have come to know this as a rule with Rolando Hinojosa: every new book—rendition or not—is novel in the adjectival sense of the word. Knowing he is dealing with his own work, the author does not content himself with a word-for-word, not even a chapter-for-chapter, re-creation. **KLAIL** has undergone a process of restructuring, of both augmentation and suppression of textual material, and there are certain changes in its narrative presentation. I will attempt to make this process transparent in the following paragraphs.

The *KCDTS* draws much of its appeal from the tension created by its fragmented story lines, challenging the reader to identify and assemble dispersed fragments. However, the side-by-side analysis of such duo serial texts as **ESTAMPAS/VALLEY** suggests that the degree of disintegration may be subject to change in the form of extensive restructuring during the process of self-translation.

This notion of reorganizing is at variance with Yolanda Julia Broyles's observation made in her article "Oral Culture and Print Culture," where she states that "Although we can only speculate as to the motivating forces underlying any narrative, Hinojosa undeniably shares with oral bards the fact of narration taking its own organic course" (Broyles 1984:126).

Considering only the source texts of **ESTAMPAS** and **CONDADO**, one is tempted to agree with Broyles's reading, which is further substantiated by a proclamation of the implied author of the texts:

> This section needed to be included here; the reason? It fits; ... Not a case of premeditation, then. In writing, there's no telling what'll come up next unless one uses 3 x 5 cards; this writer can't use cards systematically. One of those things.[1] (**KLAIL**:70)

This laconic disclaimer notwithstanding, after giving **KLAIL** a thorough reading, one can only conclude that Hinojosa may actually know how to use file cards after all. Whereas the original three sections of **CONDADO** indeed appear to be organically grown miscellanea, like an attic cluttered with a family's memorabilia, eleven years later, in **KLAIL**, shelves were put up, labeled, and objects were sorted into their proper compartments.[2]

Thus, prologue and opening remarks on heroism in **KLAIL** (7, 9) remain largely the same as in **CONDADO**, and Don Salvador's fierce orchestration of his son's wedding still provides a forceful opening but is now preceded by a table of dramatis personae, establishing right away—and thus enhancing—the piece's theatrical thrust.

"Echevarría tiene la palabra" has become "Echevarría has the floor," and since Hinojosa has dispensed with the table of contents that preceded **CONDADO**, the internal structure of this section had to be outlined on its opening page:

    A.   Choche Markham: A Cantina Monologue
    B.   Doña Sóstenes
    C.   The Buenrostro-Leguizamón Affair
          a. The Dogs Are Howling

A prime example of how the author takes liberties with his own texts by way of transporting cultural idiosyncrasies from the Texas Mexican context into his English language version can be observed on page 25 of **KLAIL**. The "Graffiti at Dirty Luke's" contains a series of sagacities that appear in **CONDADO** (40) as rhymes preceding Echevarría's monologue "Cosas de familia."

Echevarría then turns the floor over to Don Marcial de Anda, Don Aureliano Mora, and Don Manuel Guzmán whose formerly dispersed sketches now appear together under the title "The Older Generation I–III."

Except for the author's notoriously liberal adaptation of his Spanish texts, the essential points remain largely unchanged. Surprisingly, even the verses of the *corrido* bewailing the killing of Ambrosio Mora, placed at intervals in the sketch of the victim's father Don Aureliano, were converted into English, rhymes and all!

The author proceeded in the same fashion with the five fragments that deal with the theme of migrant workers, here bearing the title "The Searchers." Four of the sketches appeared in **CONDADO** numbered 6–9. In **KLAIL**, their sequence is reshuffled, and they are introduced by the formerly isolated fragment "Una conversación," in which Rafa Buenrostro eavesdrops on a conversation between two women while their husbands talk separately nearby. In **CONDADO**, the two simultaneous conversations were represented on the page in two side-by-side columns. The English-language version has been converted into two successive passages entitled "Some Women" and "Their Husbands" (**KLAIL**:46–49).

The new sequence of the fragments manifests a transparent, coherent evolution of events starting with anonymous people fretting over the disastrous drought in the Valley ("The Searchers"). As a consequence, everybody boards up their houses and gets ready for the trip north ("The Searchers II"). Having thus portrayed the community, the narrative now focuses on individual characters. In "The Searchers III" the narrative zooms in on the truck driven by P. Galindo, and eventually it cuts to a pharmacy-morgue in small-town Colorado ("The Searches IV"). A young Chicano couple has been summoned by the local authorities to claim the bodies of the woman's parents, who have suffered a fatal car accident on the long hard trip north. Especially noteworthy is the fact that this originally mixed-code text ("Un accidente" in **CONDADO**) is no longer represented through the actual use of two languages. However, through a skillful rendering of the conversation between the young Chicano couple and the small-town coroner, the notion of the couple's code-mixing is effectively preserved.

At first, "The Searchers V" may come across as an attempt to conclude this chapter on an upbeat note. The sketch portrays the good-hearted Anglo high school teacher Tom Purdy (**CONDADO**:105). Together with his wife and his two sons, he sets out to build decent housing for the Mexican harvest workers that come to southern Michigan every summer. As a matter of fact, the **CONDADO** version may actually have the reader utter a sigh of relief, welcoming the fact that not all Anglos are deprecated as selfish, exploitative racists. Upon closer reading, however, it dawns on the reader that the noteworthy singularity of the Purdy family really serves to expose the utter indifference of the better part of American society to the plight of the Mexican *braceros* and their vital contribution to U.S. agribusiness. In **KLAIL**, Hinojosa took extra care to get this point across. He added two paragraphs designed to debunk the expected reactions from growers and the public, and to hail the fortunate absence of any government participation in the Purdys' project ("The writer can well imagine what the outcome of *that* would have been . . ." [**KLAIL**:69, original italics]).[3]

Each of the first three prose works in the *KCDTS* (**ESTAMPAS**, **CONDADO**, and **VARONES**) contains a section on one of the "lives" of Rafa Buenrostro. These sections always consist of a series of miniatures of varying length and number, which narrate incidents directly pertaining to Rafa's life and surroundings. The Rafa sections in **KLAIL/CONDADO** are unusually short compared to those in **ESTAMPAS/VALLEY** or **VARONES**, and perhaps for that reason, Hinojosa chose the new title "A Few Words" for the English rendition (headed "North Ward/Corea" in **CONDADO**: 74–81). The miniatures differ only insignificantly from the original, with one of the perhaps most curious alterations occurring in the sketch that narrates Rafa's precocious courting of his future wife, Conce Guerrero. Rafa, barely fourteen, walks six miles to Conce's house and—in observance of Mexican tradition—formally asks permission of Conce's mother to keep seeing her daughter. In the self-translation, the fragment took on a slightly different quality. While the whole section is fairly faithfully rendered, this particular fragment came out quite a bit more sentimental in comparison to the dry, laconic tone of the Spanish version. The passage of years may have had a nostalgic effect on the writing of this piece that, after all, ends with a timid show of affection between Rafa and his reticent father Don Jesús, who is murdered shortly after this scene and will be glorified throughout the entire *KCDTS*. The most surprising deviation, however, occurs in the renaming of Rafa's mother-in-law-to-be. In the Spanish version, she is called Doña Modesta, while in the English recast her name is Doña Margarita. It is also open to speculation why Hinojosa dropped a sketch from the book that portrays Jehú having a serious crush on a girl called Emilia Monroy, according to Rafa a singular and improbable occurrence, seeing that Jehú is not given to emotional commitments (**CONDADO**:78).

It has frequently been noted that the *KCDTS*, unlike most works of Chicano literature, successfully captures the Chicanos' predicament without the harsh bitterness of, say, Tomás Rivera's *. . . y no se lo tragó la tierra* (1971). If it is the humor that accounts for much of the success of the Series, then it is Jehú Malacara in his capacities as narrator and protagonist who converts each of his pieces into page-turners.

The hilarious narratives featuring Jehú the *pícaro* are the icing on the *KCDTS* cake, and here in **KLAIL**, Hinojosa's skill of transposing the comedy into English, which in **CONDADO** hinges on elements intrinsic to the Spanish language and Hispanic culture, reaches an out-and-out high point, transcending the limitations commonly ascribed to literary translations.

Four of the five Jehú Malacara pieces make up the second half of the original "Generaciones y semblanzas" section in **CONDADO** (45–66). The fifth is the isolated fragment "Texto sagrado," now entitled "With Brother Imás," which has been inserted in the center of this sequence of episodes. They continue Jehú's picaresque journey where it left off in **ESTAMPAS/ VALLEY**. We remember that Bruno Cano died in the hole he had dug during his treasure hunt with Melitón Burnias.

After the incident, Don Pedro is loath to give Bruno Cano a Christian burial, but eventually he agrees on the condition that it be a fifteen-minute ceremony. This news is quickly spread over the Valley, and the funeral turns into a seven-hour fiesta with Don Pedro having no choice but to suffer through it under the prying eyes of some 4,000 spectators.

It is at this point that **KLAIL** picks up the story with the piece "Brother Imás" ("El hermano Imás"). After Anacleta Villalobos has broken a leg on account of Jehú's negligence, he decides to leave the services of the irascible priest and travel with the gentle Protestant preacher instead. The two subsequent episodes ("A Newborn Sun" and "With Brother Imás") provide a character portrait of Imás and show him together with Jehú on the road singing hymns and selling bibles. Jehú's dry, laconic narrative together with the brother's wonderful Spanish and eccentric diction, make for such a hilarious reading that the challenge of recapturing the comedy in English must have been considerable. For one, Imás's Spanish favors verbs strictly in the infinitive and features the typical absence of gender agreement in nouns and adjectives—errors, then, that cannot be rendered in English, precisely because they stem from English-language interference. In order to show how Hinojosa works his way around these snags, below I examine the short passage in which the brother offers Jehú a job as his assistant:

Jovencito, yo pasar un otro día más aquí y después yo ir a Klail City. ¿Tú querer ser mi ayudante en el trabajo de abrir almas a la alabanza y el conocimiento del Santo Señor? . . . No tener que responder ahora. Tú seguir tu trabajo y puedes me decir mañana viernes. (**CONDADO**:48)

In **KLAIL**, the corresponding passage reads like this:

> Youngster, I am spending this Friday here, and tomorrow I am on my way to Klail City. You want to be my assistant? Want you, then, to **S**earch for the **S**alvation of **S**ouls and the **S**weeping of **S**ins under the **S**oil? No, answer not as yet, you continue with your shovel work, and tomorrow you decide, for tomorrow is Friday, the **F**airest day of the **F**aithful. (**KLAIL**:85, my bold)

The principal effect created in the Spanish version is one that Spanish speakers usually refer to as the language of Indians, an impression that stems, perhaps, from the film industry's misrepresentation of indigenous peoples as incapable of learning to conjugate a verb correctly. As English is a language with few verb inflections to begin with, a similar effect is usually achieved by obliterating all articles, a measure that would seem rather inappropriate for an obviously intelligent and eloquent character such as the preacher. Instead, Hinojosa chose to highlight Imás's penchant for alliteration by capitalizing the initials (see my bold type in the above quote), by extending the passage, and by generally augmenting the oddities in the preacher's idiolect. Add a slightly quaint choice of words and diction and ring it in with an aside by Edelmiro—"(Softly) How do you like his Spanish, Jehú?"—and the effect achieved is neither heavy handed nor overdone, but rather on par with the Spanish original.

Another oddity of Hinojosa's self-translation is the omission of the fragment "Enedino Broca Lopez" from the text of **KLAIL**. When I had the chance, I brought the omission of the piece to Hinojosa's attention. He expressed surprise and insisted that he remembered rendering it in English, adding that he generally tried to include all the fragments in his new versions unless a particular piece posed a special problem (see for example the Esther Lucille Bewley fragment in *Los amigos de Becky*).

On the related subject of minor deviations between versions (for instance, such easily retrievable details as the first name of Mrs. Guerrero, or Tom Purdy's age; there are numerous examples) Hinojosa commented that this was on account of the deliberately perfunctory approach he used when working on a rendition. Eschewing close adherence to the original, the author avoids the pitfalls of literary translations. Instead, he takes a brief look at a passage and then works from memory, which may account for the alteration of the occasional small detail.

Conversely, the five character portraits that make up the last section of **KLAIL** remain largely intact. The section is entitled "Coming Home," and each of its pieces approaches the coming-home theme from a more or less oblique angle. Formerly entitled "Casa de putas," the sketch "Coming Home I" portrays the good Chicano cop Don Manuel Guzmán as a homecomer from the Mexican Revolution. "Viola Barragán" (now "Coming Home II") narrates this Belken County beauty's odyssey that has taken her to distant places and into the arms of various husbands and lovers. She too comes home to the Valley in the end. The portrait of undertaker Damián Lucero ("Coming Home III") is perhaps not so much concerned with the homecoming of its protagonist as with that of his clients. Gone to his last home also, Epigmenio Salazar ("Coming Home IV") is remembered at the graveside by his father Don Efraín. And Don Orfalindo Buitureyra ("Coming Home V"), as can be gleaned from the sketch on Viola Barragán, is the same pharmacist who, as a young apprentice, brought about Viola's first widowhood by administering the fatal prescription to Viola's husband, Dr. Agustín Peñalosa. Don Orfalindo's special coming home consists of sporadic drunken sprees, during which he solo-dances himself back to the times when he was enamored of the young widow of Dr. Peñalosa. The reader is advised not to jump to hasty conclusions.

While we can only speculate about what caused the alteration and suppression of textual material in this recreation of Hinojosa's most famous work, the reasons for adding completely new information are easier to divine. As we shall see, new material on some of the characters is bound to surface with the passage of the years, and somehow it refuses to be kept outside the new book. The most prominent examples of this phenomenon occur in the final segment with the subtly altered title "A Classy Reunion: The Homecoming." The content and format of this piece have been described above in the chapter on **CONDADO** (143 "A Class Reunion"). While the basic narrative strategies (children's rhyme and skipping ahead in time) remain the same, the recast has been done in a brand new mold, as it were. The class and race consciousness that marked the source text have been toned down, and some factual details have been treated with the before-mentioned casualness. Again, names of some specifically remembered persons are changed, such as the teacher who barred Jehú from the library, or the cousin who got married to a German woman and now has several *kinder*. Much more significant, however, is the fact that **KLAIL** was obviously influenced by other installments that were added to the Series during the eleven years that separate the source text from the rendition.

For instance, mention is made repeatedly of Jehú's job at the Bank and his previous post as a teacher at Klail High. He even comments on some of his former schoolmates and their parents' dealings with the Bank, thus providing a link between his various lives that did not emerge at all in the source text. Similarly, the members of the KBC clan like Sammie Jo, Noddy, Ibby, Freddie and their various sidekicks do not step into the limelight until the publication of *Mi querido Rafa*. Since then, however, they have played a crucial part in the *KCDTS*, and as they are genuine Valley folks—albeit Anglos—it would make sense to include them in a commentary on the Belken County social fabric.

As contradictory as it may sound, *Klail City* must be considered a remake and an altogether new book at the same time. The jurors who elected *Klail City y sus alrededores* winner of the 1976 Premio Casa de las Américas cited "descriptive vigor and use of dialectical and colloquial speech patterns" as the principal merits of the book (see Calderón 1984: 135). It seems an even greater achievement that Hinojosa managed to recast this work in English, furnishing it with such authenticity and vigor that it may never occur to readers that this book came out of a Spanish original. Indeed, given the bilingualism of many Mexican Americans, one may not realize right away that one is **not** reading a book about Texas Chicanos actually speaking in English, being witty and intelligent, grim or mean in English. Still, contextual evidence in some of the fragments rules out this possibility (e.g., the references to Brother Imás's Spanish). Viewed independently, other fragments leave room for such an "original English" reading. When I turned to the author himself for a solution to the problem, I received an unequivocal answer: "Al convertir el trabajo al inglés se entiende, que la persona es *fluent* ya que es *fluent* en español" ["Upon converting the work into English, it is understood that the person is fluent, given that she/he is fluent in Spanish already"] (letter dated April 29, 1996, my italics).

5

KOREAN LOVE SONGS

Korea Liebes Lieder (1991)

CONCEIVED as a collection of poems written in the tradition of British World War I poetry, the text has also been described as a narrative poem. Wolfgang Karrer, editor and translator of the 1991 German/English edition *Korea Liebes Lieder/Korean Love Songs,* has called it "a short novel in verse" (**SONGS**:122).[1] It was this third installment that revealed the gradual unfolding of a larger project—a series of microtexts as parts of a macrostructure, as Rosaura Sánchez has suggested (1984:76). Indeed, the signet *Klail City Death Trip* appeared for the first time on the cover of the 1978 edition of **SONGS**, ringing in the official beginning of this Texas Mexican chronicle.

In **SONGS**, the first person narrator private Rafe Buenrostro sublimates the trauma of his Korean ordeal through a poetic divulgence of the horrors experienced by himself and the group of Chicano GIs we have already met in "North Ward/Corea" (**CONDADO**:74). The action is entirely set in Korea and Japan, and while it deals with such elemental war themes as dehumanization, loss, and guilt, **SONGS** is also about Mexican Americans in an Anglo society, segregation, Anglo indifference toward Chicano contributions in this and other wars (a frequent concern in Hinojosa's books), race prejudice, and lack of social justice.

Puzzling and intriguing at once is the opening quote from 2 Kings 9:19: "And Jehu said, What hast thou to do with peace?" The particular enigma that surrounds the question stems from two distinct observations. Firstly,

Jehú Malacara, the cousin and best friend of the protagonist, Rafa Buenrostro, does not feature in any significant way in this or subsequent installments that narrate Rafa's recollections from the Korean War. The second observation has to do with the fact that the story of the biblical Jehu perfectly parallels a series of events in Jehú Malacara's life that will not emerge until the publication of some of the most recent books in the Series. What is more, the importance of the biblical Jehu story, which is here brought to our attention through the ominous quote, will never again be alluded to in any of the posterior installments that span twenty years of *KCDTS* publication history.

The biblical theme of Jehu's purging of Israel from the idolatrous Ahab dynasty is generally interpreted in the context of the Korean War as a commentary on the right to bring peace to a neighboring nation. However, the parallels between the biblical Jehu and Jehú Malacara are much too conspicuous to be dismissed. It would be impractical, though, to discuss these parallels at this point in the Series because it would entail an anticipation of events placed much further ahead in the plot. Therefore, the reading of Jehú Malacara's story against the backdrop of the subtext that is evoked by the biblical quote will be placed in the Jehú chapter in part four.

This first original English installment of the *KCDTS* has attracted relatively little critical attention. It is hoped that with the help of the recently published *The Useless Servants,* Rafa Buenrostro's Korean War journal, additional light will be shed on some of the more obscure passages of **SONGS**.

6

CLAROS VARONES DE BELKEN

Fair Gentlemen of Belken County (1986)

THE era of the literary portrait as a genre in Spanish medieval literature reached its peak with Pérez de Guzmán and was brought to a close by Hernando del Pulgar and his book *Libro de los Claros Varones de Castilla* (1446).[1] In *Claros Varones de Belken,* Hinojosa continues the dialogue with Spanish literary history he began in **ESTAMPAS** and **CONDADO**. Hector Calderón has noted "Obvious points of contact with Spanish historiography from the period of transition between the Medieval Age and the Renaissance" (Calderón 1991:20) that clearly match some of the transitory changes taking place in the Valley. And even though Hinojosa himself dismisses in no uncertain terms the notion of depicting heroes of epic proportions (see **CONDADO**:29), Calderón insists that within the narrative of the *KCDTS*, Don Jesús Buenrostro's characterization parallels the medieval Spanish genre in that it raises the murdered patriarch to the status of a popular hero and model of virtuousness:

> Both Spaniards are chroniclers of a world of feudal estates in which the older male nobility is still important, but it is a world in transition, contrasting an older warrior ethic with a newer concept of manhood associated with fame and a virtuous life. Through the biographical forms of the *estampa* and the *semblanza* based on an analogy with portraiture, historical figures and genealogies of illustrious men could be represented. Following these models, Hinojosa will be the chronicler of genealogies, of "claros varones, hombres rectos y cabales." (Calderón 1991:21)

This is the only Spanish book in the *KCDTS* of which no English rendition has been provided by the author himself. However, Bilingual Press offers Hinojosa's Spanish text with Julia Cruz's English translation appearing on opposite pages.²

As a consequence of its late publication, scholars have failed to recognize and explore the continuity of the plot that unites these first four books and that distinguishes **VARONES** as the transitional element—the missing link as it were—between the first three books and those to come.

The author himself must have been thinking along these same lines when it occurred to him to add the caption *"Atando cabos"* ["Tying up some loose ends" (**VARONES**:9)] to the title, subsequently informing the reader that he will go about this task by granting each of the four protagonists their turn at the telling of the *KCDTS* (see **VARONES**:9). Indeed, the narrative, in its familiar disjointed fashion, fills several gaps in the biographies of Rafa and Jehú; relates their return from Korea (Rafa served in the artillery, Jehú as a military chaplain), their undergraduate studies, their jobs as schoolteachers at Klail High, Jehú's position as a Baptist preacher in Flora, and the death of Rafa's wife. The third narrator, P. Galindo, bears witness to many of these events and—through his numerous anecdotal contributions on known and unknown Valley characters—prepares the canvas of contemporary Valley life on which to sketch the biographies of Jehú and Rafa. Esteban Echevarría's animated cantina monologues, due to his advanced age and afflicted liver, have given way to melancholic laments. Approaching ninety and about to be laid to rest, he is the personified voice of the Valley's oral history, which he fears he will take to the grave with him.

VARONES comes across as the least disintegrated and most structured book so far. In **ESTAMPAS** and **CONDADO**, abruptly shifting points of view and absence of transitions were the norm. In many cases, the identity of the narrator could only be guessed at. In **VARONES**, a table of contents immediately informs the reader that there is an author's prologue (13), an address to the reader (15), two chapters narrated by Rafa Buenrostro (17–60, 171–98), and another two by Jehú Malacara (61–66, 133–70). P. Galindo and Esteban Echevarría were allotted one chapter each (67–132 and 199–223, respectively).

The story launches into a fragmented account of one of Rafa Buenrostro's many lives, here entitled "Donde se ve otra vida de Rafa Buenrostro." As in the previous books, this section consists of twenty-seven mostly half-page miniatures dealing with Rafa's life after the Korean War, up to his graduation from the university. While there are such recurrent topics as war memories, academia, family matters, and Rafa's various jobs, the narrative freely roams about, exploring Valley life and history in its every facet.

Similarly, the second chapter, "Cuatro cortos pasos de Jehú Malacara" ["Jehú Malacara's Four Short Steps" (**VARONES**:60)], features four anecdotes portraying Valley characters involved in incidents of lost virginity, adultery, theft, and greed.

Chapter three, "Donde el nunca como se debe alabado P. Galindo llena ciertos huecos" ["Where the Never as He Should Be Praised P. Galindo Fills In Some Gaps" (**VARONES**:66)], is a collection of eight ("P. Galindo I–VIII") very short stories. They start with new episodes from Jehú's life (I and II) and then turn to an anecdotal story of a cuckold and his imaginative revenge (III). Four humorous character portraits focus on minor characters from the previous books (IV–VII). The chapter concludes with an introspective, life-weary Esteban Echevarría taking a stroll by the river (VIII).

In the chapter entitled "Donde se ve algo de la vida variada de Jehú en sus diferentes etapas" ["Where Something of Jehú's Varied Life May Be Seen in Its Different Stages" (**VARONES**:132)], Jehú Malacara takes the floor once more to entertain his audience at the cantina with eight anecdotes revolving around his favorite subjects: womanizing, adultery, and philandering (young Jehú, the *pícaro*, worked several jobs as a go-between). The chapter closes with Jehú's account of Esteban Echevarría's final days before his death at age eighty-seven.

Detailed physical descriptions of settings, landscapes, houses, and most characters are consistently and conspicuously absent from most of the *KCDTS*. In the penultimate chapter, "Rafa Buenrostro vuelve de Corea" ["Rafe Buenrostro Returns from Korea" (**VARONES**:170)], this pattern appears to be momentarily suspended on account of the impact that the beauty of the Valley has on Rafa upon stepping off the train after more than three years in the war. Rafa's description is that of an oasis in the desert, where the traveler stops to admire the lush vegetation and relishes the naming of all the wild plants and the Valley's crops. In the ensuing conversation between Rafa and his older brother Israel, facts and details about the Buenrostro family, theretofore unmentioned, suddenly emerge in surprisingly sentimental tones.

In similar fashion, the chapter's remaining four sketches relate Rafa's first days back in the Valley. They are filled with the recollection of people and places, particularly the memory of Conce, his wife of ten months. When Rafa was nineteen, she drowned along with her parents in a car that had gone off the road and into the river. Memories of the dead are also at the center of two sketches that relate Rafa's painful visits to the families of his friends Chale Villalón and Pepe Vielma, who did not come back from the war.

Nowhere in the entire Series is the death trip theme more tangible than in these accounts of Rafa's first days back in the Valley and in the last three fragments that make up the chapter entitled "Esteban Echevarría q.e.p.d." ["Esteban Echevarría R.I.P." (**VARONES**:198)]. Their melancholic lament of the Chicano culture dying along with its elders and its promising young being wiped out in the Anglos' wars is Echevarría's obituary as well as that of *la raza,* as it has existed since the times before the Mexican Revolution. The first fragment is another cantina monologue decrying the fashion in which the Chicano community, time and again, manages to disable itself during election time on account of their indecision and petty bickering.

The second piece is the independently published and much quoted "Con el pie en el estribo" ["With His Foot in the Stirrup" (my translation)]. In his lament of the gradual disappearance of Chicano culture in the Valley, Echevarría mourns the loss of the old ways in the famous opening passage "casas sin corredores, calles sin faroles, amigos que mueren, jóvenes que ya no hablan español, ni saben saludar. . . . ¡Je! Desaparece el Valle, gentes" ["Houses without porches, unlit streets, friends who've died away, and youngsters who no longer speak Spanish. . . . Hah! The Valley is disappearing" (my translation)].

Echevarría's last monologue, which reads like a nomenclature of mostly long-gone Valley characters, marks the end of the very generation that witnessed the beginning of the death trip, the annexation of their territory by the United States, their new existence as a minority, the loss of their lands as the basis of the agrarian society, and finally the relentless suppression of their language, without which the oral memory can no longer be.

The conclusion of **VARONES** also marks the end of a generation of *KCDTS* installments that distinguish themselves through their almost exclusive use of the Spanish language; their consistent allusion to Spanish literary history, its literary genres and narrative styles; and, perhaps most importantly, its principal concern with life *within* the South Texas Chicano community, largely irrespective—though not altogether unaware—of the surrounding Anglo society.

7

MI QUERIDO RAFA (1981)

IN many ways, this book marks the beginning of a new phase in the evolution of the *KCDTS*.[1] As early as 1984, even before the publication of **VARONES** and the 1985 installment *Partners in Crime,* Rosaura Sánchez pointed out the significant shift from a heterogeneous but static depiction of the Valley community in the early books, to an exploration of "the social and class contradictions" (Sánchez 1984:76) in the later installments. The watershed element here is obviously the Korean War experience, which serves as a catalyst in the lives of the young Chicanos. The GI Bill entitles them to a college education, setting in motion a process of upward mobility that will open up a whole new world to them.

The gradual crossover into the new setting of the Anglo world creates the necessity to employ new forms of storytelling. The shifting away from the Spanish language as the genuine Chicano idiom is indisputably the most salient new feature.

I know of no other author who has taken the idea of a realistic representation of a minority's struggle over assimilation versus acculturation to such an extreme as to mimetically reproduce the minority's linguistic evolution in his texts. And to crown this, Hinojosa, in this fifth installment of the *KCDTS*, finds the perfect form to match the Chicanos' dual linguistic existence in the mixed-code text of **RAFA**. This text—or texts—consists of a series of letters from one bilingual Chicano to his equally bilingual cousin. The writer of the letters, Jehú Malacara, all but exhausts the rhetorical possibilities of switching between English and Spanish in his commentaries on social, political, and economic affairs in the Valley.

RAFA comes as part epistolary novel and part reportage. The narrative frame is set by the moribund P. Galindo, who is interned at the same hospital where Rafa is undergoing follow-up treatment for a wound sustained in the Korean War. We are now in the early 1960s, and Jehú is chief loan officer at the Klail City First National Bank. He writes to Rafa in the hospital in order to keep him posted on political, social, and Jehú's own amorous affairs in Belken County. The plot revolves around the KBC family empire that controls the county and succeeds in gerrymandering Ira Escobar, a token Mexican, into the office of county commissioner. Jehú, through his secretive romantic entanglements and a clandestine land deal made possible by his position with the Bank, maneuvers himself into a situation of common disfavor, quits his job and disappears.

At the hospital, Rafa hands the letters over to the terminally ill P. Galindo. After his release from the hospital and with little time left, Galindo resolves to find out what the Valleyites know about Jehú's whereabouts and the circumstances of his disappearance.

Jehú's conduct—uncharacteristic of an upwardly mobile Mexican and therefore highly controversial—sparks a turmoil of contradictory sentiments in Galindo's informants. While some actually seem to have access to firsthand information, others rely completely on the Valley grapevine, and still others seize the occasion to display their views on the events as mere projections of their own positions on the Belken County social ladder. What emerges in the end is a conglomerate of voices, opinions, facts, and conjectures.

In an insightful 1985 essay, Sharon Keefe-Ugalde states that even for readers who had not been to Belken County previously, **RAFA** "offers a penetrating analysis of contemporary life in the Río Grande Valley of Texas, delving below the *costumbrista* level to an exploration of political and social structures and cultural values" (Keefe-Ugalde 1985:161). On the following pages, Keefe-Ugalde offers a perspicacious reading of the text, unraveling the intricate plot sequences revolving around the Machiavellian scheming of KBC Ranch empire mastermind Arnold (Noddy) Perkins. Noddy, president of the Klail City First National Bank and Jehú's boss, craftily uses Ira Escobar, the Mexican American candidate for county commissioner, as a pawn to exert pressure on the Anglo candidates and to mollify the Chicano community.[2] "The story reveals the author's preoccupation with a system that maintains the status quo: the political power-structure of Belken County, firmly in the hands of the *'bolillo'* elite" (162).

It would go beyond the scope of this exposition to even summarize all the astute observations in Keefe-Ugalde's article (1985). Suffice it to say that she identifies political manipulation, racism, segregation, and self-entrapment as the main targets of the novel's literary attack, with Hinojosa deploying satire, linguistic interplay, and the reader's participation ("the reader is jolted into discovering for himself" [163]), as the most powerful forces in what Hinojosa himself has once called a "comic, hard-hitting novel."

8
DEAR RAFE (1985)

UNLIKE the significant structural and contextual differences that mark the previous duo texts, the modifications that characterize **RAFE** are of a considerably subtler nature.[1] Another recast, obviously created to make the themes of **RAFA** accessible to readers not literate in Spanish, this English version once more achieves a faithful rendition of the original in terms of content, story line, themes, and motifs. The book even provides additional information not included in **RAFA**, which establishes the text's interrelation with the installment *Partners in Crime,* also published in 1985. Apparently, the author once again wanted to underscore the continuing story lines of the Series by including passages that make reference to Rafa Buenrostro's work in the Belken County Police Department (see **RAFE**:7, 9, 15).

In terms of structure, the only notable variation is the numbering of the letters in the first half of the book. The original letter 11 in **RAFA** is divided into two letters, now numbered 11 and 12, so that **RAFE** has an additional letter and the subsequent numbering of the letters is out of step.

On the whole, the main differences between the books seem to be rooted in the programmatic, contentious conception of the mixed-code source text that has, in a manner of speaking, been turned on its ear by its being translated into English. In order to substantiate how **RAFE** has, to a degree, undermined the initial thrust of **RAFA**, we need to delve a little deeper into the socioethnic make-up of the Anglo Mexican population along the U.S.-Mexican border.

The cultural and linguistic blending along the Río Grande, especially along the final 150-mile stretch commonly called the Valley, has been documented as recently as February 1996, in an issue of *National Geographic*. In the article entitled "The Tex-Mex Border," the author, Richard Conniff (1996:49–69), describes old, established landowner Enrique Madrid as "a creature of the border, Hispanic and married to an Anglo, fluent in both cultures, but not, it seemed to me, wholly comfortable in either" (61).

What is surprising in this passage is not so much the author's fairly accurate description of a *fronterizo,* but rather his mainstream wariness of bicultural and bilingual people. In his article, Conniff offers little information about the border Chicanos' true predicament, and therefore one could argue that the lines quoted above actually reflect the author's own discomfort with "creatures" who are suspiciously capable of surviving in another cultural context.

Perhaps it was this attitude that the "bicultural creature" Rolando Hinojosa wished to challenge when he penned the mixed-code text of *Mi Querido Rafa* (**RAFA**), in which the main character is not only fluent in both cultures but also quite comfortable in either. Ironically, it is **RAFA**'s faithful depiction of *fronterizos* being fluently bicultural and bilingual that creates the very phenomenon so resented by the monolingual and the monocultural, (i.e., exclusiveness, clannishness, ill-manneredness, secretiveness).

This, of course, is where *Dear Rafe* (**RAFE**) calls out for critical scrutiny. In a way, this third rendition opens a can of worms with its numerous implications regarding Hinojosa's aesthetic parameters as well as the potential artistic impact on his audience. The gap between the realistic recreation of his Chicano community on the one hand and whom it will reach on the other hand, becomes nowhere more apparent than in the juxtaposition of **RAFA** and **RAFE**, where Hinojosa's alter ego P. Galindo reiterates his preoccupation with fidelity in the reporting of his findings—especially with respect to the languages. Let us therefore consider the two corresponding paragraphs:

> *Caveat* final: ¿Sería mucho pedir que no se sorprendieran cuando los Anglos Texanos hablen inglés? Es su idioma natural y casero; se sabe que unos hablan español y cuando así suceda, el español saldrá por delante. Si se hablan ambos idiomas así saldrán también. También es natural que la raza del Valle hable más en español. Ahora, si la raza sale en inglés, así se reportará. (Hay que ser fidedigno, hay que ser etc.) (**RAFA:** 8)

["Final *Caveat*: Would it be too much to ask not to be surprised when the Texas Anglos speak English? It's their natural and domestic language; it's well-known that some of them speak Spanish, and when they choose to do so, Spanish is what you'll get. If both languages are spoken, it will be recorded accordingly. Also, it is natural for the Valley-Chicanos to prefer Spanish. Now, if they turn out to be speaking in English, that's how it will be reported here. (One must be truthful, one must be etc.)" (my translation)]

Typically, the same passage in **RAFE** departs considerably from its source text:

Final *Caveat*: Belken County *mexicanos*, aside from their northern Mexican Spanish language, speak English, by and large; the Belken County Anglo Texans, aside from their predominant Midwestern American English, also speak Spanish, by and large. Proximity creates psychological bonds and proximity also breeds children, as we've been told. The truth, then, *über alles*. (**RAFE**:8)

With undisguised sarcasm, **RAFA** lays claim to the notoriously overlooked fact that it is just as natural for a Texas Mexican to speak Spanish as it is for an Anglo Texan to speak English. In **RAFE**, the same passage has taken on the tone of a laconic admonition: the linguistic situation on the border defies the application of set patterns, and the truth—while of the utmost importance—is never simple.

Half of the two books' narratives consist of letters, and the private nature of the correspondence allows for extreme candor. This is perhaps why **RAFA/RAFE** reach a high point in unconcealed criticism of the race relations in the Valley. However, the passage quoted above is symptomatic of the fundamental difference between the two versions: both source text and rendition "hit hard" (to speak in the author's own words), but the mixed-code text of **RAFA** packs more of a punch.

In his 1993 dissertation on the *KCDTS*, Jaime Mejía (1993a) finds fault with previous critics' general failure to incorporate both versions of a serial text in their criticism. Mejía calls into question the soundness of scholarship in much of the criticism, citing many examples of textual errors, oversights, and erroneous readings, most owing to the critics' sidestepping of either the rendition or the original, and thus remaining oblivious to the additional information to be found there.

What is more, Mejía examines Hinojosa's shift to English from various angles and discovers that it coincides with a change of publisher as well as the acceptance of a teaching appointment, thus intimating that the author's shift in a different linguistic direction might be motivated by a concern for his departmental standing.[2]

Although I am at odds with the polemic nature of these extra-textual extrapolations, I do agree with Mejía in that

> perhaps the author's most significant and unique rhetorical maneuver is his production of the Series in both English and Spanish. This maneuver clearly represents an act of capturing the languages and "voices" that have met, competed, and existed in the Valley's ruptured intersection of cultures. From this intersectional position, the author can rhetorically move out and reach audiences who have been affected by and who continue using the various cultural codes found in the Valley's languages. (Mejía 1993a:112)

Surprisingly, Hinojosa himself spoke out adamantly against the idea of mixed-code narration in an interview printed in a 1987 issue of the Barcelona based journal *Quimera* (Riera 1987:115). When asked about the potential audience for literature written in a mixture of languages, he stated that there was no such thing as a novel written in "spanglés."[3] He added that he strongly advised his creative writing students against mixing languages because they minimize their audience and run the risk of becoming unintelligible to both Anglos and Mexicans. This is an unexpected viewpoint coming from an author who proudly told me that **RAFA**, against all odds, had gone into a third printing. If nothing else, we can gather from the interview the author's preoccupation with a dilemma that places the duo **RAFA/RAFE** exactly at the fulcrum point of Hinojosa's bicultural literary project: the phenomenon of a singular fictional narrative that strives to truthfully depict its bicultural personnel while resisting the temptation to preach to a multicultural choir.

9

RITES AND WITNESSES (1982)

THE transition away from Spanish as the genuine idiom of the South Texas Chicano community is made complete in **RITES**, and while bilingualism is frequently a theme, the book is written entirely in English.[1] In **RAFA**, we witnessed the shift away from an almost exclusively Chicano microcosm to a world of Texas ranch empires and big business mixed with family drama. Incidentally, these are also the staple ingredients of the TV soap opera genre, cherished by both North American and South American audiences.

While in **RAFA** the stock elements of the soap opera or *telenovela* focus on a mere contextual level, **RITES** takes the generic adjustment one step further by presenting twenty-four of its thirty-five short chapters as if they were indeed dialogues in a screenplay script. The absence of stage directions is compensated for by frequent intrusions by an omniscient narrator. The scenes alternate between bits taken from the drama surrounding the KBC family empire (board meetings, behind-the-scenes politics, family indiscretions) and flashbacks from the Korean War (Rafa in the field, in combat, wounded, hospitalized, decorated).

Again, a sort of reportage-style technique is used in the remaining ten fragments, in which the "witnesses" have their say. They are Anglo Texans bearing witness to the Texas Mexican presence in the Valley, with statements covering the full range of sentiments expected in a region where cultures clash. From straight-out, no-bones racism and soft-pedaled notions of white supremacy, to simple accounts of personal relationships and friendship across cultures, all seem to be intermingled indiscriminately with scenes from Rafa's Korean ordeal.

The juxtaposition of war scenes overseas and racial conflict back home is curiously anachronistic. The incidents in the Valley are set in the 1960s, during the time of Jehú's employment with the Bank. The Korean War took place ten years earlier. However, the somewhat strained montage achieves its goal: the scandalous ethnic inequity in the Valley is contrasted against the images of Chicano youths losing their lives in a fight for American principles of democracy.

From a group of Chicano GIs fighting against the North Koreans and the Chinese Communist Army, only Rafa—wounded and decorated—returns to the Valley. Ten years later, Jehú Malacara is the first Mexican who has moved up far enough in the business hierarchy to have gained some insight into the machinations of the actual string-pullers. It is through his eyes that we witness the rites of the wealthy power-brokers using Valley business and politics to their exclusive advantage.

The book's two final fragments are designed to give a jarring note to the otherwise satirical tone of **RITES**. Seventy-eight year old Abel Manzano's testimony, evoking the voice of his friend Echevarría, culminates in an account of a vanquished people in a Valley steeped in Texas Mexican history. José David Saldívar (1991:177) stresses the importance of Abel Manzano's testimony as a demystification of the traditional white supremacist rhetoric in the works of Texas writer Walter Prescott Webb, who glorifies the exploits of the famous (or infamous) Texas Rangers.

A U.S. Army report closes the book, dispassionately stating the wounding of Cpl. Rafael Buenrostro and the killing of his friend PFC. José Vielma after a rocket attack by the Chinese Communist Forces in Korea on September 13, 1951.[2]

10

PARTNERS IN CRIME

A Rafe Buenrostro Mystery (1985)

AS the subtitle of this next installment indicates, the *KCDTS* literary quest is taking yet another tack. So far, fragmentation of space and time, rapid shifting of points of view, and variation of narrative techniques have dominated the *KCDTS*. With the appearance of **PARTNERS**, the novelty is manifested in the implementation of the conventional crime mystery genre with a chronological unfolding of the plot, a consistent narrative format, and a stable point of view.

Rafa—or Rafe, as he is called in the English books—is now a lieutenant with the Belken County Homicide Squad. At first glance, and uncharacteristically for the *KCDTS*, the precise time of events seems to be clearly indicated in paragraph three of the narrative ("during that October 1972 World Series"). Rafa's age is thirty-seven, and he has been on the police force for eleven years, having practiced as a lawyer previously (**PARTNERS**: 6). However, this information implies that Rafa was born in 1935 and must therefore be taken with a grain of salt. Frequent incongruities regarding Jehú's and Rafa's ages appear throughout the Series. According to this omniscient narrator in **PARTNERS**, Rafa was born in 1935, while Rafa himself tells a fellow soldier in Korea that he will turn "Twenty-one in January" (**RITES**:38). Granted that Rafa can be trusted to know the date of his birth and that the Korean War actually took place when it did, it would be safe to assume that he was born in January 1929 or 1930. Hinojosa himself was born in January 1929. In view of the autobiographical nature of his writings, it is probably safe to claim that this extra-textual datum outweighs the contradictory information in the various texts.

The action in **PARTNERS** focuses on the Belken County Police Department investigating three different criminal cases. The first one is a fairly straightforward, however elaborately narrated, murder investigation. The victim is the small-time drug smuggler, Charles Darling, who is unfortunate enough to pick up David McKinlow, on day leave from the Flora Asylum for the Insane, for a casual date.

As the detectives of the Belken County Homicide Squad start to gather both genuine and misleading clues, one of their own, the prosecutor for the Belken County district attorney's office Gus "Dutch" Elder, becomes a victim of a brutal shooting at the Kum-Bak Inn, where Elder had stopped to pick up some beer on the way to his favorite fishing pond. Almost at the same time, Jehú Malacara, now vice-president of the Klail City First National Bank, receives information about a money laundering operation going on at several Klail City banks.

During the course of the novel, the omniscient narrator portrays the detectives sweating over the resolution of the murder of their friend and colleague. For the most part, their job consists of the meticulous uncovering and assembling of evidence that will take them deep into a border dispute between two gangster outfits waging war over a lucrative drug-trafficking operation.

The above summary of **PARTNERS** appears to indicate a radical swerve even for an author who is notorious for generic experimentation. It turns out, however, that the book is really not so far removed from the previous *KCDTS* installments as it may seem. Hinojosa manages to weave into his crime mystery a fair number of his already familiar ingredients. There are several short character portraits that could have been clipped straight out of any of the early prose works (John Milton Crossland [**PARTNERS**:14], Gus Elder [103], Packy Estudillo [202]). Board meetings at the Bank (116) and Sammy Jo Perkins being sexy (164) could be inserted easily into the screenplay script that makes up the major part of **RITES**. Furthermore, there are legal depositions as in **ESTAMPAS**, remarks on art and writing as we know them from Galindo in **CONDADO**, as well as the cynical debunking of corrupt, racist Texas Ranger-type Anglo sheriffs such as Big Foot Parkinson and Bowly T. Ponder (e.g., **PARTNERS**:118)—the list could be extended. Perhaps the most conjunctive passages, in terms of linking the book to the rest of the *KCDTS*, are two very succinct summaries of Rafa's and Jehú's lives and careers during the previous decade (110–11, 156–57).

In keeping with the book's false start, the respective conclusions of the various crimes are rather unorthodox, when considered against the backdrop of the mainstream crime-mystery genre. Jehú's money laundering case ends with the arrests of the corrupt bank tellers. The incident rallies a variety of law enforcement agencies from both sides of the river and takes on "an air of festivity with friends waving to friends" (**PARTNERS**:160). Unquestionably, the description bears a certain resemblance to Bruno Cano's famous funeral-fiesta in **ESTAMPAS**.[1] When Lt. Rafa Buenrostro's partners in crime finally catch the Mexican mobsters that gunned down Dutch Elder, they learn that somebody had ordered a hit on a local drug baron. Elder had simply been at the wrong place at the wrong time. I would venture to say that this is probably the only whodunit in the history of the crime mystery genre whose principal plot line is based on an absurd mix-up. In either case, though, the masterminds go untouched, the crimes remain only partly solved, and Hinojosa's concern with the day-to-day heroism of people doing their jobs as best they can has once more proved to be the driving force in his writing.

It is a curious circumstance that the great bulk of the criticism generated so far by the individual works of the *KCDTS*, while generally written in English, is dedicated principally to Hinojosa's early Spanish-language prose works, with the mixed-code text of **RAFA** taking a distant second position. **PARTNERS**, as the second genuinely English-language novel in the Series, overturns that pattern. Of the sparse criticism it has attracted since its publication in 1985—apart from the customary reviews—only one in-depth article (Bruce-Novoa 1987) is written in English. To date, two lengthy Spanish-language contributions offer the most insightful readings of **PARTNERS**. Manuel Martín Rodríguez allots an entire chapter of his 1993 book on Hinojosa to the author's program of dialoguing with various oral and literary traditions. Martín Rodríguez provides brief sketches of the conventional usage of each of the genres, subsequently demonstrating how Hinojosa appropriates them and molds them to his particular needs (on **PARTNERS** see Martín Rodríguez 1993a:114–18). However, the most comprehensive, and indeed, most inspired reading of this particular serial text predates the publication of Martín Rodríguez's book. Antonio Prieto Taboada's "El caso de las pistas culturales en *Partners in Crime*" (1991) is replete with novel, judicious commentary. The author posits, and then proves, that Hinojosa really only uses the mystery format as a vehicle for his commentary on recent societal changes that continue to make inroads into the Valley community. He goes on to discuss the book's treatment of such multifarious concerns as drug trafficking, excess of bureaucracy, alienation of the workplace, child pornography, promiscuity both hetero- and homosexual, all of which are handled in the by now well-known, nonjudgmental Hinojosa style.

The main thrust of Taboada's article, as the title indicates, hinges on the rightful assumption that Hinojosa's text makes significant use of ethnic criteria. The critic explains how in this thriller the sleuthing is headed for failure unless the investigators are capable of understanding certain cultural clues, the decoding of which depends on their thorough knowledge of the bilingual, bicultural reality of the Valley. Of course Rafa Buenrostro, the sole Chicano in the team of investigators, has the necessary background to put all the clues together in order to solve the crime. And yet, Hinojosa never falls into the partisan trap of idealizing the Chicano. In this novel, police work is a joint effort, and once more the real protagonist is a collective one. Indeed, the Valley has become a more complex place. By introducing us to a cast of genuinely respected Anglo characters, **PARTNERS** reduces the distances between the ethnic groups. By portraying Anglos and Chicanos joining forces against the bad guys, Hinojosa acts on a sentiment that Antonio Prieto Taboada has correctly identified as "Esta desconfianza ante el valor absoluto de los criterios étnicos" ["The skepticism towards the supremacy of ethnic criteria" (my translation)] (Taboada 1991:123).

11

BECKY AND HER FRIENDS (1990)

THE Spanish part of this duo, *Los amigos de Becky* (**AMIGOS**), was published in 1991. Due to the peculiar circumstances of its composition, it is problematic to establish which is the source text and which the translation. My observations in the present chapter will almost without exception obtain for both versions. Subsequently, a separate discussion of **AMIGOS** will shed additional light on the matter of the composition of the books and the textual variants.

Shortly after its publication, Antonio C. Márquez reviewed this eleventh installment of the *KCDTS*, summarizing the concept of the novel in a nutshell: "Hinojosa's tack in his latest novel is to dramatize how the community responds to *la mujer nueva*, the Chicana who eschews traditional roles and asserts her independence and individuality" (Márquez 1991:303). However, Rebecca Escobar, the central character of the novel, is not the first *mujer nueva* in the *KCDTS*, and I would like to introduce her by briefly discussing her predecessors and the attention they have received from the critics.

As early as 1984, in their essay "The Elliptic Female Presence as Unifying Force in the Novels of Rolando Hinojosa," Maria I. Duke dos Santos and Patricia de la Fuente explored the character of Viola Barragán both as that of a strong, independent, nontraditional Chicana as well as a recurrent character "whose function seems to be to intertwine the threads of different plots and characters throughout the novels" (Duke dos Santos and de la Fuente 1984:65).

The two critics then go on to discuss the character of Jehú Malacara's semiofficial girlfriend Olivia San Esteban in **RAFA** as a prototype of "the image of the new Hispanic woman in the Americas" (Duke dos Santos and de la Fuente 1984:75). They point out that Olivia appears to be directly modeled on Viola Barragán, given that both women reveal the same "deviation from the Hispanic female stereotypes" (72). Furthermore, in *Mi querido Rafa*, Olivia seems to fulfill the same unifying narrative function that can be attributed to Viola across the entire *KCDTS*.

In 1993, Manuel M. Martín Rodríguez qualifies somewhat the notion of perfect parallelism in the two female characters by adding that "una diferencia fundamental entre ellas refuerza el argumento generacional que se viene insinuando aquí al hablar de los valores tradicionales en el texto" ["a fundamental difference between them reinforces the generational argument that has been continually hinted at here, when speaking of traditional values in the text" (my translation)] (Martín Rodríguez 1993a:53). The difference between Viola and Olivia, according to Martín Rodríguez, manifests itself in the way they have gained their independence. While the younger woman, at twenty-nine, is personally and economically independent (thanks to her career as a certified pharmacist), Viola Barragán had to go through the traditional motions. She got married and was widowed while still young (the bizarre circumstances of that first widowhood are frequent narrative fodder in the *KCDTS*), then she remarried and was widowed a second time, emerging from this marriage as a wealthy woman. Using her new assets to build her own business must be credited to her independent spirit and strong character, the very traits that indeed make her a likely model for the creation of Olivia San Esteban. What is more, the younger woman, encouraged by Jehú Malacara, is determined to go back to school and study medicine. Her ambition is met with incomprehension by several male characters in **RAFA/RAFE**. Even her own brother does not support her: "I mean, she wants to *apply* to *med* school, can you imagine? Shoot, we've got enough business here already" (**RAFE**:70, original italics). To be equitable, I should add that Olivia's brother, Martín San Esteban, will change his mind upon seeing the pleasure Olivia takes in her studies (see **FRIENDS**:78).

At the time when Duke dos Santos and de la Fuente had their essay published, neither **VARONES** nor **PARTNERS** had come out yet. Surely, the critics would have added Angela Vielma and Irene Paredes to their list of nontraditional Chicanas. Angela is the sister of Pepe "Joey" Vielma, who died in the Korean War in Rafa's presence. Angela was raised in a liberal intellectual household and is very much given to swearing in her amused father's presence. Though an excellent student, she drops out of high school at sixteen, because school, she scoffs, "es una pendejada, una porquería, y una babosada" (**VARONES**:119) ["Garbage, pile of shit and drivel" (**VARONES**:118)]. As a secretary in a law firm, she works her way through college, becomes her former employer's partner and—much to people's surprise and shock—moves in with another woman.

Another strong, independent female, and Jehú's current companion in **PARTNERS**, is Irene Paredes, an assistant at the Belken County Homicide Lab. Irene's character is not nearly as elaborately drawn as those of the other women described above, but her existence in **PARTNERS** proves that Hinojosa's concern with strong, nontraditional Chicana characters is a consistent element in the *KCDTS*. I feel it necessary to make this point, since it has been argued that thoroughly developed female characters are scarce in the *KCDTS*. Particularly, Manuel Martín Rodríguez (1993a:54) suspects that **FRIENDS** was written to appease "críticas que la serie de Hinojosa ha ido recibiendo a lo largo de los años" ["criticism that Hinojosa's Series has been receiving over the years" (my translation)]. Unfortunately, he does not cite his sources, and I myself am not aware of the publication of harsh criticism from that direction. Hinojosa himself discusses his stance on feminism in clear, unequivocal terms in his interview with José Saldívar where, indeed, he does mention in a general way that "Most feminists don't even know my stance. To add to this, some critics are very selective as to what they are going to criticize—or to teach and emphasize in class. In his regard, I say to . . . my readers: Go back and reread; form your own opinions without outside influence" (Saldívar 1984b:188).

To readers familiar with the previous installments, Rebecca Escobar seems an unlikely choice for the role of *la mujer nueva*. In **RAFA/RAFE**, we knew her as the conceited wife of the sellout Mexicano politician Ira Escobar and one of Jehú Malacara's passing affairs. In fact, Becky is portrayed as the inverse image of the new Hispanic woman as exemplified by the likes of Viola and Olivia. Egged on by an overambitious mother, Becky has renounced her Mexican identity and language, and tries her best to be an Anglo girl. A music major turned housewife, Becky has her heart set on being accepted into the same social circle of the Valley's upper-class Anglos that gerrymandered her gullible, self-deluded husband into the office of county commissioner. There is nothing here, then, to herald our heroine's metamorphosis, and the theatrical opening of **FRIENDS** comes as a bit of a surprise. After a few expository paragraphs and a curt introductory statement ("The novel begins here:"), we read the stage directions that situate us in the living room of Becky and Ira's house. Becky is waiting for her husband to come home. Upon his arrival, there is a brief altercation between the spouses, which is concluded by Becky with the words, "I've decided that you are not going to live with us anymore."

In the following 160 pages of the novel, the author returns to the reportage technique he employed in the second half of **RAFA/RAFE**. An unidentified narrator—or listener—as she/he calls herself/himself, sets out to investigate the exact circumstances of Becky Escobar's divorce from Ira Escobar and her ensuing marriage to Jehú Malacara. Under Jehú's tutelage, Becky re-embraces her Chicano identity, its culture and language, denouncing, however, the oppressive aspects of the traditional Hispanic gender roles.

For the unidentified narrator/listener, the Becky Escobar incident becomes a vehicle to investigate the genealogy, history, and social activities of the Anglo-Mexican communities in the Valley. As a prelude to each of the interviews, the listener individualizes the voice of her/his informants by identifying their gender, ethnicity, profession, social standing, and—very revealing—their linguistic preference. About her/his own person, the listener is considerably less candid. In his 1993 article "Gender and the Sense of Place in the Writings of Gloria Anzaldúa and Rolando Hinojosa," Wolfgang Karrer analyzes Hinojosa's maneuver of making the listener's sex an enigma:

> His or her discourse is so carefully engendered, and the reactions of his or her interlocutors are so varied and ambivalent that it becomes a tantalizing game to read from innuendos and verbal echoes to guess the listener's sex role. The androgynous listener and master/mistress narrator of the last volume in the series to date clearly crosses the boundaries of gender and ethnicity. Though clearly middle-class and at ease with the different spokespersons in the novel, the listener seems to point at an overriding principle in the series: property and class overdetermine everything and even pave the way for the assimilation into the dominant group or gender for those who want it. But the dominant group is no longer Anglo. (Karrer 1993:243)

On September 2, 1997, the online magazine, *Weekly Wire Books,* published an article by Barbara Strickland entitled "Crossing Literary Borders." Part of the article reproduces Strickland's conversation with Hinojosa in which the author explains what inspired him to make Becky Escobar the heroine of his 1990–1991 installments. Moreover, he makes a surprising and uncharacteristically specific disclosure concerning the issue of the androgynous narrator in **FRIENDS/AMIGOS**:

He has "no idea," he says, what will happen next in the series. "I think most writers write that way, most writers start with a 'what if.'" He pauses over the cleared table. "What would happen, if a Mexican-American woman, educated, belonging to one of the first families of her town, well-off, Roman Catholic, with two kids . . . what would happen if that woman one morning decided to drop-kick her husband through the goalposts of life, as the hillbilly song says? And what if I let people from the community, who are pro and con, from all walks of life, all ages, tell the story? But, now, I have a question for you, Miss Strickland." He points a finger at me. "What gender was the writer?"

It's a trick question, right? I think fast, trying to remember Becky and Her Friends, the plot of which Hinojosa-Smith has so neatly reconstructed for me. I realize that it isn't that I can't remember—there simply is no way to know. Hinojosa's "narrator" in Becky is genderless, which Hinojosa says was his intention. "Because people say, 'Only a black can write about blacks, or only a white can write about whites. . . . Or a man can only write about men, he can't write about women.' So I said, let's see. What is the sex of my questioner—there's no narrator, really. In Spanish it was much more difficult, you have gender in Spanish. I put in one hint."

I wait, but he's not telling. "That secret," he says, "is safe with me. And with the book." And he smiles. (Strickland 1997:6)

The androgynous narrator's informants, in typical oral fashion, may begin at the beginning, jump in at midstream, or come in on the tail end of Becky's story. The account may be chronological or confused, may rehash old news or produce really surprising new details on scores of familiar—or theretofore unmentioned—Valley characters. There are, for instance, several excursions into Valley history (e.g., **FRIENDS**:107, 47) that serve as a backdrop for some new disclosures on how the Buenrostros managed to stay ahead of the Anglo land-grabbers (81–82) and how their archenemies, the Leguizamóns, sided with the Confederates during the Civil War (49). In **AMIGOS** (35) it is even insinuated that they were once slave owners.

Other references tie in with incidents that have gone almost unmentioned since **ESTAMPAS** and **CONDADO**. Lucas Barrón, landlord of the *Aquí me quedo*, gives praise to Jehú's long-forgotten great-grandfather Braulio Tapia and provides the missing link between Jehú Malacara and the stabbing of Ernesto Tamez way back in "Por esas cosas que pasan." Dirty Luke—

"el Chorreao" in the Spanish books—recalls that as a kid, Jehú was working at his Uncle Andrés's gambling house. On the night in question, he was to bring Andrés Malacara's takings to Dirty Luke's to keep them safe, during which time he came upon Baldemar Cordero, knife still in hand, and Ernesto Tamez dead on the floor (see **FRIENDS**:101).

The duo **FRIENDS/AMIGOS** is an inexhaustible source of intriguing details harking back to many earlier episodes. Indeed, it appears that the novel's leitmotif of portraying young Chicanas and Chicanos choosing a life of independence and individuality without losing touch with the Valley's history, culture, and language, has inspired the author to bring his series full circle. Hinojosa must have started work on **FRIENDS/AMIGOS** shortly after the publication of **KLAIL**. Also, around that time, initial negotiations for the brand-new editions of **ESTAMPAS** and **CONDADO** were probably under way. Definitely, the material from his early books was fresh in his mind, and thus, in his novelistic treatment of *la mujer nueva*, Hinojosa seizes the opportunity to reach across the entire Series. He recalls the traditional, self-contained Chicano community living on the other side of the tracks in the 1940s and 1950s and the gradual inroads made into Anglo social and political territory after the Korean War and the Civil Rights movement. Finally, in the 1970s world of **PARTNERS**, with organized crime, drug use, and the general corruption of society taking on new proportions, the ethnic groups (or at least some segments) move closer together in an attempt to stave off the tide.

Clearly, the duo **FRIENDS/AMIGOS** stands out as the most integrative contribution to the *KCDTS* so far; integrative not only because it portrays the dawning of an ethnically integrated society, but integrative in the sense that this particular text really only comes to life in the context of Hinojosa's larger serial project. R. L. Streng's slightly bewildered 1991 review of **FRIENDS** bespeaks the unsurpassed challenge the text constitutes for infrequent visitors to Belken County. Even the *KCDTS* experts among the critics are not in agreement on its merits. Rosaura Sánchez's Marxist-feminist reading of **FRIENDS** qualifies Becky's sudden transformation as "only partial and limited, for the most part, to the cultural sphere," and denounces the new Becky Malacara as "a business woman."

> As such, both Viola Barragán and Becky Malacara participate in exploitation like any capitalist entrepreneur, although paternalistically or rather, maternalistically, in relation to the Texas Mexican community by looking out for Chicano contractors, in a way like a Chicana "Mamá Grande." (Sánchez 1992–1996:82)

"In the end," Sánchez concludes, "Becky remains ultimately locked into the constraints of love and marriage" (83).

Wolfgang Karrer, in contrast, has opted for a less ideological reading. Karrer foregrounds Hinojosa's latest authorial feat of exploring gender conflict in the Chicano community from the point of view of a sexually ambivalent narrator. In his analysis of gender and sense of place, Karrer situates the *KCDTS* opposite Gloria Anzaldúa's complex *Borderlands* (Anzaldúa 1987) with its feminist lesbian discourse, demonstrating how both authors work autobiographically (they are both from Hidalgo County, Texas) and share "certain central features: familism, class, ethnicity, and a search for an engendered discourse that can hold the broad themes together and tie them to place" (Karrer 1993:238). Anzaldúa's treatment of gender roles in the Chicano family and the marginalization of women in traditional Hispanic society remains largely a portrait of her own liberation as a lesbian feminist in New York and San Francisco. In contrast, Hinojosa "describes female victims and strong women in the patriarchal and rural world of Belken County. They either become outsiders or dominant players by playing the men's games" (240). While Hinojosa seems genuinely concerned with his women characters, here, as in all of the *KCDTS*, he also enlists and instrumentalizes them in chronicling the historic changes of the Valley, which he sees predominantly in terms of struggle over land, notions of property and class, and the forming and maintaining of family alliances.

Both **FRIENDS** and **AMIGOS** transcend simple messages of ethnocentrism and sexism. Some of the Anglos are more at ease in Spanish than some Chicanos, and male proponents of women's lib appear opposite staunchly traditional Chicana housewives. Surprisingly, the treatment of nontraditional race and gender discourses is incorporated in a conventional, sentimental love story plot—a point that we will revisit in the following discussion of the story's Spanish-language rendering.

12

LOS AMIGOS DE BECKY (1991)

UNLIKE any of the previous duo serial texts, **FRIENDS/AMIGOS** were written almost concurrently, and differences between them are less conspicuous. Therefore, the above exposition of **FRIENDS** obtains in almost all points for both editions, whereas the following observations foreground those features that set them apart.

The duo's narrative is reminiscent of Hinojosa's early books because it is once again firmly set in the arena of the Belken County grapevine, introducing the new theme of *la mujer nueva* and presenting it against the backdrop of the Valley's social history as portrayed in **ESTAMPAS**, **CONDADO**, or **VARONES**. The partly commemorative tone of the novel is matched by the author's reverting to his unique polyphonic narrative fabric. Even the publication of an original version and the subsequent rendition is clearly evocative of the first generation of *KCDTS* serial texts. This time around, however, the first book to come out is the English-language **FRIENDS**. In view of the main thematic foci of the narrative, it comes as a surprise that Hinojosa has given preference to the English language to portray a heroine who is, after all, struggling to recapture her Chicano identity along with its culture and—extremely important—its genuine idiom. Thus, it is understandable that Manuel Martín Rodríguez and Jaime Mejía—who both place a great deal of significance on incorporating the renditions in their respective readings of the *KCDTS*—could not forgo commenting on the seemingly reversed pattern of the customary Spanish original followed by an English rendition.

Both Martín Rodríguez and Jaime Mejía claim that **FRIENDS/AMIGOS** sustain the original pattern, as the Spanish-language **AMIGOS** was written first (see Martín Rodríguez 1993a:12; Mejía 1993a:92). When I queried him on the subject, Hinojosa said that he did indeed start out by writing the book in Spanish but that about halfway into it he "hit a wall." He states that "it just didn't work. I don't know what happened."[1] Eventually, he overcame the block by writing the book in English. When he had finished **FRIENDS**, and Arte Público Press was about to publish it, the editor, Nikolas Kanellos, encouraged him to go back to the Spanish book and finish that too.

On balance, readers and critics must weigh their own criteria in order to determine which is the original and which the rendition, or else live with the ambivalence. For my own part, I believe the issue goes beyond dates or sequence of composition and publication. At the root of the matter lies the bilingual reality of the Valley, which a priori allows for an original Spanish reading as well as for an original English reading. The problem is not entirely new. It has been discussed in this study with respect to other renditions (particularly in relation to **KLAIL**) and could be solved on the grounds of contextual evidence (consider, for example, Jehú's remarks about Tomás Imás's Spanish). This evidence clearly signals that—in spite of all their textual differences—the English-language renditions are still translations. Also, Hinojosa has unequivocally identified his previous self-translations as renditions of Spanish-language originals (see the concluding remarks in my discussion of **KLAIL**).

In the present case, however, the author seems to have every intention of playing mind games with the readers by leaving certain vital questions unanswered. Just as the listener's sexual ambivalence is a clever authorial scheme, the present linguistic conundrum is, in all likelihood, no coincidence. Hinojosa deliberately exacerbates rather than allays the puzzle by having the narrator (the listener) introduce a series of interviews with Anglo Valleyites with the following remarks:

> The listener has some ideas and opinions to express. The Valley is a strange place, to begin with. The speakers that follow—Valleyites to the core—are at home, at ease, both in English *and* in Spanish. They are all Texas Anglos, and they are all bicultural, to use an old term now used popularly.
>
> There are Valley Anglos who claim they are bilingual, but aren't. It

takes work to speak as a native Spanish-speaker. Then, there are also those Anglos who say they wish they were bicultural and thus bilingual, but they're neither. This also takes time. And there are those who were born to it; it had nothing to do with work, or wanting to or wishing for it. They were at home, at ease.

As the listener insists, it's a strange place. (**FRIENDS**:80, original italics)

As a matter of fact, the linguistic situation in the Valley is referred to on a surprising number of occasions in both **FRIENDS** and **AMIGOS**.[2] The sensitivity of the subject shows in the fact that the Anglos are at pains to ascertain their bilingualism by providing accounts of how they acquired their language skills. At the same time, the Chicanos express their wonder and amusement at Becky's struggle with her newfound Spanish. But for all that, it seems impossible to pin down one particular speaker to one particular language. As mind-boggling as it may seem to readers of both versions, the interviewees may actually be speaking in either language depending on which book one is reading at the time—with one exception! In an artful display of Hinojosa's fine irony, it is the ignorance of Spanish that constitutes the most telling feature. Ira Escobar's interview in **AMIGOS** (106) is preceded by the caption "Ira. (Tomado del inglés)." By highlighting this one particular piece as the only translation in a monolingual Spanish book, all the other interviews in this volume are implicitly confirmed as Spanish-language originals. Indeed, the perceptive reader comes prepared for this move. At the very beginning of **AMIGOS**, when Becky tells the incredulous Ira in Spanish that he must move out of the house, he asks, "What?" And while this may be stretching the point, one could argue—by working back from Ira Escobar's example—that all of the other interviews in either **FRIENDS** or **AMIGOS** were actually carried out in the language that appears on the page.

Creating different realities for the respective readers of linguistically different books is rather in keeping with the implementation of an androgynous narrator, whose sex role may also be perceived differently depending on the reader. Shortly after the publication of **FRIENDS/AMIGOS**, Hinojosa stated in an interview: "I like point of view because I don't know what the truth really is half the time and it isn't what people tell me it is all the time. Everyone sees things differently" (Dasenbrock and Jussawalla 1992:274). The only certainty to cling to, then, is that trusting blindly in the values dictated by ethnicity and gender may no longer turn out to be practicable, nor desirable, in the fast-changing bicultural South Texas world.

The language issue also seemed to be the reason why the author hit a wall while he was writing **AMIGOS**. When I interviewed him, Hinojosa could not exactly pinpoint the linguistic obstacle that delayed the composition of the book, although he did remember that one particular passage—the interview with Jehú's secretary, Esther Lucille Bewley—would not turn out to his satisfaction. He solved the problem by dropping the episode altogether when he started the book over in English. Later, Hinojosa rose to the challenge and salvaged the troublesome Esther Lucille for the Spanish-language **AMIGOS** (63), thus making it the first in a series of textual changes concerning content, structure, and narrative strategies. The mixed-code fragment is admittedly intricate from a linguistic point of view, since it depicts a white-trash ranch girl speaking in vernacular Spanish. The matter is complicated even further because Esther tells the listener about a very delicate conversation she had in her office with Sammie Jo Perkins, an incident that she naturally would—and does—recall in English. The events portrayed here tie in with another interview with Esther Lucille in **RAFA** (105–6). It should also be noted that the absence of the interview creates a void in **FRIENDS**, because it is actually referred to elsewhere in the book (see for example the listener's remarks on p. 93). This could, of course, be interpreted as yet another postmodernist feature, were it not for the more pedestrian circumstances described above.

Perhaps on account of the almost concomitant genesis of the two serial texts, the structural differences are considerably less pronounced than in the previous duos. Excluding the interview with Esther Lucille Bewley, both books contain an equal number of chapters. The sequence of interviews in the second half has been slightly reshuffled, but the interviews as such remain largely the same. A longish dedication, narrating the ordeal of the Zok brothers in World War II Yugoslavia, initiates **AMIGOS**, but is absent from **FRIENDS**. Instead, **FRIENDS** is dedicated "to everyone who has wished me ill luck. As you can see, it's brought nothing but more titles to the Series." A major part of "The Opening Shot" (**FRIENDS**:9) was made into the epilogue of **AMIGOS**, entitled "Fin y rendición de cuentas" ["End and Settling of Scores" (my translation)].

As for the differences in narrative strategy, there is obviously the question of the sexually ambiguous narrator. The listener in **FRIENDS** is rather chatty—annoyingly so, as critic R. L. Streng remarked (1991:186). To cast her/him in the same loquacious role, without revealing the listener's sex, would be a feat impossible to pull off in Spanish, given that the gender of a Spanish noun is clearly marked in a number of ways. As a result, the listener is featured considerably less in **AMIGOS**. She/he is actually rather taciturn and limits her/his introductory character profiles to a minimum, while not affecting the mannerism of speaking of her/himself in the third person. The absence of crafty authorial maneuvers notwithstanding, the gender puzzle remains.

Despite the relative scarcity of structural and narrational differences, a side-by-side perusal of individual interviews reveals the notorious changes that go far beyond even the most liberal approach to literary translation. The interlocutors actually make different statements, and at times seem to utter them in a different voice, with an altered pitch. Edith Timmens, for instance, is the widow of Ben Timmens, "attorney cum public relations drum beater cum one-time state and national congressman for the KBC interests" (**FRIENDS**:86). In both versions, Mrs. Timmens laments her deceased husband's racist inclinations, shrewdly linking them to his partly Mexican ancestry.[3] However, while in the **AMIGOS** version, Mrs. Timmens comes across as an extremely Mexicanized—albeit superior upper-class Anglo woman, her English-language account smacks of the type of perfidious, latent racism that may be much harder to grapple with than her husband's blunt bigotry. When speaking in English, Mrs. Timmens, whom readers may remember for her anti-Mexican remarks in **RAFA** (88), thinks nothing of blurting out statements like: "As for Spanish, . . . Made use of the maids who raised us, of course . . . simple as that" (**FRIENDS**:87).

With E. B. Cooke, Harvard alumnus and financial mastermind of the KBC clan, it is the Spanish interview that proves more enlightening. His English account (**FRIENDS**:81) is that of an unscrupulously egotistical, imperious manager type. In contrast, **AMIGOS** (59) leaves us with a sense of *Schadenfreude* at the sight of the overbearing Texas tycoon going senile. Seventy-two-year old E. B. starts out his interview in astoundingly polished Spanish, only to get completely sidetracked towards the end. His relation fades out in what resembles a mumbling fool's monologue.

Jehú's uncle, Andrés Malacara, one-time owner of several gambling houses and a notorious philanderer, went straight thirty years ago and has turned into something of a recluse. The interview with the octogenarian is a storehouse of Valley anecdotes about both Anglos and Chicanos. One episode, though, did not make it into **FRIENDS**. In this missing episode, Andrés recalls two Anglos who came to his rancho twenty years ago, asking his permission to hunt rattlesnakes for their meat, which, according to the two gourmets, "tastes like chicken" (**AMIGOS**:39). The idea struck

56 : Chapter Twelve

Andrés as so absurd that for him it has become a symbol for Anglo eccentricities, among which he also includes eating frog legs and tomato soup. What's remarkable about the anecdote is perhaps not so much its portrayal of cultural idiosyncrasies as Andrés's funny way of telling it and his wry dismissal of people's silly ideas. Arguably, the debunking of the *bolillos*' antics panders to Mexicano ethnocentric sentiments. It is questionable, though, whether the motives for omitting the passage from the English-language text should to be sought in that direction.

Before concluding this exposition with a final look at the listener's interview with Sammie Jo Perkins, it should be pointed out that the analysis of changes in these and other duo serial texts in the *KCDTS* merits further study. There are scores of linguistic subtleties calling out for critical commentary, which must be shelved for now as they would go beyond the scope of this section. However, I cannot leave **FRIENDS/AMIGOS** without pointing to an extraneous passage in **FRIENDS** (120, absent from **AMIGOS**), which not only bespeaks Hinojosa's whimsical attitude toward his renditions, but also calls attention to the author's penchant for blurring the lines between reality and fiction. A frequent tactic of his consists of casting friends, acquaintances, or colleagues as characters in his books, sometimes openly, sometimes clandestinely. There is even a thinly disguised reference to his own person in the minor character of lawyer Romeo Hinojosa.[4]

In **FRIENDS**, his tack consists of toying with his characters' awareness of being part of a romantic plot in a fictional story. After all, on top of Jehú and Becky having found true love at last, Sammie Jo Perkins is now blissfully married to Rafa Buenrostro. And Sammie Jo displays no small amount of uneasiness at the ironically convenient turn of events.[5] Indeed, she admits that the somewhat maudlin story could indeed be right out of a "soap opera plot by a third-rate writer . . . [laughs] make that second-rate" (**FRIENDS**:120).

13

THE USELESS SERVANTS (1993)

SERVANTS is a work marked by superlatives. In Hinojosa's uncompromisingly ambitious literary project, Rafa Buenrostro's war journal is without a doubt the most uncompromising fascicle yet.[1] In **SERVANTS**, Hinojosa has singled out the one most cataclysmic experience in the life of Rafa Buenrostro and made it into a haunting, disturbing book. Set entirely in Korea and Japan, it is the narrative farthest removed from the Valley, and yet it may harbor one of the most vital clues for a deeper understanding of the *KCDTS*. Lamentably, in the context of the flaw-riddled publication history of the *KCDTS*, **SERVANTS** is marred by the most destructive editorial negligence imaginable, as we shall see presently.

Rafa's tour as a sergeant in the Korean conflict never goes without mention in any of the installments. It is touched upon briefly in the first two prose works, **ESTAMPAS** and **CONDADO**. In **VARONES** the war theme grows more poignant. We witness Rafa as he returns from the war and sees the Valley through different eyes. In **RAFA**, we are again reminded of the war, for Jehú's letters reach Rafa in the hospital, where he is undergoing follow-up surgery on his old war wounds.

In these books, the Korean War is but one of several recurrent themes the narrator cannot stay away from. At intervals, however, he feels the need to utterly purge himself of the horrible images of war. This occurs in three installments that form a kind of Korean trilogy within the *KCDTS*. It begins with *Korean Love Songs* (1978a), continues with *Rites and*

Witnesses (1982a), and—for now—ends with *The Useless Servants*.

Both **SONGS** and **RITES** are set in the Anglo military world and narrate events that occur in an exclusively English-language context. Consequently, these two books constitute the first genuinely English-language installments for which no Spanish-language renditions exist. **SONGS** is Rafa Buenrostro's poetic sublimation of the horrors of war, and although it is entirely set in Korea and Japan, it uses its particular perspective to examine the predicament of the Chicanos as a subaltern group in the mainstream culture of the military environment. As we have seen earlier, **RITES** mixes the screenplay genre with a reportage-style technique. The genre switch successfully contrasts the action in Korea against the tense racial situation in South Texas during the 1950s and 1960s.

SERVANTS opens with the famous passage from Plato's *Republic* that describes shackled humans unable to perceive the world other than as shadows thrown against the firelit walls of their cave. Thus, Hinojosa alerts his readers to the treacherousness of sensory perception and the pitfalls of artistic representation. And indeed, Rafa Buenrostro starts out his journal acknowledging the difficulty of the task after a mere two paragraphs ("but I'm telling this all wrong" [**SERVANTS**:15]).

Among many things, Rafa's journal is an attempt to establish some kind of order in the chaotic events following the North Korean aggression on June 25, 1950. However, in order to fully appreciate Rafa's journal entries, some additional background information of the United States' engagement in Korea is essential. Below, I combine a brief outline of the events portrayed in the novel with additional historical details from Morris's *Encyclopedia of American History* (1982).

The news of the Northern Korean offensive finds Rafa in Japan, where he has been training with the 219th Field Artillery Battalion since February 1949. Two friends from Belken County, Joey Vielma and Charlie Villalón, are serving in the same unit. On July 3, Rafa's unit lands in Pusan, Korea, and two days later he sees his first action. On July 10, he suffers a mild injury, getting hit by shrapnel above his left eye. On August 2, the United Nations army blows up a bridge crowded with refugees. So far, this is the worst experience of misery and pain witnessed by Rafa and typically evokes thoughts of home (**SERVANTS**:37).

Between August 6 and September 15, 1950, Rafa's unit is almost constantly engaged in action. North Korea has launched an offensive that drives UN forces back to their southernmost line of retreat, the Pusan Perimeter. On September 15, with the help of newly landed UN troops, a counteroffensive sweeps across the peninsula, capturing Seoul on September

26. When U.S. forces cross the 38th parallel, Communist China enters the war (October 24). General McArthur's "end-the-war" offensive occurs on November 24, provoking an immediate Chinese counteroffensive on November 26. Between December 5, 1950 and February 9, 1951, frenzied fighting in bitter-cold North Korea constitutes another climactic ordeal for Rafa, culminating with the confirmation of Charlie's death on January 5 (**SERVANTS**:116). On January 28, Rafa's whole gun crew is killed in an ambush. Rafa gets away with mild injuries (119).

On February 18–19, Rafa is assigned to a gruesome death count detail (**SERVANTS**:134). The impact is momentous, and for the first time, introspection creeps into Rafa's daily account, which so far has been virtually devoid of emotion.[2] After a UN counteroffensive leads to the retaking of Seoul in March 1951, Rafa, Joey, and a few other men are pulled out of the line and flown to Japan to show groups of fresh recruits the sights (see "The Baby Sitters" [158]). While in Japan, Rafa and Joey visit with another Valley Chicano, Sonny Ruíz, who has gone AWOL and has married a Japanese schoolteacher.[3] On April 26, the men leave for Pusan since they are due back with their unit the next day.

The opening of the next—and crucial—chapter, "And the Rocket's Red Glare" (**SERVANTS**:165), finds Rafa in a Tokyo hospital, talking to a psychiatrist. Following Dr. Perlman's advice, Rafa puts down on paper what he recalls of the North Korean rocket attack that kills Joey Vielma and two other soldiers, and injures Rafa once again in the face.[4]

Although the doctor recommends that Rafa be assigned to duty away from the front line, Rafa requests to return to his unit because "that's home for now, and home is what I'm looking for" (**SERVANTS**:168). It is in this passage where the destructive editorial negligence occurs that I have referred to earlier. Six crucial pages were inadvertently omitted from the first edition of *The Useless Servants*. These pages were subsequently published in fall 1993 in *Southwestern American Literature* with an introductory article by Jaime Mejía (1993b:57–62). The missing pages are to be inserted on p. 168, between the third and fourth paragraphs from the bottom, following the words "I doubt I'll ever be angry anymore" ending with: "This last, Dr. Perlman, is not an afterthought."[5] They contain Rafa Buenrostro's final notes to Dr. Perlman where he puts down in writing what is quite literally unsayable for him. In the entire *KCDTS*, this passage constitutes the one single instance of truly introspective, meditative writing, writing as emotional discharging. It is a strange coincidence, and an ironic one too, that this particular passage should have been lost.

With cruel sarcasm, Rafa relates how, after the bitter fighting during the winter 1950–1951, the patrolling soldiers blame the early spring thaw for the sudden appearance of thousands of human bones all over the beautiful Korean countryside. Bones, the majority of which turn out to be civilian ("a woman's skull half hidden by her cheap blouse and peasant skirt mingled with smaller skulls all strewn around" [in Mejía 1993b:60]). "Frozen during the winter, no doubt," the patrols say in a hopeless attempt to deflect the horrifying truth. "That's what happens when you have an early thaw. You just can't rely on people to stay hidden from view, can you?" Rafa asks, issuing a surreal reproach to the changing of the seasons and to the dead for bothering the survivors with the unrefutable proof of their violent deaths. Because "it's a static picture, one you'll remember longer" (59), Rafa relentlessly goes on to write on paper what he's carried in his head for too long: the atrocious efficacy of their own improvised land mines; the prophylactic shooting of potentially booby-trapped corpses by the roadside; and despairing young soldiers disabling and hugging their weapons as if that might stop the fighting.

Back in the Valley, Rafa receives a series of letters, the most memorable of which are from Rudy Hernández. They bring the narrative back to Belken County, indeed back to the very beginnings of the *KCDTS* and to an interesting aspect of the Valley's social infrastructure. Rudy, a World War II vet who had joined the Korean War toward the end, asks Rafa to look up his parents in Bascom, Belken County. Rudy's parents are sharecroppers on the land of a familiar *KCDTS* personage, Rufino Fisher Gutiérrez (see **RAFE**:94).[6] In his first letter, Rudy Hernández tells Rafa that he wants to stay in the Army instead of taking over the family farm. Aware of the Buenrostros' friendship with his parents' landlord, he asks Rafa to use his good name as a Buenrostro in order to go and break the news to Rodolfo and Paula Hernández ("Your family is well known and I'm banking on that" [**SERVANTS**:186]). From Rudy's second letter, we gather that Rafa not only managed to put the Hernándezes at ease about their son's decision, but also made some kind of arrangements to lighten the burden of the elderly sharecroppers ("Well old Valley friend, many thanks for helping my mother and my father. I think he's getting too old to farm" [187]).

Allusions to familiar *KCDTS* topics are not limited to these final pages. Rather, they are omnipresent throughout the journal. We have already seen how, in the face of the utmost horror, seeking mental refuge in the Valley prevents Rafa from losing his mind. But the Chicanos have also brought the Valley with them to Korea. The presence of Chicanos and other minorities in the Army is duly noted. Frequent occurrences of blatant racism are placed in the context of ethnic and linguistic controversy back in Texas (e.g., **SERVANTS**:41, 63, 79, 80, 114, 118). Perhaps the most striking incident, reminding the Chicanos of the significance of the Alamo in Texas Mexican history, is a statement from a high-ranking general. In an ill-guided attempt at cheering up the troops, he belittles the Chinese Communist commitment in Korea by comparing it to that of Mexicans in the defense of Texas (87).

Due to its fairly recent publication, **SERVANTS** has received little critical attention. As a rule, engaged war fiction written by veterans—as is the case with Hinojosa's work—never fails to receive praise for indicting war's atrocities, for its stark realism, for its timelessness, for being powerful in a general sort of way. But two of the reviews of **SERVANTS** go beyond that pattern. William Anthony Nericcio has published on Hinojosa before, and his 1995 analysis is clearly informed by a deep insight into the author's literary project. He sets **SERVANTS** apart from Chicano war novels "which *picture* the ravaging, alienating consequences of ethnocultural warfare," (Nericcio 1995:140, original italics) because here war is not a "synecdoche" for ethnic conflict but simply a plain rendering of a Chicano in the war.

Also in 1995, Susan Doyle offers her reading of **SERVANTS** within the macrocosm of the *KCDTS*. She briefly explores the themes of home and death, concluding that both remain too visceral, too complex, and thus almost inexplicable for Rafa. Up until the moment when Rafa finally spills his guts in his notes to Dr. Perlman, description of death has culminated in the unsaid, because "to write about it in too much detail, even to yourself, is to expose yourself too deeply to fear, and beyond that lie the dragons of madness" (Doyle 1995:123). She goes on to foreground the forceful implementation of the typical Hinojosa discourses: sense of place, ethnic self, death, and the elusive nature of reality:

> Similarly, the meaning of Texas falls on his Army psychiatrist's sympathetic but deaf ears. Even tying that term—home—to the doctor's Jewishness evokes no response. *Home* is one of those words that must be understood in a context: tried and tested over time, mellowed and enriched by our distance from them. Much like the extended life stories of the Buenrostro and Malacara families, which fold and unfold like the pleats of a skirt, words like *home* and *death* test our understanding of the nature of language.
>
> For a life, as Hinojosa knows, is the sum of its parts. Segments can be resurrected, reconstructed, deconstructed, forgotten, fabricated—

sometimes all in the same instant. There are epiphanies; there are discoveries that do not meet the intersection of light and fruition for years.

This understanding, of the piecemeal nature of life—utterly postmodern in its construction—is evident throughout *The Useless Servants*. (Doyle 1995:123, original italics)

Finally, Doyle uncovers a completely new aspect of Rafa's war experience, which she believes to be of the utmost relevance for the direction Rafa's life—and the *KCDTS*—have taken.

If not expressly drawn, parallels between war-torn Koreans and war-riddled Texas Mexicans are inescapable. Despite the white power structure never letting Rafe and his buddies forget their conquered status, they have crossed a border: they are part of the forces of the oppressor. Rafe finds the history of his own people enacted in front of him: the contested borders, the confused refugees who die to serve the greater good, the battle police who herd the refugees, the taking and retaking of land. (Doyle 1995:124)

Doyle draws a compelling picture of Rafa discovering his calling as a chronicler of his people's history, starting out with his log of the Korean War at age 20, and compulsively recording ever since. And here, Doyle convincingly claims, lies a great part of "the mystery of Rafa Buenrostro," who, after graduating from law school, becomes a policeman rather than a lawyer. "Lawyers," Doyle says, "must choose sides; police record the facts and act on them."

The title *The Useless Servants* is taken from Luke 17:10: "Well, will we then be like the useless servants who did nothing more than that which was commanded of us?" (**SERVANTS**:184). William Anthony Nericcio interprets the biblical motto as a lamentation of war's senselessness and futility (Nericcio 1995:140). His answer to the question posed in the quote is a tragic "yes," and while that is certainly one valid reading of Rafa Buenrostro's Korean documentary, the biblical passage that contains the quote is actually not about uselessness at all. Instead, its theme is man's relation to God where man's part is that of a humble servant who is not to expect a reward for his service. Rather, he is to seek fulfillment through obedience to God. Actually, *The New Oxford Annotated Bible* (May and Metzger 1977:1271) chooses "unworthy" instead of "useless." In this version the quote runs: "So you also, when you have done all that is commanded of you, say, 'We are only unworthy servants; we have only done what was our duty.'"

Rafa remembers the words from a Sunday mass held by a military Chaplain in 1949, on the third Sunday before Lent ("Septuagint [*sic*] Sunday" [184]). Joey Vielma, Charlie Villalón, and Rafa Buenrostro are training in Japan, not yet aware that there is really going to be a war. After the service, Joey scoffs at the passage, countering with another quote from Luke: "And be content with thy wages," adding, "Well, screw that, you guys."

Given that the three young Chicanos attend church service and can actually cite scripture, it is unlikely that they would sneer at the kind of religious faith expressed in the passage from Luke. Rather, as the immediate context and the reference to the national anthem in the chapter's title would indicate, they seem to be referring to the service they are rendering to their country (here Texas—and by extension—the United States). In a chain of associations typical of the stream-of-consciousness technique, Rafa reports the loss of parts of his journal, then immediately chastises himself for even considering this a loss in the face of all the lost lives. Faced with anguish too immense to cope with, he falls into his usual safety net, his sense of self and thoughts of home, of "who and what [he is]: a youngster from Texas, from the Rio Grande Valley" (**SERVANTS**:184). It is this sentiment that triggers the memory of the three Valley boys (with Rafa as the sole survivor) attending mass together where they hear the words from Luke "only to have Joey finish the quote that made all of us laugh on the way to noon chow." Hereafter, the passage gathers even more momentum and meaning as Rafa dedicates his writing to his two dead friends and to "all the other useless servants, the CCF, who *also* fought for their masters in a foreign land" (184, my emphasis).

"Screw that, then," is really the Chicanos' contemptuous response to their home state, which they have come to look upon as a "master" who has dispatched them to fight "in a foreign land," presumptuously taking for granted even their ultimate sacrifice. This is the same Texas that has a long history of abusing and mistreating Rafa's folks who came to Texas with the first Spanish expedition in 1749. And yet the Chicanos' love-hate relationship with their home state continues, and Rafa closes the chapter by returning to his thoughts of Texas as described by his father, the late Don Jesús Buenrostro: "Texas, our Texas, that slice of hell, heaven, purgatory and land of our Fathers."

14

ASK A POLICEMAN

A Rafe Buenrostro Mystery (1998)

THE second book in an emerging series of murder mysteries within the *KCDTS*, **POLICEMAN** portrays the Belken County Homicide Squad's investigations during one hot, rainy month of August in the early 1990s, roughly twenty years after the events reported in **PARTNERS**. We remember that a mysterious character named Dr. Juan José Olivares had ordered a contract on the life of Mexican drug lord "El Barco" Práxedes Zaragoza, to be carried out at the Kum-Bak Inn on the Texas side of the border. The hired killers, however, had mistakenly executed criminal prosecutor Dutch Elder, who had simply been in the wrong place at the wrong time. It is left to the reader to deduce that Dr. Olivares is really Capt. Lisandro Gómez Solís, director of *orden público,* in Barrones, Tamaulipas. Making his escape with the proceeds from the sale of 226 pounds of cocaine, Capt. Lee Gómez, alias Dr. Olivares, had bought a new home on Padre Island off the Texas Gulf Coast for his young wife, his sons, and himself.

Typical of Hinojosa's segmented, unchronological narration, some of the details hinted at in the 1985 **PARTNERS** are not brought to light until the surprise opening of **POLICEMAN** in which Lisandro Gómez Solís is skillfully sprung from the Klail City Court House jail shortly after his arrest at his condo on Padre Island. Lisandro's jailbreak occurs on Chief Inspector Rafa Buenrostro's first day of duty after what seems to be a longish sick leave due to a severe shoulder injury that is hinted at repeatedly and ominously but whose exact circumstances will probably not be disclosed until the next *KCDTS* installment.

In the weeks that follow, a twisted tale of perversion, patricide, and savage revenge unfolds. During the investigation, Rafa Buenrostro, Sam Dorson, Peter Hauer, and Ike Cantú work closely together with Maria Luisa Cetina de Gutiérrez—the new, efficient, and incorruptible *Directora del orden público* in Barrones, Mexico. The break comes when Gómez's ranch-hand Tiburón Morales turns himself in to the Klail City Police asking for protective custody and reporting a series of killings on the ranch grounds in Soliseño. Rafa's men stand by as the Barrones Police crime lab examines dozens of corpses that evidence both a dispute within the Gómez family and the killing spree of a single avenger coming from the outside. In the end, the sole surviving Gómez, the deranged twin José Antonio, remains at large. He is eventually cornered in a Mexican-standoff tableau with Lu Cetina and Gómez aiming at each other at point blank range.

The above synopsis retells only the bare bones of Hinojosa's tale of U.S.-Mexico border crime, but it must be placed here since it provides the foundation on which my ensuing discussion will rest. While **POLICEMAN** fairly closely follows the format of the murder mystery genre, the author weaves into his principal narrative a series of subplots and motifs that are designed to make subtle, but forceful, commentary on political and social conditions in the embattled bicultural border region. The incorporation of these elements showcases Hinojosa's writerly control because they neither interfere with the core crime-mystery plot, nor do they take on the form of lectures on racial and social affairs in the Valley.

MILITARIZATION OF THE BORDER

The first of these subplots revolves around Rafa's ongoing struggle with the district attorney, Florencio "Chip" Valencia, over a budget increase from the federal government that Valencia is lobbying for in order to buy automatic rifles and a minitank. Forever campaigning, Valencia swoops down like a vulture on every piece of news about violent crime in the Valley. With a barrage of press releases "about all the violence he could get on either side of the river," Valencia intends to get the public and office holders to "push his request for an increase in fire power" in order to combat "the systematic violence that some of the undesirable element from across the river has been visiting upon us" (**POLICEMAN**:158). Yet even without Valencia's minitank, much of the border resembles a military stronghold already. Chapter eight of the novel, in which detective Peter

Hauer goes to see an official at the U.S. Immigration Service headquarters, is replete with allusions to border matters, the most telling of which is the description of "Immigration's main building" as a "fortress-like structure" (32).

The general subject of militarizing the border and its disastrous repercussions on Mexican American civil rights is a frequent concern in recent Chicano scholarship. It is a topic that deserves to be investigated in the diachronic context of Texas history and will hence be revisited in my chapter on Rafa Buenrostro as a revisionist chronicler of the Texas Mexican perspective on Valley affairs. With respect to **POLICEMAN**, though, it is essential to note that Rafa Buenrostro, as chief inspector of the Belken County Police, is obviously in a pivotal position with sufficient clout to oppose Valencia's projects. He can issue his own press releases and thus create a forum for public debate on armament and its dangers. Of his colleague Peter Hauer, who has volunteered to use his contacts with the local press, he asks:

> And Pete . . . call that new editor of the *Enterprise*. Take her out for coffee. We need publicity on the unneeded budget increase and the high risks in the use of the AK-47s, the Uzis, the lot. How much this would cost the taxpayers. Mention the mini-tank, the County budget, the need for improvement of county roads, pour it on. (**POLICEMAN**:44)

In his usual oblique fashion, Hinojosa asserts that the antagonism over firepower is not so much a racial as a political matter. In the D.A.'s office we note "the photo of the smiling Chip shaking hands with Reagan and another of Valencia with Bush. The present incumbent was missing" (89). Due to Valencia's lack of familiarity with the network of old and trustworthy Valley families (see 177–78), we can infer that he must be second or third generation Mexican American—a Johnny-come-lately by Valley standards. In other words, in his characterization of the D.A., Hinojosa draws a picture of a social climber who has forgotten his roots and instead joins forces with the conservative Republican camp that has little love for "wetbacks" and "shoebiters" from across the river, and who prefers to chime in with the moral majority's heckling against immigration, affirmative action, and social services for undocumented workers. By exposing Valencia as a character who is not only despicable for his views but also a dupe whose antics are easily deflected, Hinojosa makes an unambiguous political declaration. Moreover, the chief inspector has allies in the D.A.'s own office, like Gwen Phillips, who alerts Rafa when Valencia intensifies his lobbying (see 178). Buenrostro's position is also clearly delimited by outside voices. Such is the case when he runs into the new editor of the *Enterprise* at the grocery store. After introducing herself, Marcia Ridings says: "I've not met an anti-gun cop before," adding, "I received two faxes from the D.A.'s office today. One for increased armament and one against. But you do carry a gun don't you?" (58). Clearly, the indictment of both violence and revenge takes center stage in **POLICEMAN**, and a reading of some of the pertinent passages will eventually result in a closer inspection of the title of the book.

Reading and Rereading

On a somewhat personal note, I must confess that after my initial, perhaps too cursory, reading of **POLICEMAN**, I was taken aback both by the quantity and the graphic nature of the violence depicted in the novel. Even though I had duly noted the clear stand the book takes on armament and militarization, I was disappointed momentarily that the author would resolve the plot of his book by virtually killing off all the bad guys. But then it struck me that that was perhaps a desired effect. When I went back to the book, my attention was soon caught by the abounding references to the treacherousness of first impressions. In fact, the text intones a mantra of reading, close-reading, rereading, checking, double-checking, scrutinizing, looking for patterns, contradictions, and missing pieces (see, e.g., **POLICEMAN**:54, 117, 119, 138, 142).

Once again, Hinojosa does not limit himself to merely telling readers about the significance of accurate investigation, but rather he makes readers enact the ritual of the quest. Criminals are not stupid, and clues in an investigation are rarely offered on a silver platter. Accordingly, the text demands the same careful screening and probing of evidence that Chief Inspector Buenrostro requires of his detectives. The picture that emerges after a closer reading is that of a Rafa Buenrostro who has physically suffered the violence that is an inescapable attribute of his job. And even though he is daily reminded of it by pain and scars, he will not succumb to its corrupting force. An ongoing intellectual struggle against the enticement of vengeful thoughts is suggested by Rafa's reading Greek Tragedy on his first day back on full duty (see **POLICEMAN**:17). Whatever it was that has happened to him, it must have been a violent incident in the line of duty, as desk sergeant Art de la Cruz indicates: "We nearly lost the chief inspector some time back, . . . and we have to be careful" (28). Whether he took a bullet, or sustained some other injury, it has neither made him bitter nor vindictive. And unlike some of his colleagues, he is never tempted to "forget" checking his gun with the customs officials when he goes to Mexico on police business (24, 65, 165). This integrity of character is regarded with a strange mix of admiration and contempt by Eduardo Salinas, himself a strong believer in the virtue of his vendetta ("Do I have a choice?" [165]).

The climactic passage that narrates Rafa's encounter with Eduardo Salinas in a cane field by the Gómez Ranch has the theme of revenge at its core. Rafa correctly guesses that Eduardo is the avenger who killed Felipe Segundo and Juan Carlos and that Eduardo is unaware that Lisandro has been dead for weeks. Rafa also has insight into the young man's code of honor, and he is positive that Salinas will come back to finish the job, unless he is given a reason to stop. In the ensuing conversation, the chief inspector makes it known to the young man that while he understands his code of honor and does not judge him for what he has done, he does not endorse these acts of revenge either. In turn, Eduardo honors his father's respect for Rafa Buenrostro, and seeking his approval, he asks, "Is your father alive, jefe inspector?" (**POLICEMAN**:164). The question prompts Rafa to think back on the murder of his father, Don Jesús Buenrostro. Jesús's brother Julián shared Eduardo's antiquated warrior ethic that would not let him rest until he had confronted and killed Alejandro Leguizamón in one-on-one combat.[1]

Rafa, however, has learned something that young Eduardo has not, namely that vengeance will only perpetuate violence. The passage at hand represents one of the many instances that bespeak the Faulknerian legacy in Hinojosa's work. (Faulkner's influence on Hinojosa's work will be discussed in-depth in part three.) In William Faulkner's 1934 novel, *The Unvanquished,* when Bayard Sartoris, just like Eduardo Salinas, is called upon by his peers to continue fighting his dead father's wars, he says, "I am tired of killing men, no matter what the necessity and what the end. Tomorrow, when I go to town and meet Ben Redmond, I shall be unarmed" (Faulkner 1960:175). Unlike Salinas, both Rafa and Bayard have fought in wars and have distinguished themselves as soldiers. With no urgency to prove their valor, they have learned that the only way to combat violence is to break its vicious circle. And in effect, even as Sam Dorson and Rafa accompany Lu Cetina to face the armed and dangerously deranged José Antonio Gómez at the close of the story, the narrator is most definitely paying homage to Faulkner when he simply states: "They were unarmed" (**POLICEMAN**:193).

Chapter Fourteen

Reconstructing Peace in the Valley

The motif of breaking the dynamics of revenge is taken up in its historical context when Rafa goes to visit his ailing father-in-law in the hospital. Noddy Perkins, the economic and political mastermind of the KBC ranch and Bank empire, which literally owns five-hundred Mexican families (**RITES**:8), has a long record of manipulating and subjugating the Belken County Mexicans. (For a thorough discussion of the significance of the KBC Ranch and its real-life model, the King Ranch, please see the section on Jehú Malacara in part four.) The KBCers were also the closest political allies of the Leguizamón clan who bought up all the land surrounding the Carmen Ranch. As a last resort against the Buenrostros' staunch resistance, they had Rafa's father murdered. Noddy has elsewhere vehemently denied any KBC implication in the murder of Don Jesús (51). But now he senses that what he is going to ask his Mexican son-in-law is nothing short of asking to be pardoned for a life led as a racist and opportunist. Knowing this, Noddy takes a long time in getting around to the critical question: "Son, I want to be buried in the Old Families cemetery by the Carmen Ranch, on your brother's land" (**POLICEMAN**:19). Having to seek this absolution from a Mexican, Noddy has undoubtedly met his nemesis. Notions of guilt and absence of guilt are reflected in the body language displayed by the two men. While the usually sprightly, imperious Perkins is fidgeting, running "both hands across his face as if washing and drying it at the same time," Rafa is "sitting comfortably and relaxed in the straight back chair" with no intention to make things easier for the all but prostrate Perkins. At the same time, Rafa knows that this is no time for vindictiveness. Instead, he says: "It's not too much to ask, Noddy." Perkins can muster just about enough humility to say thank you "in a half-whisper," and before the emotionally charged situation can go overboard, Rafa allays it with a joke:

> Our cemetery's a state-designated landmark. That means the state of Texas takes care of it. That also means you'll be a ward of the state for eternity. (**POLICEMAN**:20)

This encounter that occurs early on sets the stage for a whole series of conciliatory messages in the novel. Alliances and antagonisms, bonding and friction occur almost completely independently of ethnicity in **POLICEMAN**. Militarization is favored or rejected both by Texas Mexicans and Texas Anglos; incompetent FBI agents turn out to be Hispanic Americans; Anglo *fronterizos* like Peter Hauer are foregrounded for their bicultural and bilingual upbringing; even the Belken County jet set mix happily across ethnic lines when they celebrate their cocaine parties on expensive yachts, as long as they belong to the same class of the well-to-do.

Certainly, Hinojosa neither denies nor belittles racial strife along the border, but in his prognosis, the true conflict in South Texas will be a class conflict that manifests itself in exclusionist tendencies against the poor—Mexican or otherwise. This is also why Rafa Buenrostro, son of *El Quieto*, comes very close to losing his legendary cool when Chip Valencia is lining up votes to step up armament along a border that has never ceased to be a battle zone and a dividing line between the affluent and the underprivileged. Where the D.A. exacerbates the conflict with new arms, Rafa tries to de-escalate it. But even Rafa, with his even temper, has to struggle to maintain his poise in the face of Valencia's utter foolishness (see **POLICEMAN:108, 178**).

Perhaps the best illustration of cross-ethnic bonding, apart from his happy marriage with Sammie Jo, is Rafa Buenrostro's social and professional relationship with Sam Dorson, which is characterized by absolute trust and understanding. "They'd worked together for fifteen years and talk in the court house was they could read each other's minds" (**POLICEMAN: 183**). Both are described in the novel as bicultural and bilingual borderers, and ethnicity is never an issue between them. Instead, their familiarity with each other's thought processes runs so deep that Dorson can divine his friend's thoughts ahead of time and is able to spare him awkward situations. Such is the case on the last page of the text where Rafa cannot avoid answering Lu Cetina's question, "Who killed the people out at the ranch, Rafe?" When he gives her Eduardo Salinas's name, she wants to know whether he would have told her if she hadn't asked. Rafa, though, had promised Eduardo Salinas that there would be no need to tell the directora, as she would, in time, find out by herself. Now he realizes a truthful answer could jeopardize his excellent working relationship with his Mexican colleague. Dorson, however, is on the ball and saves the uncomfortable moment by diverting the directora's attention:

"Would you have told me if I hadn't asked?"
Dorson stepped in. "Ask a policeman."
Puzzled, she asked "What's that?"
Sam Dorson, smiling, sang out:

> *"Every member of the force*
> *Has a watch and chain, of course*
> *If you want to know the time,*
> *Ask a p'liceman!"* (**POLICEMAN:195**)

Chapter Fourteen

The "silly piece" that makes Lu Cetina laugh and forget about her question is—as Hinojosa has explained to me—from an English music hall play, and its implicit significance, apart from amusing Lu Cetina, lies in the fact that English policemen did indeed wear a watch and chain—but no gun!

15

A CONCLUDING NOTE

WITH **POLICEMAN**, the *KCDTS* has succeeded in spanning a twenty-five-year-long history of Belken County chronicles. In many ways, the book perfectly exemplifies Hinojosa's agenda as a teller of engaging stories, as a revisionist tejano historiographer, and as a visionary of the Valley's immediate future. Moreover, it proves beyond a doubt that each book is designed, and can be appreciated, as an independent work of literature. At the same time, each assumes its rightful place as one integral segment in an ongoing literary project whose entirety is much larger than the sum of its parts. It is precisely this overall aesthetic design, resting on the dichotomy of individuality and union, which is the central concern of this study. The previous expositions were written with the intention of portraying each of the fourteen installments in its generic originality, its individual—always purposeful—architectural construction, and to highlight how each installment is linked to the larger project without forfeiting its distinctiveness. With this, a foundation has been laid that will enable the subsequent discussion to move away from the idea of individual books. Instead, the *KCDTS* will be read as one continuous novelistic project whose fragmented, disjointed representation is employed by Hinojosa to recreate the mimesis of a traditionally oral community. For the readers, the constant shifting of genres, points of view, and temporal and spatial settings would pose an insurmountable challenge were it not for the unifying force of a restricted succession of central narrational authorities.

Before we can turn to these characters/narrators, an excursion into literary theory is called for in order to establish the position of the *KCDTS* in the continuum of literary styles and movements that aspire to a renewal of artistic concepts and ideologies vis-à-vis the traditional realistic forms of narration. The author's unmistakable renunciation of chronological plots, static narrative perspectives, moral positions, and clear-cut generic boundaries in the *KCDTS* have prompted a number of critics to apply the terms "postmodern" and "postmodernist" to Hinojosa's work. However, a thorough exploration of Hinojosa's work in terms of postmodern ideology and aesthetics has not yet been undertaken. Consequently, in the following chapter, I propose to challenge the prevailing attribution of postmodern status to Hinojosa's work. Especially in view of the integrative and conciliatory tendencies in Hinojosa's recent works, which we have had occasion to observe in **AMIGOS/FRIENDS** and **POLICEMAN**, it is imperative to examine the author's agenda against the background of both the prevailing and more off-beat contributions to the postmodern debate.

PART TWO

Rethinking the Postmodern: Gender,
Ethnicity, and Language in Belken County

L IKE "the Toyota of thought, produced and assembled in several different places and then sold everywhere" (Rajchman in Zukin 1991:26), the concepts of "postmodernity" (a general social condition) and "postmodernism" (its attending aesthetic ideology and cultural style) have become blanket terms for any number of theoretical constructs, sociopolitical movements, and aesthetic innovations. Although postmodernist thought advocates challenging the established canons of "high culture" and including experiences of difference and "otherness," the intellectual acrobatics of its proponents and critics have converted the postmodernist debate into an exclusionary, strictly high-brow domain of academic scholarship.

Inexorably, cultural theorists in general, and intercultural theorists in particular, have been appropriating postmodernism as a catchall for a wide range of sociocultural models:

> While we do not need yet another definition of what the postmodern or the postcolonial really is, it seems clear to me that U.S.-Mexico borderland sociocultural theorists . . . are emphatically implicated in any attempt to map out the specificity of postcontemporary culture, history, literature, and society and thus to gauge this culture's distance from what might be called the culture of "high modernism." (Saldívar 1997:20)

As we shall see presently, postmodernist concepts of thought can be applied to such intercultural literary productions as Rolando Hinojosa's *KCDTS* through a number of conflicting, even downright antithetical approaches. Although Hinojosa's critics frequently fall back on the concept of postmodernism in order to characterize his work, postmodernist thought and aesthetics are not at the center of any of the studies that I will cite below. Therefore, after a brief survey of what might be called seminal postmodernist readings by various Hinojosa critics over the past fifteen years, I propose to widen the scope by placing models of thought by major postmodernist theorists at the center of the following chapter.

16

THE CRITICS AND THE QUESTION OF THE POSTMODERN

IN his 1991 book, *Chicano Satire: A Study in Literary Culture,* Guillermo Hernández contends that a successful transit from oral to literary discourses "requires familiarity with those conflicting planes of discourse at which the Anglo and Mexican cultures meet" (Hernández 1991:86), a challenge for which no one could be better prepared than someone with Hinojosa's background. In addition to being a product of an Anglo-Mexican marriage, reared as a rural *fronterizo,* and invested with impressive academic credentials in both English- and Spanish-language disciplines, Hinojosa possesses the authorial acuteness to guarantee the successful transit from orality to literacy, as evidenced in the fragmented, polyphonic narrative fabric of his Belken County chronicles.

In traditional fiction, Hernández explains, narrative constitutes a self-contained entity. Essential aspects of meaning and characters' motivations are to be found within the text. In such a narrative, according to Hernández, "it would indeed represent an authorial failure to omit essential clues" (Hernández 1991:86). Conversely, in a true oral performance, as well as in quotidian conversation, "oral transmitters frequently dispense with fundamental contextual data," which is possible due to the "community of experience of poet and audience."[1]

Curiously, the *KCDTS* fits the descriptions of both orality and literacy. In any given illocutionary situation within the *KCDTS* essential clues may be omitted. Still, the Belken County chronicles constitute a largely self-contained entity precisely because those seemingly missing clues are placed elsewhere in the fragmented, discontinuous narrative fabric. Hernández identifies this simultaneity as a postmodernist appearance (Hernández 1991:86), conceived to accomplish a mimesis of an oral society couched in a plot of literary fiction.

Here, as in many other instances where criticism has centered on the particular type of generic experimentation in Hinojosa's work, we can note a tendency to recur to the terms "postmodern" and "postmodernism." Owing perhaps to the vast, heterogeneous fusion of concepts in this "Toyota of thought" (utterly postmodern even in its genesis), Hernández, as well as the other critics I will cite below, stop short of a thorough exploration of Hinojosa's *KCDTS* in terms of postmodern ideology and aesthetics.

Other Critics' Voices

One testimony, which actually concurs with Guillermo Hernández, is that of José David Saldívar. In his 1984 contribution to *The Rolando Hinojosa Reader*, in which he correctly pinpoints Hinojosa's rejection of traditional forms of narration, he hesitates to pigeonhole the *KCDTS* as either modernist or postmodernist:

> It [*Klail City y sus alrededores*] is a virtual textbook of ethnopoetic and folkloric techniques, one that displays all of Hinojosa's literary talents as the text drives itself to the limits of (post)modernist narrative form: collage and metafiction. (Saldívar 1984a:52)

The parenthesis saves him from having to revoke his judgment in his 1990 essay "The Limits of Cultural Studies." Principally, he enters the debate in order to challenge a particular postmodernist cultural study of minority literatures.[2] Almost as a by-product of his retort, Saldívar delimits his stance on the postmodernist issue relative to Hinojosa when he draws on *Claros Varones de Belken* as an example of "different strategies for those interested in the positive practices associated with cultural studies" (Saldívar 1990: 255). Launching into a discussion of "the chronicle" as a superior form of historiography, he claims:

> Although written in fragmented and decentered postmodernist narrative, *Claros Varones de Belken* is, in fact, a chronicle, written within certain formal generic constraints. . . . What thus **appears to be**

fragmented and postmodern in Hinojosa's *Claros Varones de Belken* is really formal and generic. (Saldívar 1990:256, my bold)

Many critics, however, are not in the least doubtful that the semblance of a postmodernist narrative in the *KCDTS* is matched with a corresponding postmodernist ethos. Erlinda Gonzalez-Berry, for instance, in her introduction to *El condado de Belken: Klail City,* sums up a discussion of Hinojosa's fragmented narrative and "polyvocality" with the conclusion that it is "Hinojosa's distrust of the authority of 'received' truths that makes his work so utterly postmodern" (**CONDADO**:11). John C. Akers feels that "Hinojosa seems to be trailing a postmodernist discourse where the discovery of the fictional world remakes the real world that inspired him" (Akers 1993:101). Without further addendum, Hector Calderón simply mentions "the postmodern *cronicón* of Hinojosa" in the concluding summary of his 1991 article on Texas border culture (Calderón 1991:25, original italics), while Susan Doyle seems more heedful when she labels Hinojosa's "understanding of the piecemeal nature of life" as "utterly postmodern in its *construction*" (Doyle 1995:123, my italics).

Lastly, there is Antonio Prieto Taboada's brief, but judicious, commentary on the issue. In the opening paragraph of his insightful 1991 essay "El caso de las pistas culturales en *Partners in Crime,*" he emphasizes the book's postmodern vision with respect to the power structure that seems to determine the relationship of the minority culture vis-à-vis the mainstream culture. Taboada submits that Hinojosa's achievement lies in offering an alternative, reconstructive way of dealing with the failure of the radical projects (literary, political, ethnic) of modernity (Taboada 1991:130).[3]

17

POSTMODERNISM REVISITED

Initiatory Debates and Recent Criticism

AS the foregoing examples illustrate, the terms "postmodern" and "postmodernist" have been used in relation to the *KCDTS* as a whole and many of its individual installments. In the present chapter, I submit my own critical analysis of the *KCDTS* based on a selection of readings from postmodernist theory. I contend that while the surface structure of much of Hinojosa's text is admittedly postmodern in appearance, the true postmodern nature of his work remains controversial. I feel that the striking difference between genuine postmodernist fiction on the one hand, and Hinojosa's authorial program on the other, is not so much one of form, but rather a careful opposition of moods and attitudes. In contrast to the exhilarating, liberating use of aleatory writing that has become a trademark of postmodernist fiction and that clearly shuns responsibility towards its subject, Hinojosa's work is informed by a genuine concern for the people and the culture he writes about. Thus, we need to achieve a clearer understanding of whether the concepts put forth by postmodernist critics are indeed pertinent to Hinojosa's South Texas chronicle. I therefore propose to structure my argument along the lines of what I believe the three eminent debates generally associated with the term "postmodern" are:

1. The distinction between modernism and postmodernism.
2. Closing the gap between high culture and low culture.
3. The loss of the distinction between the real and the illusory.

I will outline these debates as briefly as possible, and after each one, I will call into question its applicability to a postmodernist reading of the *KCDTS*. In a next step, I will define my understanding of the particular ethos that distinguishes Hinojosa from the established postmodernist rhetoric, as well as from the current postmodernist celebration of "otherness" and plurality. In fact, much of recent Chicano literature and criticism seems to focus on strictly essentialist ethnic and gender discourses. There is, however, a radically divergent tendency in recent postmodernist criticism to reject essentialist notions of race and gender. Incidentally, Hinojosa's most recent books are replete with passages that are obviously designed to reveal the pitfalls of narrow, constricted notions of identity.

In mapping a discourse that clearly resembles the critique of essentialism currently formulated by postmodernist thought, Rolando Hinojosa proffers an alternative vision, refusing to trust blindly in the values dictated by gender and ethnicity. I will cite a number of examples that are particularly suitable for illustrating an ever-increasing conciliatory and integrative attitude that is becoming more and more apparent with each new installment of the *KCDTS* and that is particularly evident in Hinojosa's latest mystery novel *Ask a Policeman*.

Modernism and Postmodernism

The chief controversy surrounding the term "postmodernism" concerns its distinction from the term "modernism." In its essence, postmodernism is based on the assumption that the principal ideals advocated by the modernist project such as progress, rationality, truth, or scientific objectivity are no longer tenable as they make no provisions for the manifold contingencies in a world where cultural values are always local and particular. This debate started to gain momentum in the late 1970s, when Jürgen Habermas charged that postmodernity is really *anti*-modernity, i.e., it prevents the so-called Enlightenment project from reaching completion (Habermas 1993). Taking issue with Habermas, Jean-François Lyotard (1993) proclaimed his fundamental distrust of what he calls the metanarratives or Grand Narratives. These all-inclusive, totalizing, "objective" models for explaining human existence (e.g., Christianity, Marxism, modern science) are illusionary constructs, according to Lyotard. They only serve to suppress the fact that we live in a makeshift world where everything is provisional and temporary.

Another practicable approach to delineating the position of postmodernist literature vs. modernist literature focuses on fundamental differences in narrational moods and attitudes. Both the modernist's and the postmodernist's image of contemporary life is one of fragmentation and discontinuity. Both tend to manifest their rejection of traditional realist narration through generic experimentation, polyvocality, and discontinuous plots. However, modernist artists generally exercise these new forms of expression with a rigorous, ascetic discipline that bespeaks their nostalgia for a past "when faith was full and authority intact" (Barry 1995:83). Conversely, postmodernism revels in this new freedom from the "claustrophobic embrace of fixed systems" that is generally associated with the Enlightenment. One particularly illustrative feature of this postmodern revolt is a radically eclectic manner of artistic presentation, often identified with the use of so-called aleatory forms, such as collages literally pasted together from random newspaper clippings or the pastiche made up of textual bits and pieces taken from different genres and periods.

Incidentally, Rolando Hinojosa's generic experiments include the use of fabricated news clippings, seemingly arbitrary footnotes, and fictitious quotations; that is, postmodern features that need to be scrutinized for their true postmodernist spirit. It is certainly true that Hinojosa's choice of narrative devices should be understood, if not as a rejection, at least as an alternative to the traditional modes of narration—the formula novel as he called it in his essay "The Sense of Place" (Hinojosa 1984a:22). What is more, the generic experimentation described above is really characteristic of both modernist and postmodernist aesthetics, and thus does not provide a sound basis for distinguishing modernism from postmodernism. It is only when we examine *how* he implements his experiments that a modernist rather than a postmodernist attitude emerges. In fact, the stories in the KCDTS are imbued with the Enlightenment's pledge for freedom, justice, and equality. In accordance with Habermas's "moral imperative" (1985:97), Hinojosa invokes an ideal of a rational, informed, and—wherever possible—learned dialogue. His attitude toward such dichotomies as truth/falsehood, reality/illusion, serious/nonserious is one of modernist skepticism, rather than postmodernist indifference. Moreover, there is a distinct modernist nostalgia in Echevarría's wistful laments, in the glorification of Don Jesús's character, and in Rafa's old-fashioned code of honor and conduct. And those who would claim that Hinojosa's generic experimentation challenges modernist ideas of unity, order, and the rational need only take a close look at **VALLEY** and **KLAIL**, Hinojosa's English renditions of his first two novels. These new, thoroughly restructured—one could almost say organized—versions illustrate Hinojosa's taut, disciplined execution of his writing. Hinojosa himself professed that "few writers have the chance to rewrite their own work. I was lucky because I went from one language to the other" (my interview with Rolando Hinojosa on September 17, 1996). Certainly, this is a far cry from the postmodernist's susceptibility to aleatory impulses.

High Culture and Low Culture

In his article "Mapping the Postmodern," Andreas Huyssen (1993) gives an account of the debate that is concerned with the deconstruction of the no longer tenable distinction between mass culture and high culture. In the 1960s, one of the main protagonists, Leslie Fiedler, postulated the emancipation of popular culture, thus challenging the canonized high art and the elitism of its "higher discourses." Fiedler's proclamation of a "post-white," "post-male," "post-humanist," "post-Puritan" era can perhaps be seen as the beginning of a new development within postmodernism that refutes any kind of ethnic, gender, moral, or class segregation in art (see Huyssen 1993:122). Huyssen points out though, that in spite of Fiedler's populist call "to cross the border and close the gap between high art and mass culture," his constant attacks on the modernist dogma betray the same oppositional high vs. low dualism—only heading in the opposite direction.

Hinojosa's *KCDTS* does indeed assimilate mass culture subgenres such as the detective novel and the soap opera, placing them side-by-side with traditional oral styles and medieval Spanish genres. Thus, it would initially seem that Fiedler's call to "cross the border and close the gap" has been heeded. And yet, the methods and designs used by Hinojosa in the process of adaptation are at variance with Fiedler's expectations. Fiedler, after all, proposes an "uncritical" assimilation in order to achieve a radical democracy in the arts.[1] In contrast, Hinojosa's use of popular forms is deliberate and driven by a purpose. Each new form he implements serves his quest for an adequate portrayal of his South-Texas Chicano community. Indeed, the spotlight in Hinojosa's murder mystery *Partners in Crime* does not so much illuminate the grisly details of murder and mayhem, but rather it focuses on the day-to-day work of the Belken County Homicide Squad, which consists of the persistent collecting, screening, and ordering of information. The more information that is gathered, the higher the probability that a pattern can be teased out of it. Intellectual acuteness, rationalism, and knowledge of the culture you live in constitute the open-sesame of the vaults of truth.

Similar observations can be made about Hinojosa's adaptation of the soap opera genre. The title *Rites and Witnesses* points ahead to a tightly constructed novel that enacts the same quest for truth and truthfulness. We observe the rites and indiscretions of the Texas money-elite as we know them from the most popular TV shows, only to see their trivialities and superficialities brutally unmasked when contrasted with a group of Chicano GIs in Korea who are putting their lives on the line for American principles of democracy. The witnesses, Valley folks who subsequently give testimony, are scrutinized for at least some awareness of the appalling truths. Here, the triviality of the televised mass culture is stripped bare, exposed, or deconstructed, if you will. Eventually it is incorporated precisely into one of those "higher discourses" whose existence and validity are renounced by postmodernism.

The Real and the Illusory

In 1981, when Jean Baudrillard's book *Simulacres et simulations* came out, the French theorist coined the phrase "the loss of the real" and gave the postmodernist debate a new thrust (see Baudrillard 1993:346). In our postmodern world, according to Baudrillard, our understanding of reality is constituted of a constant bombardment of images from the mass media. As a consequence, we exist in a state of "hyperreality" where the distinction between the real and the imagined, or between surface and depth, is no longer possible. In his essay "The Precession of Simulacra" (Baudrillard 1993:346), he insists that in our contemporary life it is more probable than not that the surface of an image is only an indication of other images layered in its depth. In a succession of four steps, as shown below, the image will reach a stage of complete emptiness:

1. The image is the reflection of a basic reality.
2. The image masks and perverts a basic reality.
3. The image masks the absence of a basic reality.
4. The image bears no relation to any reality: it is its own pure simulacrum.

Disneyland, a typical third-order simulacrum (it marks the absence of a reality) is generally taken to be an imaginary, exalted version of America. In reality (if that figure of speech is still operative!), it is a religious, panegyric reveling in the real America. Disneyland, then, masks the absence of a genuine American reality. Likewise, prisons conceal the fact that society as a whole isn't any less restricted. And as a final example, Watergate was a conspiracy that fostered another insidious simulacrum:

Watergate is not a scandal: this is what must be said at all cost, for this is what everyone is concerned to conceal. (Baudrillard 1993:354, original italics)

The true scandal is that Watergate was a simulated moral panic attack on the part of U.S. politicians and the media, contrived and constructed solely to solidify the public's belief in a simulacrum—here, justice, ethics, and morality do exist in the political world and in the media.

Critics of Baudrillard's (admittedly intriguing) impression of the postmodern condition take exception to the simulacra theory on the grounds that it pulls the rug out from under all literary theory.[2] After all, the interpretation of literature entails the exploration of images and what they mean. There is also the question of the author's responsibility for, and attitude toward, his/her literary subject matter. With nothing worth believing in, why write, or—for that matter—read? Once more the problem boils down to the question of purpose, conviction, and attitudes.

Unquestionably, Baudrillard's compelling essay "The Precession of Simulacra" brings the reader face-to-face with the callousness of Western capitalism. Also, it is probably one of the gloomiest, most cynical analyses of our contemporary society and the perfidious nature of its representation. Nothing is what it seems, everything is surface, images race ahead of their own precluded realities, doomed to a hollow existence as images of images of images; implosion is imminent. In order to get over the postmodern hangover, readers may actually find the *KCDTS* to be a potent remedy, because it portrays a celebration of life rather than a lamentation of death.

Could we read Hinojosa's books as a series of simulacra? For a start, the fact must be stressed that Baudrillard's classical simulations (Watergate, Religion, Science, Justice, even Disney) above all have one thing in common: they all stake their claim for truth. Only then can they fulfill their mission to "rejuvenate . . . the fiction of the real" (Baudrillard 1993:352).

Even if it may come as an anticlimax at this juncture, I must presume that readers of the *KCDTS*—just like most readers of critically engaged literature—have long ago gotten wise to the ontological uncertainties of virtual reality. Perhaps that is why they turn to storytellers such as Hinojosa, who sell fiction as just that: fiction. The *KCDTS* neither simulates nor conspires, nor does it stand wide-eyed before the radical skepticism of the postmodern. Instead, the narrators and characters are in cahoots with the readers. With a wink to the audience, they frequently step over the line between fiction and reality, thereby exposing it—making it all the more visible. Baudrillard's elaborate unmasking of counterfeit truths appears redundant and repetitive vis-à-vis Hinojosa's effortless play with fact and fiction.

In 1973, the California publishing house Quinto Sol elected Hinojosa's first novel as the winner of its annual literary award and decided to publish it as *Estampas del Valle y otras obras*. One member of the jury, who actually chose this title, was Professor Octavio Romano from the University of California at Berkeley. In Hinojosa's second novel, **CONDADO**, one of the principal narrators of the *KCDTS*, P. Galindo, tells us about the professor: "Octavio Romano, catedrático de la Universidad de California (Berkeley), cuenta que se fue a vivir a un pueblo oscuro de Belken County por un par de años; fue a formar parte íntegra del pueblo y a raíz de esta experiencia, cambió, si no su vida, a lo menos la dirección de ella" ["Octavio Romano, professor at the University of California (Berkeley) recounts how he went to live in an obscure town in Belken County for a couple of years; he came to form an integral part of the town and, on account of this experience, changed, though perhaps not his life, at least its direction" (My translation)] (**CONDADO**:98–99). Surely, no one knows better than Octavio Romano that Belken County is a fictional place, and yet he was one of its first visitors.

There are other curious examples of Hinojosa's propensity for inserting references that clearly allude to a metafiction that transcends, and sometimes overlaps with, the Belken County reality. One such maneuver features the author's *Hitchcockian* cameo appearances as the honest lawyer Romeo Hinojosa in many of the installments. In fact, the middle initial in Rolando R. Hinojosa-Smith actually stands for "Romeo." The lawyer made his first appearance as Baldemar Cordero's attorney when the Series was initiated with **ESTAMPAS** (78), and he handled Becky Escobar's divorce proceedings in **FRIENDS** (23). A comparison of Rolando's handwriting with Romeo Hinojosa's signature at the bottom of the legal document in **ESTAMPAS** (78) will erase any doubts—if there ever were any—about Romeo Hinojosa's true identity. Similarly, in **FRIENDS**, Sammie Jo Perkins muses about the script writer who brought her and Rafa Buenrostro's love story to a happy ending. No doubt it is with a stealthy, conspiratorial glance in the direction of the audience that she confesses that she can't quite make up her mind about whether he's a "third-rate" or a "second-rate" writer (**FRIENDS**:120).

These are only a few examples of how characters within the fiction are uncannily aware of an existence outside of the fiction—and vice versa; and one might be inclined to read Hinojosa's writerly maneuvers as perfect examples of a postmodern blurring of reality and fiction. However, where Baudrillard says "to simulate is to feign what one hasn't" (1993:344), Hinojosa counters with a "WORD TO THE WISE (GUY): What follows, more likely as not, is a figment of someone's imagination; the reader is asked to keep this disclaimer in mind" (**VALLEY**:10). The cliché of calling a spade a spade comes to mind. It is precisely the straightforwardness of this fiction that makes it real and truthful.

In the final analysis, neither Lyotard's break with the Grand Narratives, nor Fiedler's call "to cross the borders and close the gap," nor Baudrillard's rhetoric of "simulations and simulacra" may be brought to bear in a convincing way on Hinojosa's agenda as a storyteller. No doubt Belken County is a modern microcosm that leaves much to be desired. But rather than a postmodern world beyond repair, its future seems to be auspicious, especially when considered in terms of postcolonial sociocultural aspects as the examples below appear to suggest.

Postmodern Otherness

A more recent strain in the postmodernist debate, which celebrates difference and "otherness" in terms of gender and ethnicity (see, for example, Saldívar 1997:20–21), poses a singular challenge when applied to the work of Rolando Hinojosa. I, for one, am puzzled by the unique narrative strategies that are implemented by Hinojosa in his recent books. Yet, there can be no doubt that they are especially designed to target the issues of gender and ethnicity and of Spanish as a minority language.

For instance, in 1990 Hinojosa took up the gender issue with force in **FRIENDS**, and in its 1991 Spanish-language version **AMIGOS**. This reportage-style novel portrays a young woman's successful recapturing of her Chicano identity, while at the same time eschewing the traditional constraints of Mexican patriarchal culture. Aside from consolidating the portrayal of strong Chicanas in his previous works, Hinojosa presents subtle but forceful commentary on the limitations of the gender discourse by implementing an unusual strategy: the gender of the narrator remains an enigma throughout both versions of the novel. (See also my in-depth analysis of this feature in my discussion of **AMIGOS** in part one, as well as my remarks on the treatment of languages in the same section.) Such is the effect of this ambiguity that it may actually foster diverging interpretations depending on the gender ascribed to the narrator by individual readers. More importantly, Hinojosa pulls off the feat of breaking up the male-female binary opposition within a book that carries an essentially feminist discourse.[3]

A similar phenomenon, which so far has escaped critical notice, can be observed in the treatment of language in Hinojosa's most recent duo texts **FRIENDS/AMIGOS**. In the early books **ESTAMPAS, CONDADO,** and **RAFA,** the Chicanos spoke predominantly Spanish. Later their Spanish was rendered through English in **VALLEY, KLAIL,** and **RAFE.** The texts themselves never left a doubt as to which were the originals and which the translations, or renditions as Hinojosa prefers to call them. Now, with the latest duo, **FRIENDS/AMIGOS,** we are faced with a riddle similar to that of the androgynous narrator. Both books underscore the fact that all interviewees are bicultural and bilingual borderers. Indeed, when reading the testimonies of Anglos and Chicanos in both novels side-by-side, it appears that they may actually be speaking in either language, depending on which novel one is reading. Here, Hinojosa has broken up the Spanish-English binary upon which the majority-minority discourse has traditionally been structured.

The pattern continues in his latest work, *Ask a Policeman,* the 1998 sequel to his 1985 mystery, *Partners in Crime.* In **POLICEMAN,** notions of ethnic identity are challenged through a number of contextual strategies. Anglo policemen, raised on the border, make funny asides in fluent Spanish; that is, the showcasing of Hispanic culture as a quintessentially Chicano domain—representing the "Other" from an Anglo perspective—is inverted in a number of passages. And perhaps the most striking occurrence is when Noddy Perkins, the mastermind of the KBC-ranch-and-banking empire, asks his son-in-law Rafa to bury him in the Mexican cemetery on the land of the Buenrostros. This is a tall order, considering the KBC history of landgrabbing and the KBC's alleged involvement in the assassination of Rafa's father, Don Jesús Buenrostro. Rafa, however, takes it in stride.

Unquestionably, race relations in Belken County are undergoing an evolution. Hinojosa's protagonist in the recent books is a Chicano community that no longer considers the Anglos the dominant group. Valley Texans may be bilingual and bicultural regardless of their ethnicity. Obviously, Hinojosa's recent work suggests that gender, ethnicity, and language are issues that must be addressed. And yet at the same time, Hinojosa aptly instrumentalizes the individual discourses in order to deconstruct programmatic notions of ethnicity while charting his own, more conciliatory and integrative vision of diversity and multiculturalism. And here, I do in fact see an opening for a possible postmodernist reading of the *KCDTS*. As the black feminist critic, bell hooks, has pointed out in the context of the black liberation struggle, postmodernism may actually contribute to critical scholarship about difference and "Otherness" by pushing the boundaries of class, race, and gender:

> The overall impact of postmodernism is that many other groups now share with black folks a sense of deep alienation, despair, uncertainty, loss of sense of grounding even if it is not informed by shared circumstance. (hooks 1993:514)

In his recent books, Hinojosa offers an alternative vision to current essentialist concepts of ethnicity; a vision that corresponds to bell hooks's postmodernist critique of outmoded notions of identity. Thus, there is hardly a better statement to conclude this chapter with than bell hooks's pledge for a radical postmodernism that "calls attention to *those* shared sensibilities *which cross the boundaries of class, gender, race*, etc., that could be fertile ground for the construction of empathy—ties that would promote recognition of common commitments, and serve as a base for solidarity and coalition" (1993:514, my emphasis).

PART THREE

"Fooling Around with Time and Space"

THE fundamental objective of this study is to show that despite its fragmented nature, Hinojosa's work is a constructive project striving for cultural restoration and revision of historiography. Part one and part two were concerned with the disintegrated, fragmented, multigeneric nature of Hinojosa's opus. Conversely, the latter half of my study proposes to consider the totality of Hinojosa's production and to read the *KCDTS* as one unitary, integrated text. To this end I have divided my discussion into part three and part four. Part three will lay the theoretical groundwork for a successful exploration of the text as one extensive, continuing novel while part four will constitute the actual close reading of the *KCDTS* as *one* text consisting of four fragmented sections.

In a first step, we will take a closer look at the way in which Hinojosa uses the portrayal of an operative oral society to counteract the eroding influence of contemporary culture. Subsequently, I propose to employ Juan Bruce-Novoa's topological paradigm as a model of analysis that will allow us to explore the constructive power of Hinojosa's writing technique (Bruce-Novoa 1990b:155). Finally, before moving on to the actual reconstruction of the four scattered sections of the *KCDTS* in part four, I will explain how the study of Faulkner's *The Sound and the Fury* prompted me to read the *KCDTS* as a tale told from four different viewpoints.

18

THE DEATH TRIP

A Quest for Life

IN recent years, the portrayal of oral cultures in modern literary texts has attracted extensive scholarship for its use as a vehicle of cultural criticism. In 1990, the interdisciplinary research project based in Freiburg, Germany, *Script Oralia,* published a collection of articles entitled *Mündliches Wissen in neuzeitlicher Literatur.* Editor Paul Goetsch, who in the preface describes the main focus of the studies as "areas of conflict and transition between orality and literacy" ["Spannungsfelder und Übergänge zwischen Mündlichkeit und Schriftlichkeit"] (Goetsch 1990:7) comes to conclusions that will serve as guides in my subsequent reading of the *KCDTS* as a cultural topology of oral traditions.

According to Goetsch, oral knowledge—as opposed to literate knowledge—may be used in literature to symbolize the polarity between remembering and forgetting, and by extension—between life and death. In literary representation, a healthily functioning oral culture may be juxtaposed to one where oral interaction is suffering breakdowns. Therefore, in a context of cultural criticism, Rolando Hinojosa's death trip must ultimately be understood as a quest for life in the face of constant impending danger to the Chicano cultural identity. The fictional world of the Series charts a culture of proximity and closeness, a largely unalienated, homogeneous society. The menace of alienation, of forgetting, of speechlessness and—ultimately—of death, is combated by staunchly clinging to a way of life that stands for intimacy, telling, remembering, and thus, persevering.

The fictional Belken County oral memory, though it may suffer an occasional breakdown, is safely stored by the chroniclers of the *KCDTS*. These chroniclers perform their service to the community in that troublesome transitional period each minority culture is bound to go through on its path to integration. The oldest of the chroniclers, the venerable *anciano*, Esteban Echevarría, belongs to the first generation of Texas Mexicans who were born as U.S. citizens after Texas was admitted into the Union in 1845. In a way, his birth marks the birth of a minority, the beginning of its subjugated existence, the gradual demise of the ranch society, the loss of land, and the impending disappearance of the culture along with its language.

Echevarría's death, as reported by Rafa in **VARONES** (166), would signify the end of the death trip, resulting in the death of the Chicano culture, were it not for the new generation of chroniclers like Jehú and Rafa. In Rolando Hinojosa's fictional South Texas world, they are models for a new class of young Chicanos whose ethnic self-assertiveness prepares the ground for their successful integration into mainstream U.S. society as upwardly mobile professionals, without renouncing, subduing, or even soft-pedaling their Mexicanness. They are at ease with their ethnicity, fluent and literate in Spanish, and while theirs is a contemporary, all-American success story, they appear to draw their strength to prevail from the rich sources of Chicano culture. As we shall see, the better part of the Belken County reality is conveyed to us through the filter of Jehú and Rafa's remarkably auspicious perspectives.

Below, I will delineate Bruce-Novoa's reading of a *KCDTS* text that testifies to this optimistic and prophetic vision. Subsequently, I will appropriate his model of analysis that compellingly demonstrates how Hinojosa's Belken County microcosm operates as a world of "ordering experience" (Bruce-Novoa 1990b:152).

19

THE CHARTING OF CHICANO LITERATURE

IN his 1990 article "The Topological Space of Chicano Literature," Juan Bruce-Novoa expressed his discomfort with the still-prevailing practice of pigeonholing Chicano writing exclusively as a protest literature. At the peak of the excitement that came with the Chicano Movement, the relationships between works within the new field of Chicano literature were largely defined in terms of ideology:

> Up to the mid-seventies, attempts to characterize Chicano literature were narrowly, but vaguely topographic. That is, they described individual works superficially, hardly ever entering into detailed analysis. Efforts to relate works on a broader spectrum usually took the form of attributing to them a radically anti-establishment political ideology. Yet, careful reading raised doubts as to the validity of that claim. (Bruce-Novoa 1990b:147)

In order to overcome the difficulties in accurately describing Chicano literature beyond mere notions of shared ethnicity and a common sociopolitical predicament, Bruce-Novoa suggested the application of topological parameters in the investigation of "Chicano literature as a space to be charted through successive mappings of the works in constant and dynamic relation" (Bruce-Novoa 1990b:146). "Topology," Bruce-Novoa explains, has a double meaning. First, in its more general usage, it is largely synonymous with topography, i.e., the accurate and detailed description of a place, or any entity such as a system, the mind, or a particular discipline. Second, topology as a mathematical discipline studies those properties of geometric figures that remain unchanged even when under distortion.

The first of the two concepts was introduced by Bruce-Novoa as early as 1974 (see Bruce-Novoa 1990a:93). Since then, various attempts at precise description, classification, and charting of Chicano literature have been undertaken in a notable number of publications. However, the second proposal constitutes one of the more recent and innovative approaches and—as we will see shortly—may prove extremely useful when applied to the extensive corpus of Rolando Hinojosa's oeuvre. Following George Steiner's observations in "Topologies of Culture" (Steiner in Bruce-Novoa 1990b:147), Bruce-Novoa stresses the usefulness of topological parameters for the understanding of literature. Similar to certain invariant, constant properties that survive distortion in geometric figures, the manifold shapes of literary expression may actually be understood as "a sequence of translations and transformations of constants."

In order to demonstrate the usefulness of Steiner's cultural topology when applied to literature, Bruce-Novoa traces the recurrent motif of the farm worker through a variety of works in Chicano literature (see Bruce-Novoa 1990b:149–52). He concludes that a topological study "not only discloses common elements, but reveals the differences present from author to author, work to work." Furthermore, his analyses of some of the Chicano classics reveal "that at the surface level of content the following situation was consistently repeated: some element, with a key orienting function for the Chicano community, was threatened with disappearance." Bruce-Novoa goes on to furnish a brief list of works that fit the above diagnosis. He shows how the Chicano realities portrayed in these texts are on the brink of a potential breakdown because certain ordering, unifying central elements of the culture are at risk of being lost. He contends that

> whatever the form, it functioned like a traditional *axis mundi*: it created the sense of cosmos by ordering experience. Its loss, which could appear anywhere in the text's diachronic development, would throw the community into the opposite state, that of chaos. (Bruce-Novoa 1990b:152)

In all the examined works, he found what he called a "topological constant in the form of a deep structure." The threat to one of the community's central elements is opposed in the narrative by recalling, and thus salvaging, the chief characteristics of the endangered element.

This charted paradigm, used by Bruce-Novoa to represent the abstract concept, turns out to be particularly useful because apart from illustrating the pattern of the process, it also reflects its dynamic tension (Bruce-Novoa 1990b:153):

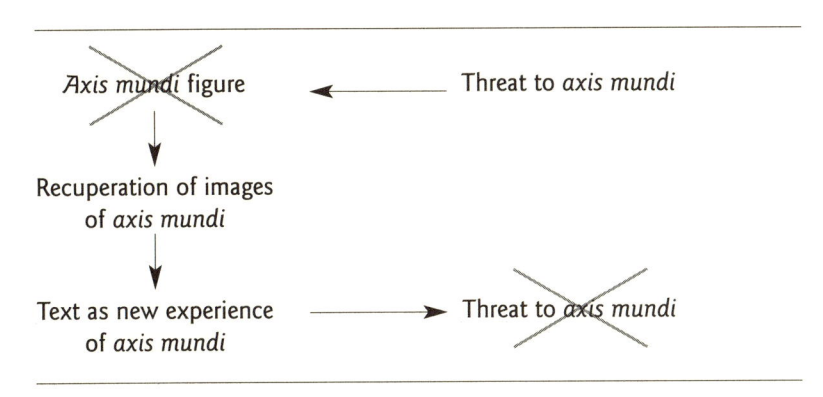

```
A̶x̶i̶s̶ ̶m̶u̶n̶d̶i̶ figure    ←————   Threat to axis mundi
        ↓
Recuperation of images
     of axis mundi
        ↓
Text as new experience  ————→   Threat to a̶x̶i̶s̶ mundi
     of axis mundi
```

From the previously analyzed works, Bruce-Novoa then singled out Tomás Rivera's *. . . y no se lo tragó la tierra* (1971) and Rolando Hinojosa's *Estampas del Valle*, and subjected them to a close topological reading. In order to gain an understanding of Bruce-Novoa's topological paradigms that will subsequently guide us through the present chapter, it will suffice to follow his analysis of **ESTAMPAS**.

According to Bruce-Novoa, **ESTAMPAS** "begins with an identity loss that bodes ill for the community" (Bruce-Novoa 1990b:154). In the book's first sketch, "Braulio Tapia," the initially unidentifiable first person narrator who much later will be revealed as Jehú Vilches receives Roque Malacara, the suitor of his daughter Teresa, at his house. Roque has come to ask for Tere's hand in marriage. Jehú Vilches, facing Roque on the porch, is reminded of himself as a young man, standing on the porch of his father-in-law, Braulio Tapia, asking for the hand of Matilde. As Jehú Vilches asks Roque inside, he is painfully reminded of the fact that both he and Braulio were already widowers at the time their daughters got married. This chain of associations is implicitly continued by the question that closes the sketch, "¿A quién vería don Braulio en el umbral cuando él pidió a su esposa?" ["Who did don Braulio see when he walked up these steps to ask for **his** wife's hand?" (**VALLEY**:12, my bold)] (**ESTAMPAS**:26).

The question is not a marginal one. Jehú Vilches is Jehú Malacara's grandfather. At the heart of the issue is the protagonist's maternal lineage and his familial relationship with the other central character, Rafa Buenrostro. The family tree below illustrates what Jehú Vilches may, or may not, remember:

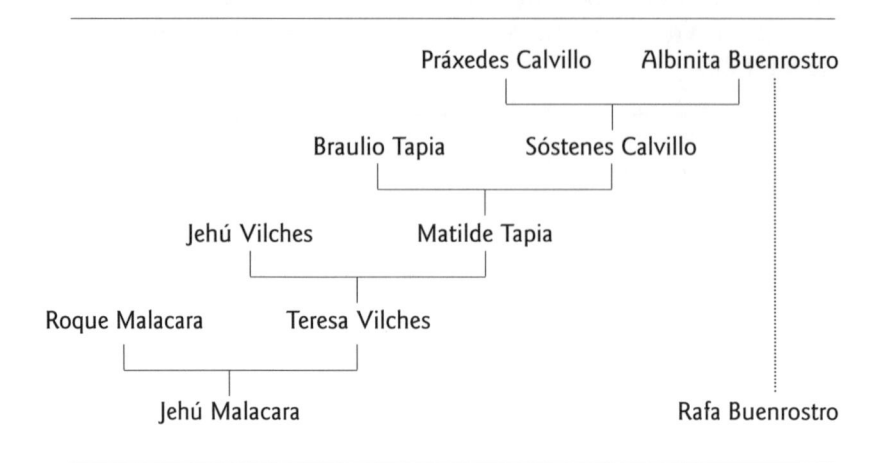

```
                              Práxedes Calvillo   Albinita Buenrostro
                              └─────────┬────────┘
                    Braulio Tapia   Sóstenes Calvillo
                    └────────┬───────┘
         Jehú Vilches    Matilde Tapia
         └──────┬────────┘
  Roque Malacara   Teresa Vilches
  └───────┬────────┘
      Jehú Malacara                              Rafa Buenrostro
```

The fact that Jehú Vilches's question is answered at a much later point in the book and in a completely different context (see **ESTAMPAS**:92), is considered by Bruce-Novoa an affirmation of the text's salvaging of the threatened element. This, in turn, proves the validity of his topological paradigm:

> A young man has come to ask an older one for the latter's daughter's hand in marriage. This simple action assumes ritual status when the older man recalls that he had come in the same manner to do the same thing. Continued observance of a traditional ritual proves the health of communal customs. However, when the old man wonders whom his father-in-law dealt with when he played the suitor's role, we glimpse a potential breakdown in the oral tradition, a ritual as central to communal health as betrothal. As the reading progresses, and we realize that at the heart of the testimony-like conversations making up the text lies the matter of genealogies, the original question assumes the significance of primal mystery. It must be answered. The text proceeds to enact numerous oral performances, creating for the reader the role of traditional youth, that is, a listener/rememberer, a future storehouse of tradition. And since in South Texas, of which this and all of Hinojosa's subsequent novels treat, genealogies are often the way one distinguishes between those to be trusted and those who have

99 : The Charting of Chicano Literature

sold out to the Anglo Americans, the information gathered is of vital importance to communal preservation. Answering the first question symbolizes the community's ability to protect itself from further betrayal and displacement. (Bruce-Novoa 1990b:155)

Sense of place is a pervasive theme in Hinojosa's books. He has reiterated time and again that sense of place rests on familiarity with the people who populate the place and how they are related. Hence, one ordering force (*axis mundi*) in the Belken County microcosm is the knowledge of genealogy. Oral performance and collective memory are the vehicles that carry this knowledge, which in turn secures the community order. The texts of the *KCDTS* act out the successful transmission of genealogical information, as long as the reader participates in the completion of the oral rituals. Bruce-Novoa's charted paradigm illustrates this process. The charted paradigm below is the first of a series that will appear in the subsequent chapters. I will insert such a chart whenever I consider it a helpful illustration of a particular deep structure in the Belken County Chicanos' traditional culture:

PARADIGM I:

~~Oral traditional ritual and genealogical community order~~ ← Breakdown of oral traditional ritual and fall into forgetfulness

↓

Recuperation of familial voices in oral performance

↓

Text as new ritual of information transmission and source for genealogical data → ~~Breakdown of oral traditional ritual and fall into forgetfulness~~

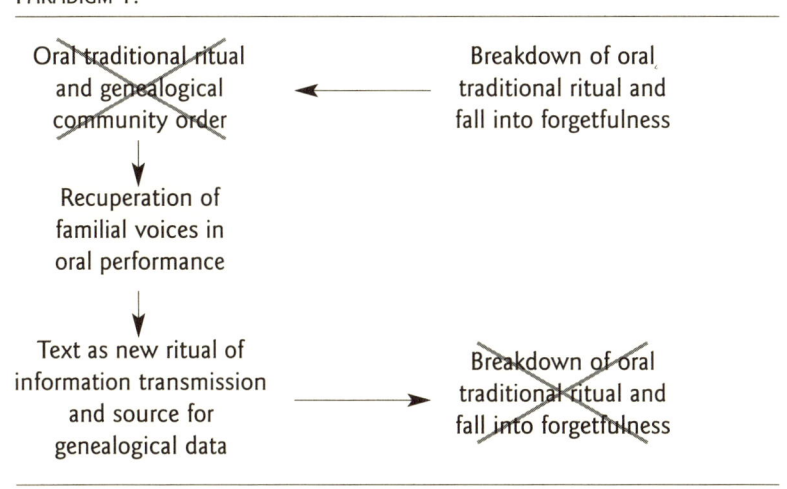

Bruce-Novoa's topological analysis, together with the charted paradigm as applied here to the passage from **ESTAMPAS**, succeeds in making visible a singular achievement in Hinojosa's fiction that has so far eluded the descriptive skills of Hinojosa scholars. Bruce-Novoa concludes that his topological analysis reveals how "Hinojosa *shows* the community healthily practicing its oral memory" (Bruce-Novoa 1990b:156, my italics). However, Hinojosa goes far beyond *showing,* beyond a mere didactic exemplification; he engages the reader to *take part* in the oral rituals. And Bruce-Novoa's model allows us to trace and make transparent the numerous instances of potential breakdown or gaps in the chain of interlocutory acts across the whole of the *KCDTS*—gaps and breakdowns that, ultimately, must be filled or restored by the reader.

The notion that the text invites the reader's active collaboration in the performance of traditional oral ritual, has been stated and explored elsewhere (see Martín Rodríguez 1993a). The novelty here lies in the fact that the charted paradigm provides us with an effective tool for the investigation of deep-structure topological patterns across an extensive body of texts. This usefulness, which Bruce-Novoa has demonstrated in an example from **ESTAMPAS**, will prove even more pertinent when applied to other examples of oral ritual that are not necessarily initiated and completed within one serial text, but rather—as is wont to occur in Hinojosa's books—are spread out across several volumes. At the same time, the charted paradigm affords a visual aid that will lay bare exactly how Hinojosa implements topological elements such as genealogy, segregation, dispossession, struggle over land, loss of cultural identity, and linguistic choices, to name a few. What is more, all these themes are presented along a diachronic continuum. Cultural, societal, and political configurations are subject to change, as recent entries in the *KCDTS* indicate: In other words, the constant elements of the Valley's bilingual/bicultural reality virtually call out for a perusal of their unchangeable properties under the distorting forces of historical change.

In a close union with the topological exploration, I propose to demonstrate that in spite of the text's fragmented, disjointed appearance, the *KCDTS* maintains the narrative cohesion of a novel in installments thanks to its consistent plots and characters. As we shall see presently, additional cohesion and transparency can be achieved by reconstructing the fragmented text in a way that echoes the structure of William Faulkner's *The Sound and the Fury.*

20
A FAULKNERIAN LEGACY

CRITICS seldom fail to mention the parallel between Belken County and Faulkner's Yoknapatawpha (and, of course Márquez's Macondo) and the fact that both are thinly disguised versions of Hinojosa's Hidalgo County and Faulkner's Lafayette. Mark Busby's 1984 article, "Faulknerian Elements in Rolando Hinojosa's *The Valley*," all but exhausts the subject by drawing attention to the use of mythical counties and the strong factual sense of place in the works of both authors. Furthermore, Busby points out the historical dimension of the Civil War in the work of the Mississippian that he equates to references to the Mexican Revolution in the *KCDTS*. In both oeuvres, the motifs of military strife and bloodshed invariably resonate with the poignancy of endurance in the face of hardship and misery. Busby also launches into a brief exploration of the use of humor, and he highlights the similarity of techniques in the portrayal of certain characters. And finally, the critic finds that there is a common tendency to shun traditional novelistic practices of carefully unraveling the plot in a chronological narrative told from a consistent point of view. It is this last feature that I appropriate and apply in a very specific sense of my own in order to organize my discussion of the large disjointed textual body of the *KCDTS*.

In his 1929 masterpiece *The Sound and the Fury*, William Faulkner tells the story of the Compson family, dividing his narrative into four sections, each controlled by a different narrative voice. What is more, throughout the book, but especially within the first two sections, Faulkner radically departs from the practice of chronological narration. Rather, the Benjy section reflects its narrator's distinctive mode of perceiving past and present as one, ordering memories not according to chronology but based on the associative powers of sensual perception. While Benjy has no notion of time, his brother Quentin is obsessed with it. His account is so thoroughly dominated by his alienation from present realities, that it is almost as confounding as Benjy's. Still, one feels that from each section to the next, Faulkner seemed increasingly inclined to reward the hard-taxed reader with a slightly less demanding, more transparent textual conception. Indeed, to the reader who has managed to labor through the puzzling stream-of-consciousness style in the Benjy and the Quentin sections, the interior rantings of the niggardly, embittered Jason Compson come almost as a relief in terms of textual coherence. The persevering reader has the gratifying experience of encountering in the final section (frequently referred to as the "Dilsey section," in spite of its being related by an Olympic narrator who does, however, implement the black servant's moral point of view) a direct description of the Compsons' gradual degeneration from their lofty position in the grand old Southern Aristocracy. At this point (or perhaps after reading the appendix added by Faulkner in 1946), any reader not completely callused against this impassioned quest for complete and utter writerly penetration of the true story of the American South, will have to turn back for a second, more informed, reading. Similarly, Hinojosa's chronicle of the South Texas Río Grande Valley requires readers to invest a significant amount of patience and effort.

Although the inner workings of confused, troubled, or mean minds are evidently not at the center of Hinojosa's particular literary quest, any one of the installments of the *KCDTS* leaves the reader with sensations akin to those produced by a first reading of *The Sound and the Fury*. Closer examination confirms that generic experimentation is clearly not motivated by an eagerness to dazzle with contrived artistic originality. Put in the words of Jean Paul Sartre, "It would be a mistake to regard these irregularities as gratuitous exercises in virtuosity" (1987:253). Rather, they reflect an arduous struggle for new forms of authentic expression that may come to grips with the universal themes emanating from their respective regional *sujets*.[1]

In a 1978 interview with Bruce-Novoa, Hinojosa—always laconic when speaking of his accomplishments—dismissed the notion of generic originality: "*Estampas* is a novel and that's it. There's a bit of fooling around with time and space, but the plots are there" (Bruce-Novoa 1978:110). I write the following chapters on Jehú Malacara, Rafa Buenrostro, Esteban Echevarría, and P. Galindo to shed some light on how exactly Hinojosa *fools around with time and space*.

PART FOUR

The Four Sections of the
Klail City Death Trip Series

WHILE Faulkner used new forms of expression in order to take us into the confusing labyrinth of the Compson brothers' mental processes, Hinojosa employs his generic experiments to recreate the interlocutory practices of a vigorously functioning oral society. However, both writers have opted for a similar solution to lend unity to their seemingly disjointed, fragmented narrative through a restricted succession of central narrational authorities. In *The Sound and the Fury,* these authorities dominate and direct each of four clearly demarcated blocks of narrative. The innocent, neuter Benjy; the repressed, obsessive Quentin; the vicious, resentful Jason; and the imperviously upright Dilsey, each tells the same story from their particular attitudinal perspective (with Dilsey's filtered through the implied author's viewpoint).

In much the same way, the four narrators of the *KCDTS* also constitute unifying forces in an extremely fragmented narrative. Rafa Buenrostro, Jehú Malacara, Esteban Echevarría, and P. Galindo (*the writer,* who is eventually replaced by a close relative, the nameless androgynous *listener*) share in the telling of a common story. And, like the Compsons, they can be distinguished by their attitudes toward life, which will lend individuality to their respective accounts of the Belken County chronicle. Guillermo Hernández has already adequately characterized Jehú as "an extrovert who is resourceful, ironic, and controversial, while Rafa, an introvert, has a balanced, endearing, and gracious personality" (Hernández 1991:99).

The old-timer Echevarría, who most critics agree personifies the collective memory of the South Texas Chicano community, is portrayed in the early novels as a mixture of respected sage and belligerent old drunk with a propensity to wildly hold forth against Anglo oppression and Chicano inertia in front of half-intrigued, half-scornful cantina audiences. Over the years, Echevarría's drunken rage over the injustices inflicted on *la raza* is replaced by gloomy temperance after witnessing the gradual disappearance of the Valley culture of which he has been a part from the beginning. After his death, foreshadowed by his jeremiads at the end of **VARONES**, other members of his generation fill his place, although always as poor substitutes for a man who "could tell you everything. Todo. From A to Z. Yes" (**FRIENDS**:48).

Unlike Jehú and Rafa, Echevarría and P. Galindo are of minor importance as characters in the unfolding of the plot. Yet, as narrational authorities, they add historical depth and sociological breadth to the fictional setting of the chronicle. And while Echevarría's is a virtually unwitting contribution, Galindo betrays an uncanny awareness of the fictional project he is involved in.[1] In an interesting narrational maneuver, Hinojosa places Galindo at a metafictional point where he is at the same time inside the fictional Belken County world and in the real-life world of Chicano letters. He associates with *KCDTS* characters and actual nonfictional people alike, thus functioning as a mediator between the Belken County community and the *KCDTS* readership. In dispersed passages spread across the Series, he continually reiterates that his mission is the impartial, truthful recording of what Valleyites do and say, without passing judgment. His eagerness to salvage the oral knowledge of his community in order to define his sense of self and place (see **KLAIL**:55–56) reveals much of what Hinojosa's literary project is all about.

In 1986, the overdue fourth installment, *Claros Varones de Belken,* was published by Bilingual Press. Never before or thereafter has Hinojosa come closer to the Faulknerian model by ostensibly instrumentalizing his four narrators as structural guides in the narrative. In six specifically marked-off sections, Hinojosa assigns each of the four narrators his turn at the telling of the *KCDTS,* duly conceding two extra turns and twice the space to the protagonists Jehú and Rafa. Careful examination reveals that the surface structure of **VARONES** is actually identical to the deep structure of the entire Series. Any textual fragment in the *KCDTS* can be made to bear upon the particular narrational agenda of at least one of the four narrators/protagonists discussed above. This is not to say in any way that the Series was conceived or planned in sections. While careful planning must surely have been part of the composition, Hinojosa no more scrambled a prefabricated chronological text than Faulkner wrote a conventional version of *The Sound and the Fury* and then went and hacked it into little pieces in order for it to fit his aesthetic conception. We must imagine the process more like Faulkner described it in connection with the story he considered his "finest failure," which began with the image of children playing in the water and suddenly the entire story "seemed to explode on the paper before me." Nevertheless, the idea of the four sections of the *KCDTS* emerges as a useful stratagem on which to base a complex literary analysis of a large disjointed, multigeneric body of fiction. I therefore propose to read the complete text of the *KCDTS* as a narrative consisting of four *scattered* sections and to organize my discussion accordingly. Thus, in each of the chapters in part four, an initial step will consist of collecting the scattered information necessary to chart the characters' biographies. The reassembled biographies will then serve as a platform on which further analysis can be conducted with an enhanced degree of coherence and transparency.

The first section will have Jehú Malacara at its center. Starting out by sketching a reconstructed version of his exploits as a *pícaro*, I will seize the chance to chart the evolution of the picaresque novel and to discuss some of the current theories regarding that genre. A second, fragmented subplot relates to Jehú's rocky career at the KBC-controlled Klail City First National Bank, particularly his successful foiling of a KBC attempt to gobble up a large portion of Texas Mexican land. Owing to the extremely disjointed presentation of these events across several volumes, this stretch in the life of Jehú deserves a thorough examination before moving on to take a look at Jehú as husband, stepfather, and vice-president of the Bank.

21

JEHÚ MALACARA

A Moral Delinquent

THE genre of the picaresque novel, or romance of roguery, originated in sixteenth century Spain (see Heidenreich 1969; Parker 1967; Rosenthal 1983). Generally, the anonymously written *Lazarillo de Tormes* (1554) is considered the first picaroon (Span. *pícaro*), followed by Mateo Alemán's *Guzmán de Alfarache* (1599). Especially the latter became the model for a line of successors, establishing a tradition that, in Spain, reached its peak with Francisco de Quevedo Villegas's *La vida del buscón* (1626). In France, Alain René Lesage, the best known of the several translators of *Guzmán*, created his own rogue with *Gil Blas de Santillane*, whose adventures appeared in three volumes (1715, 1724, 1735). In England, a number of works took up the idea of the orphaned, transient rogue, among them Thomas Nashe's *The Unfortunate Traveller* (1694), Daniel Defoe's *Moll Flanders* (1722), and Henry Fielding's *Tom Jones* (1744). And incidentally, the first German picaresque novel and the last Spanish book of that genre have the same setting, namely the Thirty-Years War. Thus, in 1669, Grimmelshausen's *Der abentheuerliche Simplicissimus Teutsch* initiated a tradition in Germany that in Spain had already come to a close with *Estebanillo de González* in 1646.

In the course of four centuries, the picaresque novel has undergone considerable transformation, yet both the classical and the modern picaresque novel feature a (sometimes comic) anti-hero who journeys from one master to the next, "satirizing their personal faults, as well as their trades and professions" (Chandler quoted in Rosenthal 1983:13). While the classical

Spanish *pícaro* does not undergo any significant personal development, since he chiefly serves as a vehicle to denounce certain reprehensible traits of the respective society personified by his various masters, the modernist picaresque novels of American literature (e.g., Ralph Ellison's *Invisible Man* and Saul Bellow's *Augie March*) show the makings of the *Bildungsroman*. They portray the hero in the quest for his true self, while discrediting traditional roles and the values of the society he lives in. This quest is taken even further in American postmodernist literature (Thomas Pynchon's *Gravity's Rainbow,* John Barth's *Sot-Weed Factor*) that, at its most extreme, calls into question even the desirability of the concept of the true self. The postmodernist *pícaro,* having to choose from a multitude of positions, may experience "an increasing indifference towards his initial quest for the self resulting in a complete diffusion of identity" (Rosenthal 1983:152). Interestingly, both the classical and the postmodernist picaresque novel favor a lack of narrative conclusion and an open-ended plot, which sets them off from the above-mentioned modernist representatives of the genre, for whom at least the possibility of contentment looms at the end of their quest.

In light of the fact that the *KCDTS* is the brainchild of an author well-versed in both the Spanish- and the English-language literary traditions, it will prove advantageous to discuss Jehú's childhood wanderings against the backdrop of earlier picaresque heroes and to establish Jehú's position vis-à-vis his predecessors. As we shall see, the influence of medieval Spanish literature in particular had a palpable impact on the drawing of the Jehú Malacara character.

Orphaned and on the Road

Jehú's story starts before his birth, and so does the *estampa,* "Braulio Tapia," which in fact inaugurates the *KCDTS*. A number of critics have singled out this particular sketch since it lends itself well to scholarly explorations of Hinojosa's principal discourses. Aside from scholars Bruce-Novoa and Hernández (whose readings of "Braulio Tapia" were discussed on the foregoing pages), another prominent Chicano critic, Luís Leal, has analyzed "Braulio Tapia" and highlighted it as an example of how in Hinojosa's fiction "present action brings to mind the past" (Leal 1984:103).

In Leal's interpretation, Jehú's memory initially goes no further than two generations into his family's past, but eventually he retrieves the complete genealogy of the Tapia family and charts it in the fragment "Los revolucionarios" (**ESTAMPAS**:92). What is more, Jehú now displays detailed knowledge not solely of his own family history, but also the histories of all the elderly in his barrio and their participation in historical events. Thus, Jehú really represents the young Chicano gradually discovering "a historical conscious of a regional society that has not had the fortune of having a written history" (Leal 1984:104). It is this gradual awakening and commitment to his calling as one of the Belken County chroniclers that will be at the center of the following exploration of Jehú Malacara's picaresque journey.

However, an incision must be made in order to touch upon a problematic point in the Tapia family genealogy. If we are to believe the chronicler of "Los revolucionarios," Braulio Tapia was born in August 1883 and married in 1910 (**ESTAMPAS**:92). Although Jehú Malacara's year of birth is nowhere mentioned, based on various snippets of evidence sprinkled over remote passages of the *KCDTS*, we can assume it to be around 1929 or 1930.[1] The problem that arises from these considerations is that Don Braulio is only fifty years older than his great-grandson Jehú Malacara, allowing a mere twenty years for three generations of progeny between Braulio's marriage in 1910 and Jehú's birth in 1930.

This example is only one in a series of discrepancies in Jehú's and Rafa's genealogies. In the course of this discussion, further inconsistencies will emerge that must ultimately be attributed to a lack of precision in oral traditions or to the unreliability of the narrators.

It is in the third sketch of **ESTAMPAS/VALLEY** that the character Jehú Malacara is mentioned for the first time. Roque Malacara remembers how his late father-in-law, Jehú Vilches, used to go fishing with his grandson. The fish the two were after were the "sly Río Grande gray-cat" and "each had the patience to bait and hook the trickster feeding in the tules" (**VALLEY**:14). Clearly, at age seven, Jehú is already the cunning, resourceful image of his grandfather.

Jehú's mischievous disposition comes to bear in typical fashion on his facetious account of his relatives, the Briones family. The *estampa*, "Mis primos" (**ESTAMPAS**:31), is illustrative of one major difference between Hinojosa's original Spanish-language texts and their renditions (here the corresponding sketch, "About Those Relatives of Mine" in **VALLEY** [18]). In this piece, Jehú paints a vivid picture of an idiosyncratic Hispanic custom: the giving and changing of colorful sobriquets [see also **VARONES** (213) and **RAFA** (14)]. The English version is considerably longer and wordier, because it has to fill in some details of the cultural background that are known by a reader literate in Spanish. The significance, for example, of cousin Pepe's nickname, *El Mión,* is immediately apparent in Spanish, and even though Hinojosa translated it into Wet Pants and inserted two explanatory paragraphs in the sketch's English version, somehow it does not quite seem to render the dry humor of the Spanish original.[2]

Curiously, there is a marked dichotomy between the comical tone of the piece and the significance of the events narrated there. The Briones family history has a direct bearing on the preceding piece "Huérfano y al pairo," where we learn that the deaths of Jehú's parents occurred in short succession. For even as Jehú pokes fun at the antics of his Aunt Chedes, his Uncle Juan, and their offspring, he sketches in deft, economical strokes the dissolving of the family that might have taken him in after the death of his parents. Hinojosa establishes the link between the two fragments through common thematic elements: Aunt Chedes's temper tantrum and the presence of a traveling carny troupe in town. Both Jehú and his cousin Vicky leave Klail City after joining up with the circus people, and both provoke one of Chedes's frequent fits—albeit for different reasons. While Chedes is dismayed at her daughter's decision to join the circus, she seems equally dismayed at the prospect of having to take charge of the orphaned Jehú. Thus, upon regaining her composure, she performs on her nephew an astounding, magic ritual:

> The house was quiet, and she hadn't said a word in about five minutes. Placing the glass on the ironing board, she dipped that middle finger in the cold water, made the sign of the cross in the air and then on my forehead: Drink this, she said, drink this whole glass of water, Jehú. All of it, now, and don't stop till you do. While you're doing that, I'm going to say an Our Father backwards for today's the day you're to meet your new Pa.
>
> I looked at her, but she wouldn't start until I started to drink. Standing there, mouth agape, I didn't know what to do, but—just in case—'cause you never can tell, I took the glass and began to drink as she half-hummed, half-sung out: Amen, evil from us deliver and . . .
> (VALLEY:16)

This is the crucial point in his life that marks the start of his journey as an orphan. Jehú intuitively recognizes the subtle rejection intimated in the odd procedure. And although he is perplexed by the unlikely ritual that combines superstitious folklore with the Lord's Prayer, at age seven he takes his life into his own hands and, as prophesied by Chedes, meets his new father in the person of Don Víctor Peláez, proprietor of the Peláez Tent Show and veteran of the Mexican Revolution.[3]

As Elaine Dorough-Johnson has pointed out in her exhaustive thematic study of *Estampas del Valle,* the picaresque elements emerging in Jehú's biography include the orphaning (factual and spiritual), the theme of the journey, and a narrative in the form of an episodic (auto-)biography (Dorough-Johnson 1978:72). Indeed, we encounter Jehú and Don Víctor for the first time together in the sketch entitled "On the Road: Hard Luck, Hard Times." Jehú, in the typically transient position of the *pícaro,* acquires new skills, like changing a tire, pitching a circus tent, acrobatics, advertising the show, and—most importantly—reading (**VALLEY**:21, 24, 25, 27). Part of this is told in the form of an autobiography, while in some instances a third person narrator steps behind Jehú and tells the story from his removed point of view, thus achieving some distance in the narration (**VALLEY**:23, 24, 25).

The classical picaroon soon finds out, "first, that no help is to be obtained from one's fellow-men and that the only course to pursue is selfishly to look after one's own interests; and secondly, that what rules in society is hypocrisy" (Parker 1967:29). In contrast, Jehú's first master, Don Víctor, is a benevolent man for whom Jehú has only esteem and affection. Each is anxious that the other not hurt himself while changing a flat tire, and when Don Víctor dies in the town of Flora, Jehú is disconsolate ("I broke down and cried about as much as when Ma died, and just as heartfelt" [**VALLEY**:33]). Attended by the members of two other carny troupes, Víctor's funeral becomes a grand affair. As we shall see presently, this event will serve as another transitional element leading over to the events portrayed in the subsequent *estampas.*

Flora, which is introduced in the next sketch so entitled, will crop up all over the *KCDTS* as a city of fools and rogues, much like the English village of Gotham, or the German city of Schilda. But while the tricks of the Gothamite and the *Schildbürger* in the end turn out to be directed at themselves, the Flora Mexicanos now and then manage to pull a trick on someone who had it coming, as it were. The victim, for example, in the prank related in the final story of the Jehú section entitled "Bruno Cano: Lock, Stock, and Bbl [*sic;* "Bible" instead of "barrel"]" is Don Pedro Zamudio, a fine specimen of the hypocritical clergyman, that ubiquitous stock character of picaresque fiction (see **VALLEY**:35; or "Al pozo con Bruno Cano," **ESTAMPAS**:46).

After virtually causing, and explicitly welcoming, the death of Bruno Cano, Don Pedro refuses to give Bruno Cano a Christian burial (see **VALLEY**:35). In my exposition of **KLAIL**, I provide a shortened account of how the Belken County people exploit the Bruno Cano incident in order to teach their despotic priest a lesson in humility, who at least momentarily has to succumb to "the people's latent capacity to prevail over entrenched authorities, antagonistic to their interests" (Dorough-Johnson 1978:28).

Jehú's involvement in this episode is not revealed until **CONDADO** (45; **KLAIL**:79) where we learn that he is the same acolyte who narrates the Bruno Cano incident. Eventually Jehú tops it off with a piece of roguery of his own that will send Don Pedro's temper over the edge and Jehú running to catch up with his new master "El hermano Imás" ["Brother Imás"].[4]

This change of masters is significant in a number of respects, the most striking one being the fact that Jehú trades Catholicism for Protestantism in a traditionally Catholic Mexican community, a lasting decision as we shall see. (For more details on the Flora Protestant community, Jehú's religious convictions, and his stint as a Baptist pastor in the Flora mission see **VARONES**:67–75.) The point here is that Jehú does not care what creed his master belongs to and that nontraditional and unconventional experiences may very well signify a turn for the better. And indeed, after leaving the tyrannical, uncompassionate Catholic priest, things improve for Jehú.[5] His new master is a gentle, caring man who acts on a genuine calling. His funny Spanish and his colorful background make him a bizarre outsider in the Valley. He shares his oranges and the profits from his Bible sales with Jehú, who in return offers his knowledge of the Valley:

> Now here, in Belken County, it's too hot for door-to-door selling, as I told him. You've got to get folks in a crowd, bunched up, see, like on Sundays when they come in for the groceries and such. So, after my spiel, I'd step down and hawk the stuff face-to-face. (**KLAIL**:99, compare **CONDADO**:123)

In his sales pitch, Jehú can apply the skills acquired as a barker for Don Víctor's carny troupe: "Jehú Malacara shows himself a master of that skill so highly prized in oral culture: verbal improvisation. He compensates for his lack of familiarity with the Bible, for example, through frequent, random biblical quotations, which he quickly weaves into the flow of his sales pitch, bending and breaking their meaning without hesitation" (Broyles 1984:116). The following sample is significant in that it showcases Jehú's improvisational verve and his lack of respect for scripture and for his customers. Much later in **RITES** (32), when Noddy Perkins is making arrangements to use Jehú for politics, his aptitude as "a good speaker; a preacher almost" is considered especially valuable:

> Repito: el idioma no importa. Lo que importa es el gesto, gente, el gesto

y el rasgo y no la mera traducción que la providencia perpetua proviene para nosotros por puentes largos y angostos y si no, ahí está la respuesta de Job a Eliphaz: 'No eye shall see me. And he puts a veil over his face. He digs through houses in the darkness.' Permítanme traducir: El ojo (eye) que mire (see) pondrá (puts) buena cara (face) a las casas (houses) que tengan este texto (darkness). (**CONDADO**:122–23)

[To repeat, it doesn't matter if it's in English; not at all. What *does* matter is the *act;* the act, the grand gesture, *not* the translation the Perpetual Providence Provides for us as we walk those-oh-so-long-and-narrow bridges to the ETERNAL HELL, but why listen to *me?* Let me read what Job says to Eliphaz: 'No eye shall see me; And he puts a veil over his face. He digs through houses in the darkness.' Here, here, here allow me to translate: "El ojo (eye) que mire (that sees) pondrá (will put) buena cara (a good face) a las casas (to the houses) que tengan este texto (of darkness)."] (**KLAIL**:98)

Jehú's rather liberal translation is not entirely innocent from the point of view of the trusting customers. The cryptic Job quote takes on a much more purposeful meaning in Jehú's Spanish version: "The eye that watches over you will look favorably upon those houses that possess this text" (my translation). Alexander Parker, in his book *Literature and the Delinquent*, discusses the etymology of the word *pícaro* and contends that the term "delinquency" is the key to defining the genre of the picaresque:

> Philologists are still not agreed on the etymology of *pícaro*. The word is first documented in 1525 with the sense of 'kitchen boy,' but twenty years later it already meant 'evil living.' The first Dictionary of the Spanish Academy in 1726, which reflects the usage of the seventeenth century, defines the *pícaro* as 'low, vicious, deceitful, dishonorable and shameless.' . . . 'Rogue' seems to me now quite inadequate as an equivalent for this; I prefer the term 'delinquent' as being the word that in current usage best expresses the *pícaro* of Spanish seventeenth-century literature. By this I mean an offender against the moral and civil laws; not a vicious criminal such as a gangster or a murderer, but some one who is dishonorable and anti-social in a much less violent way. (Parker 1967:4)

Ironically, the character of Jehú Malacara pinpoints both the merits and the shortcomings of Parker's definition. Jehú is indeed an offender against the moral laws, and—less frequently—against the civil laws. In most of the later novels, Jehú's constant womanizing becomes a consistent motif that serves to depict intimacy across racial and social lines and disrespect toward the latent laws of racial segregation. A similar purpose is served when Jehú, in **RAFA/RAFE**, is caught in a dubious land deal that is antagonistic to the interests of the Bank Jehú works for. Seen in a historical perspective, however, Jehú's machinations are nothing compared to two centuries of Anglo landgrabbing.

The two examples above already hint at the shortcomings of Parker's classification. While Jehú really does disrespect moral and civil laws, he is never actually "dishonorable and anti-social," not even in a "less violent way." On the contrary, Jehú always displays a keen sense of justice, fairness, and loyalty. The parameters of civility and morality in Belken County are obviously not identical with Jehú's, which is why he craftily undermines those laws, and why—much like Huckleberry Finn—Jehú Malacara is a moral delinquent, to coin a phrase, and a true picaroon after his own fashion. Jehú's particular brand of delinquency will serve as a yardstick in defining Jehú's position in the lineup of picaroons and rogues and will shed more light on his biography as we proceed.

Probably the foremost roguish feature of Jehú is his way of telling his own and other people's stories. The details he chooses to relate are more often than not aimed at bringing out the facetious, the droll, and the bizarre. The way his cousins earn their nicknames and later turn the embarrassment into a source of pride ("About Those Relatives of Mine" [**VALLEY**:18–19]), his gleeful, but nonetheless loving description of the amateurish Peláez Tent Show (**VALLEY**:15, 26), or the mirthfully depicted funeral scene in "Bruno Cano" all prove that Jehú takes a humorous, yet always sympathetic, view of his fellow Texas Mexicanos.

The first occasion on which actual fault can be found in his behavior is his negligence with respect to Bruno Cano's hole, which results in an accident and induces Jehú to skip town. While this is a rather harmless incident, his hawking Lutheran Bibles in English to Catholic Mexicanos is not,[6] and it is the first in a sporadic line of more severe instances of delinquency. Jehú, however, soothes his conscience by the fact that the Bibles were "good quality" and at a "fair price" (**KLAIL**:99).

After Brother Imás is attacked by a rattlesnake, Jehú once again loses a surrogate father, though luckily, the dramatic events following the preacher's mishap do not end with one of Hinojosa's frequent funerals. The snakebite is referred to on numerous occasions across the Series. In **RAFA** (83), for example, Rufino Fischer Gutiérrez shows P. Galindo the field where it happened. The episode, related in **VARONES** (77–83), explores a side of Jehú that is of the utmost relevance for the characterization of this *pícaro* and his relationship with his masters as it highlights Jehú's devotion to Brother Imás when the boy—previously described as uncommonly ophiophobic—snatches the rattler away from the preacher's leg, strangles it, and stomps on its head until he is dragged away by farm workers. While the preacher is recovering from the amputation of his leg in the hospital, the badly shaken Jehú is trying to rid himself of the sickening sensation of the hateful reptile in his hands. For eight days, Jehú is incapable of touching any sort of food. Finally, he is taken to the preacher's house in the hope that Imás will know what's best for the boy. What happens next has a twofold significance with respect to the relationship between Imás and Jehú. First, the still ailing preacher expresses his deep affection for his acolyte when he tenderly washes Jehú's hands; and second, he demonstrates his acute insight into human nature in general and Jehú's in particular by telling the boy that the cleansing and the prayers won't take effect unless Jehú continues his fast for another forty-eight hours. And just as Imás had foreseen it, Jehú's unruly nature immediately begins to rebel.

> el Hermano bien sabía que Jehú—al ponerle la rienda de no comer por cuarenta y ocho horas—ya le había pasado el susto. Las riendas ya las rompería Jehú por sí solo; el Hermano no sería un santo, no, pero conocía a Jehú mejor que nadie. También sabía que Jehú, desde que se habían conocido en Flora en aquella primera ocasión, tenía un miedo indecible a cualquier tipo de víbora. Andar Jehú con él cruzando zurcos y veredas a pesar de terror era algo que le podía al Hermano.
>   Cuando sintió los picotazos vio que Jehú cogió la víbora con sus propias manos; el Hermano Imás, como nadie, también reconoció el valor, en cualquier sentido, del muchacho.
>   Tentando en la mesita dio con el Nuevo Testamento de la Biechner Publishers para buscar aquello donde San Juan habla del amor más grande que hay. (**VARONES**:83)

[the brother well knew that for Jehú—by placing upon him the restriction of not eating for forty-eight hours—the nausea had passed. Jehú got over it on his own; the brother might not be a saint, of course, but he knew Jehú better than anyone. He also knew that Jehú, ever since they'd met in Flora that first time, had an indescribable fear of any kind of snake. Jehú's going around with him through the rows of cotton and paths in spite of his terror was something that had impressed the Brother.

When Brother Imás felt the two snake bites, he saw that Jehú grabbed the rattler with his own hands; Brother Imás, like no one else, recognized, too, the boy's bravery.

Reaching over to the little table, he found the Biedner Publisher's New Testament and looked for the part where Saint John talks about man's greatest love.] (**VARONES**:83)

The passage described above takes on an added significance when read as an ordering experience, and when it is represented as a topological paradigm. In previous passages we have observed a series of events in Jehú's life that denoted experiences of rejection. He is only seven years old, when his mother dies, and even though the barrio women do accept their obligation toward the distressed child, their actions are carried out without comforting warmth and empathy:

The women of the neighborhood were standing in the middle of the street waiting for me: Don't go home, now, Jehú; we'll call you. In the meantime, you go on over to Gelasio Chapa's barbershop. (**VALLEY**:15)

Similarly, at the time of his father's death only two years later, his closest relatives, the Briones family, refuse to take charge of the orphan. The community's ability and willingness to protect their own suffers a breakdown and the traumatic ordeal is clearly taking its toll on Jehú's ability to grieve and to show affection. The passage in **ESTAMPAS**, which narrates his mother's death, leaves no doubt as to Jehú affective hardening: "Por papá no pregunté hasta el día siguiente; me avisaron que llevaba dos días en la cantina de Cano y que sería mejor si no fuera a verlo. Así fue" ["I didn't ask for daddy until the following day; they warned me that he had been in Cano's cantina for two days and that it would be better if I didn't go to see him, and I didn't" (my translation)] (29).

And yet, the text of the *KCDTS* will, in due course, underscore the importance of communal solidarity through a series of episodes in which genuine acts of mutual devotion and fondness are displayed. After the snakebite, it is members of the small Chicano community who make their—albeit clumsy—efforts to cure Jehú's affliction; and it is they who finally entrust Jehú into the preacher's hands, knowing that their love for one another will help overcome Jehú's fright. In fact, the text of the *KCDTS* enacts the construction of an entire net of adoptive fathers for Jehú, including Don Víctor Peláez, Don Celso Villalón, Don Manuel Guzmán, the Buenrostros, and Tomás Imás himself. And finally, in a splendid display of Hinojosa's ability to carry a motif across the entire scope of the Series, he makes Jehú Malacara, the orphaned foster child, into the loving foster father of Becky's two children from her first marriage.

The text perpetuates and projects into the future the people's willingness to nurture a child's capacity to give and receive affection. Threats to the traditional *axis mundi,* as Bruce-Novoa labeled those elements with their key orienting function for the Chicano community (Bruce-Novoa 1990b: 152), can occur anywhere in the diachronic development of the narrative. The text however, responds to the threat by recalling and re-enacting the characteristic elements, thereby letting the reader participate in the completion of the ordering experience. As the following chart illustrates, the *axis mundi* that appears under erasure (here: the crossed out element "Traditional virtue of paternal love as part of the community order") is salvaged through the efforts of the fictional community in the text. Bruce-Novoa explains: "The recuperation of *axis mundi* images cannot bring the object itself back—as representations, words can only mark the absence of what they name. However, the text itself is a real object, just as reading is a real experience, and together they can fulfill the same world-centering function as the threatened object." The theme of orphaning and the need for foster parents pervades the *KCDTS* (see, for instance, Beto Castañeda, **ESTAMPAS**:102). It is an integral element, a deep structure of the traditional Chicano community that is fictionally recreated by Hinojosa. At the end of the process, the *axis mundi* that was placed under erasure is recuperated by the text, and the threatening element itself is placed under erasure:[7]

PARADIGM 2:

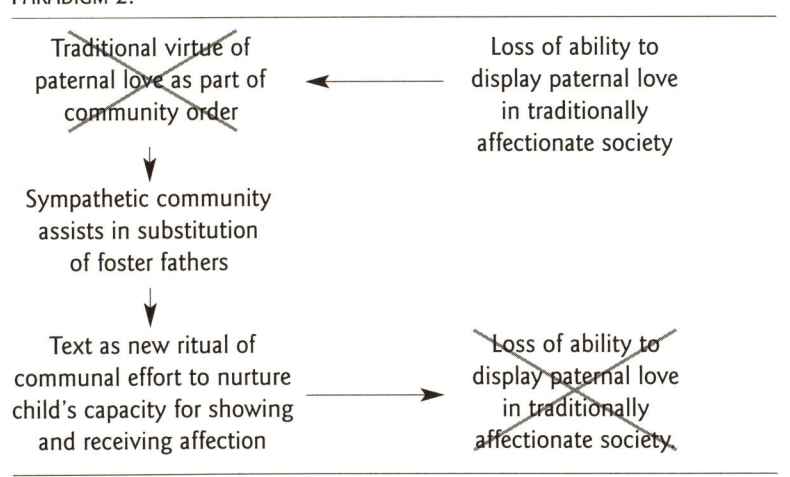

~~Traditional virtue of paternal love as part of community order~~	←	Loss of ability to display paternal love in traditionally affectionate society
↓		
Sympathetic community assists in substitution of foster fathers		
↓		
Text as new ritual of communal effort to nurture child's capacity for showing and receiving affection	→	~~Loss of ability to display paternal love in traditionally affectionate society~~

Meanwhile, on account of the brother's misfortune, Jehú is forced to take on an assortment of honest jobs. Although he is only in his early teens (see **CONDADO**:123), he works the nightshift at his Uncle Andy's gambling hall (**KLAIL**:102), he sweeps the floor at the Chagos's barbershop (105), he herds goats at Don Celso's ranch (104, 108), and he even works as a go-between for the notorious Don Javier Leguizamón (**VALLEY**:88, 99). In all of these jobs Jehú is exposed to certain aspects of Valley life and mores. While carrying messages to Don Javier's mistresses and meeting Uncle Andy's illegitimate offspring, Jehú is sufficiently exposed to Mexican *machismo* for it to have a lasting effect on him.

Places such as Uncle Andy's gambling hall and the Chagos's barbershop represent the typical news centers in a rural community where gossip is traded and spread all over the barrio. Here, the *pícaro's* journey from master to master serves as a motif rather than a theme. The hero's quest is not at the center of the narrative, his character remains static, and personal change does not become evident. This stasis in the portrayal of Jehú's character coincides with a lack of delinquency. Upon entering high school, however, a peripety is reached, a new phase of delinquency begins, and conflicts will bring about a growth in Jehú's character.

INTERRACIAL SCHOOL DAYS

In high school, Jehú is introduced to a predominantly Anglo environment for the first time and to the feeling of being a minority, and consequently, to trouble. Delinquency, here, is clearly spelled out along the lines of racial conflict, and it is not limited to Jehú's person, but rather is part of a general antagonism experienced by Chicano youths attending a racially mixed institution. The majority of these incidents do not appear in Jehú's own narrative. Instead, they are documented in Rafa Buenrostro's chronicles (**VALLEY**:43–54; **KLAIL**:70–78).[8] Jehú is mentioned as a member of a small group of Mexicanos who have transferred from the 100 percent Mexican North Ward Elementary to Klail's Memorial Jr. High. Here, they are surprised to encounter other Mexicanos who are "different from [them], somehow. Jehú Malacara . . . called them 'The Dispossessed'" (**KLAIL**:70; "los desposeídos," **CONDADO**:74). Obviously, Jehú, Rafa, and their friends are confronted with a brand of Valley Mexicano who, in the process of assimilation, have reached a stage that leaves them isolated between the Anglos and the ethnically self-confident Texas Mexicans, whose English may not be up to the mark, but who have retained a strong pride in their ethnic identity. It is this confidence, combined with their self-respect as American citizens, which catalyzes the Texas Mexicans' brazen behavior:

> The shit who handed out the balls and gloves in physical education was called Betty Grable, by us, and to his face. Blond and a bit short in the leg, and a Mexican hater; plain as Salisbury. At first it seemed as if he'd save the worst equipment for us, but after a couple of weeks we were sure of it.
>
> A word to the wise had not been sufficient. Three of us decided he needed convincing that we weren't ready or willing or able to take shit from him or anyone else. The American way. (**KLAIL**:71)

The problems that arise from interracial schooling in a largely segregated society are here placed in the context of Jehú's moral delinquency. The subject will be revisited in the chapter on Rafa, where I discuss it in the context of the segregated culture of South Texas during the period from 1920 to 1940. At the center of these passages are the mechanisms that affected—and still affect[9]—countless Chicano children all over the Southwest. Those who do not profit from classes conducted in English are placed in separate schools and thus deprived of the opportunity to assimilate. Jehú becomes the victim of the same system. An avid reader, Jehú is banished from the very institution that would further his acquisition of the English language. But Jehú, ever resourceful, has his cousin Timo Vilches check out the books for him (see **KLAIL**:142). The incident, however, illustrates how a character less alert and determined than Jehú is likely to succumb to the obstacles thrown in his way.

Jehú remembers his banishment from the library on the occasion of his high school reunion, which concludes both **KLAIL** and **CONDADO**. A remarkable feature of this particular piece is the way in which Hinojosa creates the semblance of an authentic conversational ambience. Jehú, who narrates the incident, casually mentions that this is the kind of thing that would normally be told by Rafa, only that "[h]e never got round to it, and so, I'm filling the void; as it were" (**KLAIL**:138). However, the switching of narrators here is not as random as it may seem. This is the "Twenty-Second Class Reunion" (**KLAIL**:138), and Jehú is now in his mid-thirties. Both Jehú and Rafa have come a long way since their initial shock upon changing from an exclusively Mexican elementary school to the integrated Klail High. With the civil rights movement in full swing,

Jehú's contemplation of his former classmates evokes painful images of the segregated atmosphere in a racially mixed Texas high school in the 1940s. Compared to the even-tempered, impartial Rafa, Jehú is a much more confrontational character, and therefore his mordant account of the reunion aptly represents the antagonisms experienced by many Chicano youths and the grudges they may have unsuccessfully tried to bury. In subsequent installments, both Jehú and Rafa will recall the lasting dislike and contempt in which they held most of their Anglo colleagues (see e.g., **VARONES**:51). Much later, when Jehú learns that his particular enemy, Elsinore Chapman, has been killed in a car accident, he is overcome by the struggle between regret and rancor: "I felt slightly ill; I couldn't explain it to anyone then or now, and I imagine that may be a natural enough feeling. I didn't care for her that much, but I was saddened by the news, all the same" (**RAFE**:24). The quote leaves no room for doubt as to the evolution of Jehú's character across the long succession of *KCDTS* texts. And while he will always be a *pícaro* of sorts, the journey of the orphaned Belken County Lazarillo is brought to a close by his decision "to give it [his] level best at Klail High" (**KLAIL**:101).

In the final analysis, two aspects of Jehú as a picaresque hero deserve special consideration. First, the design and function of Jehú's character in **ESTAMPAS/VALLEY, CONDADO/KLAIL**, and **VARONES** is similar to that of the classical Spanish rogue in that his journey does not always represent a quest. The journey provides a fragmented framework within which a number of facets of Belken County life are depicted at various points in time from different perspectives. In addition, Jehú gradually emerges as a moral delinquent who disobeys the restrictions that a discriminatory society has placed upon him. In the beginning, he moves in an exclusively Chicano world: barrio life, family history, Mexican history, religion, superstition, humor, violence, and death are some of the themes touched upon as the journey proceeds. Then a completely new world is added to the scope when Jehú becomes aware of the Anglos in the Valley. Gradually, conflicts such as the history of Anglo immigration, landgrabbing, Anglo politics, racially mixed schools, the university, and the military take centerstage and remain there for the rest of the *KCDTS*.

It would do his character injustice if Jehú were simply viewed as a comical rogue without emotional depth who merely served as an authorial device. Jehú Malacara is not a flat character, as Rosaura Sánchez claims, arguing that Jehú "appears to be congealed in the good-humored rogue role" (Sánchez 1984:90). A noticeable depth of character is more than just hinted at in the elaboration of the loss-motif in the sketches "Lying to with Sails Set" and "But Since He Died." Careful rereading of a number of passages that may appear trivial at first prove that Jehú is troubled by an unresolved conflict concerning his father's memory. The implications of this conflict will shed some new light on the significance of Jehú's and Rafa's telling surnames.

La mala cara y el buen rostro

The two most devastating events in Jehú's life were the loss of his mother and Don Víctor ("I broke down and cried about as much as when Ma died, and just as heartfelt" [**VALLEY**:33]). And it certainly would have turned out to be equally disastrous if Brother Imás had not survived the snake bites. Yet, mention of his father's death is made in a downright nondescript fashion: "one day—and I mean, one-two-three, just like that—when one day, as I said, he died as he was telling a joke" (**VALLEY**:15). Although Jehú does mourn his father, he remembers him "as an older brother" rather than a parent (16).

At this time, it has already been asserted that Roque Malacara is very poor ("I've no money for sponsors" [**VALLEY**:12]), that his wife is overworked and harassed to the point of complete exhaustion ("I'm bushed, beat, and dead to the world" [13]), and that Jehú, when he needs his father most, is virtually intercepted on his way home by the neighborhood women and "fed and tucked *but not in [his] house*" (15, my emphasis), because his father has "been drinking for the last two days." Lastly, there is Aunt Chedes's mysterious behavior on the day of Roque's funeral, obviously resulting from the fact that she did not hold him in particularly high esteem. Jehú notes that "my memories of him must've been quite different from those of Aunt Chedes' and of that I am certain" (16).

Eventually, we learn from Rafa (**KLAIL**:71–72) that Jehú's father "died owing money" and that "had [Jehú] got word of this, [he] would've died from shame." It is also documented that Don Víctor taught Jehú everything he knew and even left him provided for (see **VALLEY**:32), while the only legacy Roque Malacara left him was his ill-boding surname (*mala cara*—'the bad face').

All this culminates in the observation that while Jehú, as a Vilches-Malacara, is the product of "a good mix of blood" (**FRIENDS**:54), nobody ever mentions Roque Malacara's part in the business. On the contrary, Andrés Malacara, who "knew Jehú's parents, both of them," recalls the shame Teresa Vilches had to bear when she was forced to work as a maid in order to make the family's ends meet (see also **ESTAMPAS**:27). Significantly, Roque's person is conspicuously absent from Andrés's account. Roque's failure to provide for the family is an obvious embarrassment. People are much more inclined to point out Jehú's kinship with the Buenrostros (*el buen rostro*—'the good countenance'), a family of excellent repute whose uprightness is perhaps *the* principal theme in the KCDTS.

The protagonists' telling names have generated considerable critical reflection. Elaine Dorough-Johnson (1978:75) has come to the conclusion that Jehú and Rafa fuse into one single character "providing a more authoritative narration than would otherwise be possible." The names, she suggests, "[i]mply the dual nature of the reality which they relate." I find this unconvincing, especially since she compares Jehú and Rafa to the "frowning mask of tragedy and the smiling mask of comedy" in classical drama. After all, Jehú Malacara is the smirking rogue, and Rafa Buenrostro is the serious character; and besides, both characters are clearly contextualized, each in his own realistic setting, with a place of birth, a family history, and a biography.

These observations are also at variance with Rosaura Sánchez's theory, who suspects an "intent . . . to present Jehú and Rafe as two sides of the same coin" that failed because "their voices are often not distinct" (Sánchez 1984:91). Admittedly, the two characters are perhaps not always immediately distinguishable by their speech or diction. However, in general, Rafa's wry, laconic humor is sufficiently set off against Jehú's mordant irony—different dispositions of character that can be convincingly linked to the semantic connotations of their family names. Moreover, in all of Hinojosa's books a pervasive concern is the question of origin and the past, of descent, family history, and the cycle of generations. In a rural society like Belken County—particularly in the Mexican culture of extended families—people are not predominantly viewed in terms of personal individuality. Rather, the ever-recurrent questions are those concerning time of birth, place of birth, parents, spouses, offspring, relations, and finally death—who, where, when, how? Questions that are answered by a person's family name; i.e., Malacara and Buenrostro. Both their blood runs in Jehú's veins, and both their names carry meaning. *Meaning*, however, must be understood here on both the contextual *and* on the semantic plane. The key, then, to a coherent reading of the telling names lies in the combination of the two.

Thus, in the tradition of the *pícaros*, Jehú is an ambivalent character. He is a moral delinquent. As his tale unfolds, the social make-up of the Valley is captured, just like the episodic biographies of *Lazarillo* and *Guzmán* serve to capture sixteenth century Spain. But unlike them, Jehú is never separated from his roots. He moves about in Belken County, where people know his name, his family, and his hometown. They know who he is, and—more importantly—he knows, too!

The quest, if there is one, is the quest for a place in a bicultural world that doesn't sacrifice one's identity as a Chicano. In these early years of Jehú's life, the stage for this conflict is merely being set, anticipating a sharpened awareness that comes about when Jehú invades traditional Anglo turf, such as the university and executive circles.

Preacher, Teacher, Banker

In the passages of the *KCDTS* that relate the events of the early 1950s, Jehú the *pícaro* takes a backseat to Rafa the war hero. Jehú's exploits in the Army are literally reduced to a footnote in the opening pages of **VARONES**. Jehú has recently vacated his position as a Baptist preacher in the infamous town of Flora (**VARONES**:75). While filling out the forms at the recruiting office, Jehú puts down religion as one of his aptitudes. The Army responds with uncharacteristic humor; they have him sweep the camp chapel (15). However, Jehú now makes good use of his free time in the Army by studying religion seriously. In fact, when Jehú is in his early twenties, the Reserve finally calls him to Korea where he will serve as a military chaplain. Evidently, Jehú's inclination towards religion is a legacy from his travels with Tomás Imás and is adroitly used by Hinojosa to make the transition from Jehú's picaresque journey to the grim locale of the Korean War, where caring for the troops' spiritual welfare may be considered one of the more useful ways of rendering patriotic service.

After the war, like Rafa and many other veterans, Jehú makes use of the GI Bill and enrolls at the University of Texas at Austin. In "Donde se ve otra vida de Rafa Buenrostro" (**VARONES**:17–41), Rafa divulges some of the details of his and Jehú's academic life. Mostly, the cousins keep aloof from the rest of the Valley Mexicanos who are at least five years younger and "todos—pero todos—estudian farmacia" ["and all of them—and I do mean all—were majoring in pharmacy"] (**VARONES**:28) Also they don't mix too much with Chicanas on account of the strong "tufo a casorio" (**VARONES**:29) ["the wedding-related air" (**VARONES**:28)].

In order to supplement the money coming from the monthly GI Bill check, both cousins work a variety of odd jobs including writing term papers for frat boys and working at the library, a job that has the added bonus of giving them the chance to pick up *bolillitas* (Anglo girls, see **VARONES**:29).

After graduation, there is a gap of some three years that is largely unaccounted for. Rafa mentions that he worked a number of odd jobs during that time, and we can assume that Jehú did the same. Both then apply for teaching jobs at their old high school in Klail City (see **VARONES**:51), and both end up hating the job and the other staff, which at the time consists mainly of Anglos.[10] One of them happens to be the same Elsinore Chapman who kept Jehú barred from the library for loud talk in Spanish. He muses over these events when he sees his former schoolmates and ex-colleagues at their twenty-second class reunion. At the time of the party, Jehú has already given up teaching and is newly employed at the Bank.[11]

A telling incident at the crossroads of these rapidly ensuing stages in Jehú's life can perhaps be better appreciated when considered as a chain of interlocutory acts across several *KCDTS* installments, which become more transparent when illustrated by means of the charted topological paradigm shown below. The incident occurs when both Rafa and Jehú return from Korea as GI Bill vets. In order to assure their legal right to get an education with their GI Bill money, they have to see a VA adviser who has his office in the Klail Court House. Incomprehensibly, the man discourages them from going to college, and backed up by his Chicana secretary, tries to persuade them to train as boatbuilders. The episode is mentioned very briefly and obliquely by Rafa in **ESTAMPAS** (127), and then more extensively in **VALLEY** (53). When Rafa and Jehú start their first semester in Austin, they meet another Valley boy by the name of Bob Peñaloza who turns out to be the brother of the advisor's secretary (**VARONES**:25). Apparently, no one had tried to dispatch him off into boatbuilding.

At first glance, the episode seems to be yet another example of ingenuousness on the part of *la raza pendeja,* as Hinojosa labels his fellow Chicanos whenever he detects their gullibility vis-à-vis Spanish speaking Anglos or Chicano sellouts. But this only accounts for part of the scandal that will emerge years later when Jehú Malacara starts working at the Klail First. There, he learns that both Bob Peñaloza and his sister work for the KBC, which raises Jehú's suspicion enough to dig into old Bank records where he soon discovers who had owned and financed the boatbuilding schools back in the 1950s. "Not surprising, the KBC was not involved directly," Jehú says, but involved they were (**RITES**:55):

125 : Jehú Malacara

PARADIGM 3:

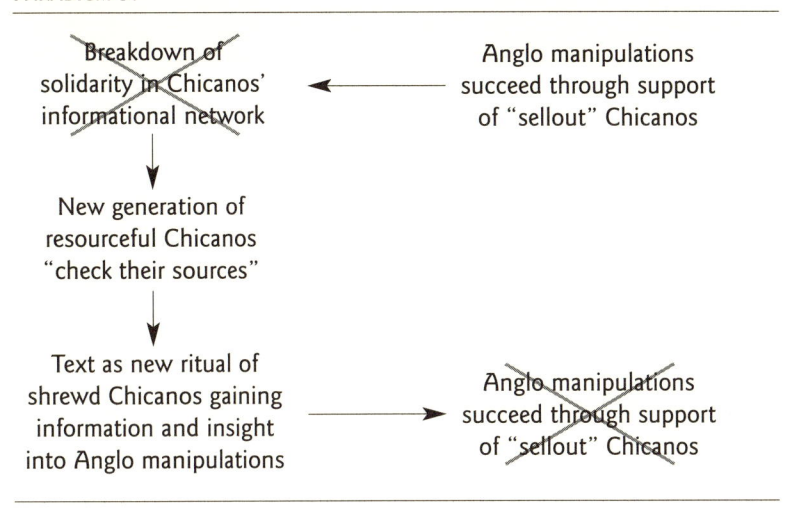

~~Breakdown of solidarity in Chicanos' informational network~~ ◄──────── Anglo manipulations succeed through support of "sellout" Chicanos

↓

New generation of resourceful Chicanos "check their sources"

↓

Text as new ritual of shrewd Chicanos gaining information and insight into Anglo manipulations ──────► ~~Anglo manipulations succeed through support of "sellout" Chicanos~~

Here, we glimpse the potential collapse of the information-network that enables the Chicano community to see through the confusing Anglo bureaucracy. The protagonists frequently make decisions based on the advice of trustworthy persons. We witness a momentary breakdown of this crucial element in the traditional community, but in due time the text uncovers the systematic Anglo scheming that lies behind it. The reader participates in this discovery and thus participates in the elimination of the threat.

A CLOSE SHAVE WITH POLITICS

The Bank, which will provide the main arena for a new and exciting episode in Jehú's life, is the Klail City First National Bank. It is owned by the KBC family empire that controls the major part of Belken County politics and finance. There can be little doubt that Hinojosa's KBC Ranch is directly modeled on the King Ranch in Kleberg County. As David Montejano describes, the town of Kingsville, placed in the middle of the King Ranch, was serviced by a complete infrastructure of companies owned by the King-Kleberg family, including the Kleberg Bank, the King's Inn, the Kingsville Ice and Milling Company and so forth (Montejano 1987:111). Incidentally, Hinojosa was teaching at a Kingsville high school when he received the Premio Casa de las Américas. The Texas Mexicans who lived and worked on the Ranch were identified so thoroughly with it that they were known as "Los Kiñenos." Notice how Hinojosa occasionally refers to the close to five hundred (!) Mexican families that live on the KBC Ranch as "KBC Mexicans" or "Ranch-Bank Mexicans" (**RITES**:8, 20, 64). Even the names "Klail-Cooke" seem to echo "King-Kleberg;" and the German-sounding names of both Kleberg and Belken County are probably no coincidence, either. The Kenedy Ranch and the Kinney Ranch are also likely archetypes, but the King Ranch is the one that best matches its fictional counterpart, the KBC, for the role it plays in Texas folklore. Richard King's life-long dream was "to own all the land between the Nueces and the Rio Grande, to own, in other words, the disputed strip of land over which the United States and Mexico had begun a war" (Montejano 1987:63). When he died in 1885, King had not fulfilled his dream, but he did own 500,000 acres of South Texas land. David Montejano (63–67) gives a fascinating account of the rapid expansion of the King Ranch in nineteenth century South Texas, underscoring the unfavorable competitive position of Texas Mexican landowners in the booming cattle market, which enabled King to buy up most of the Texas Mexican ranchos within his reach. King's widow, Henrietta King, together with her son-in-law Robert J. Kleberg, continued the practice. Montejano provides a detailed list of King Ranch land purchases from 1854 through 1903. When Robert Kleberg died in 1932, the King Ranch had the staggering expansion of 1,250,000 acres. One more piece of evidence for the King-Klail equation: Richard King's motto "Buy land and never sell" (see Montejano 1987:63), is also ascribed to Rufus T. Klail (**RITES**:55).

In his 1993 dissertation, Jaime Mejía points out the significance of the letter "K" as it appears in the name of Klail City's fictitious founding father Captain Rufus T. Klail. According to Mejía, the letter "K" in "Klail" is not only notable for its evocation of the name "King," but also because, in view of its absence from the Spanish alphabet, "its presence will always signify an Anglo presence" (Mejía 1993a:99–100). It is precisely this historical backdrop of unrestrained Anglo territorial expansion and political control versus Texas Mexican land loss and disenfranchisement, which provides the canvas on which the following events are painted.

The principal details are spread out across the texts of **RITES** and **RAFA/RAFE**, with additional information emerging later in **AMIGOS/FRIENDS** and **PARTNERS**. Hinojosa's technique of divulging small bits of miscellaneous and contradictory data is of a deceptively random nature. However, considering the complexity of the events, it is more likely that the general outline of plot was conceived of first and subsequently adapted by the author to his general aesthetic concept.

Hence, the curious maneuver of letting the curtain rise on the opening scene in the 1982 comedy, **RITES**, rather than the 1981 epistolary **RAFA**. The script takes us directly into the board meeting in which the Bank's president, Arnold (Noddy) Perkins, persuades the family to hire Jehú Malacara as their first Mexican employee. However, the significance here is not limited to Jehú being a Mexican. The family protests because Jehú is not "one of [their]" Mexicans, meaning a KBC Mexican or a Leguizamón (KBC allies and the Buenrostros' arch enemies). To make matters worse, Jehú is kin to one of those few Mexican families in the Valley that have been able to resist the KBC's unrelenting greed for more land. As would be expected, Fredericka (Freddie) Blanchard, E. B. (Ibby) Cooke, and Rufus T. Klail V. Junior (Junior) are suspicious when Noddy Perkins proposes to bring a Buenrostro into their inner sanctum:

"*Is* there a problem, Noddy?"
"Not really."
"How much of a Not Really?"
"Ibby, it isn't a problem."
"What then?"
"Well, he may be related to the Buenrostro family."
"He's *what?*"
"To them?"
"Go on, Noddy."
"I think he's related to the Carmen Ranch Buenrostros, and . . ."
"Well! The Leguizamóns are really going to be tickled, won't they?"
(**RITES**:8–9, original italics)

An interesting aspect in the KBCers' way of thinking is their mistrust of anybody who is not a blood relation, a trait revealed in the fact that Sammie Jo Perkins must second her father's motion. After all, Sammie Jo is Blanche Cooke's daughter, and therefore she is family, while her father, Noddy, is not. With his daughter's support, Noddy's motion goes through, Jehú becomes the first Mexican in the Bank, and through him we are treated to an inside view of the political and financial machinations of the South Texas ranch dynasty. The pawns on Noddy's chessboard are:

1. Democrat Texas Congressman Hapgood Bayliss, brother of Edith Timmens, who is the wife of the KBC affiliated lawyer Ben

Timmens. Hap and Edith's father, the late Osgood Bayliss, was a KBC veterinarian.

2. The lawyer Roger Terry (also called Morse Terry in **RAFE**), a Democrat who runs for County Commissioner.

3. Ira Escobar, son of Javier Leguizamón's favorite niece and the Bank's candidate for County Commissioner "place four."

The KBC needs to control this seat in order to tip the scales in their favor in the five-member commissioners court, which constitutes the central body of government in Texas counties (see Montejano 1987:293–95).[12] Ironically, Escobar was chosen because it became obvious that Jehú was not going to "work out" for politics (**RITES**:28). Between the lines, it is insinuated that Jehú is too honest and not malleable enough to be "our boy."

The story more or less begins when Sammie Jo turns a love locket over to her father, Noddy, saying that she found it by the pool. The locket holds the photos of Sammie Jo's husband, Sidney Boynton, and Congressman Hap Bayliss. Sammie Jo omits the fact that the locket was really found by Jehú in her room at the Ranch. Noddy is not to know that his daughter is having a torrid affair with Jehú Malacara, let alone that she is hopelessly in love with Rafa Buenrostro (**RITES**:47). With Hap Bayliss's homosexuality becoming a political liability, Noddy thinks up a plan to retire Hap and to gerrymander another KBC trustee into Bayliss's congressional seat.

Since Roger Terry seems a sure winner in the race for Commissioner, Noddy figures that Terry can run successfully for a seat in Congress as well. First, however, Terry has to be brought into the fold of the Bank. Thus, by running Ira as the first Mexican candidate in Belken County against Terry (see **RITES**:28), the KBC kills several birds with one stone. Firstly, the prospect of having a Mexican American in the commissioners court will go over well with *la raza*, and it "will divert the mexicanos' attention away from the congressional seat vacated by Hap."[13] Secondly, with the Mexican vote on his side, Ira Escobar is a very strong contender in a race that Terry considered as good as won. Thirdly, when Escobar wins the democratic primaries, Terry finds himself under unforeseen pressure, both politically and financially. As he refuses to give up and decides to run as an independent candidate, he is stuck with organizing his own campaign. Suddenly, everything is turning against him. His wife is harassed by the local sheriff, his campaign posters are misprinted, and legal clients are threatening to take their business elsewhere. He can't raise the money to step up his campaign, and when he finally turns to the Bank for a loan, he is summoned directly to the Ranch. There, in the presence of Chief Loan Officer Jehú Malacara,

Noddy drops the bomb on him: withdraw from the Commissioner's race and run **for us** as Congressional candidate (**RAFE**:41–43, original emphasis). Jehú writes to Rafa: "you *were* right about MT [Morse Terry] dropping his pants and bending o." (42, original italics).

While this Machiavellian scheme is running its course, Jehú has his own agenda. Though he refuses to become one of Noddy's pawns on the chess board of Valley politics, his growing expertise as chief loan officer and his popularity with both Mexican and Anglo clients makes him irreplaceable at the Bank. His insight into the Bank's manipulations grows along with his steadily increasing responsibilities. Eventually he comes to understand that the political alliance between the Leguizamóns and the KBC—consolidated by Ira Escobar's position as county Commissioner—is coupled with a secret land deal in Dellis County. The Leguizamóns have their eyes on a big piece of land adjoining their own. When the owners, the Landín family, inform the other neighbors of their plans to sell to Noddy Perkins, Rufino Fischer Gutiérrez comments:

> That's fine with us, and business is *geschafte* [*sic*] as my German grandpa used to say. But! What we didn't like or want or *need*, was for Perkins to share that land deal with the Leguizamóns. Those bastards are plain, bad neighbors; always have been. (**RAFE**:95, original italics)

The deal, then, consists of Noddy Perkins stepping forward as a buyer. Once the title is in his hands, it will be turned over to the already sizable Leguizamón land holdings.

During an informal get-together in the house of Enriqueta Vidaurri, a mutual relative/acquaintance, Jehú alerts Rufino Fischer Gutiérrez of the deal. As a consequence, instead of selling Noddy all the land, numerous Mexican families from Dellis County step in to buy, partition, and resell the land, thus making it impossible for the Leguizamóns to make a major addition to their property.[14] Jehú uses his insight into the Anglo power structure to counteract the KBC's large intelligence machinery that ordinarily enables Noddy Perkins to enter every business transaction with an informational head start. It is thus the young, upwardly mobile, though incorruptible Chicano (the moral delinquent) who manages to erase a small fraction of two hundred years of predatory Anglo practices. The episode illustrates how the old and upright Valley families are gradually getting wise to the game, thanks to the astuteness and professional achievements of their younger generation.[15]

In their 1984 essay, "The Elliptic Female Presence as Unifying Force in the Novels of Rolando Hinojosa," Maria Duke dos Santos and Patricia de la Fuente call attention to another facet in this contest where access to information makes all the difference. In **RAFA**, they note, the action develops predominantly on three levels: banking, politics, and personal affairs. They go on to explain that

> on each of these levels, Jehú is intimately involved with a woman: Sammie Jo, the frivolous daughter of Noddy Perkins, on the business level, Becky Escobar, Ira's wife on the political level, and Olivia [San Esteban] in his personal world. (Duke dos Santos and de la Fuente 1984:73)

In the long run, Jehú's relationships with these three women are not just significant within the context of scheming for land and power. They also function as catalysts that drive the story onward and that will eventually effect a vital change in Jehú's life. His relationships with Sammie Jo and Becky Escobar *at that time* must essentially be regarded as Jehú's notorious forays into forbidden territory. The serious nature of his relationship with Olivia nonetheless suggests that the orphaned *pícaro* is finally looking for stability and security in his emotional life. Surprisingly, it is Becky who will eventually provide both and capture his heart in the end. Becky Escobar is generally viewed as an insincere socialite and not at all the type of woman one would expect Jehú to seek a serious relationship with. More than ten years will pass before that happens, though, and both Becky and Jehú will have come a long way by then.

At the present time, Jehú's situation at the Bank is getting more and more precarious as the election draws nearer. He stands by as Noddy harasses, intimidates, and pushes around both Ira Escobar and Roger Terry; he realizes that as long as he works at the Bank, he cannot fool himself into believing that he is just an innocent bystander:

> One last thing: I don't think I'm going to last here much longer; I don't have the stomach for it. Por pendejo que sea Ira [although Ira's a jerk], he's still a human being. (RAFA:38)

With the arrival of election day, though, the decision is made for him. Noddy's plan works out flawlessly, and he asks Jehú to a formal celebratory dinner at the Ranch. When Jehú gets there, he realizes he's been set up. Dinner is already over, and Noddy makes a big show of embarrassing

Jehú in front of the other guests by asking him to resign from his job at the Bank. Forever a politician, Noddy finds that simply firing Jehú would mean wasting a perfectly good occasion to make a point. Hence, by staging his castigation in front of the Terrys and Escobars, he issues a warning as to what will happen to those who cross him.

The real reason for his being fired, Jehú assumes, is that Noddy has heard rumors about his trysts with Sammie Jo but that there is no proof.[16] Therefore, after a day's deliberation, he decides to see Noddy in his office and bluff it out. Instead of letting himself be humiliated, he turns around and acts outraged at Noddy's firing him for having an affair with Ira's wife, *Becky*, thus diverting Noddy's attention away from his daughter, Sammy Jo. Jehú's risky ploy works out, and he keeps his job, only to quit on his own terms three weeks later in order to go to graduate school in Austin. Naturally, when word gets out, people pounce on the story, clearly favoring the version in which Jehú gets fired. After all, the year is 1962, and Jehú is twenty-six years old when he walks away from a job that no ambitious, upwardly-mobile Mexican American in his right mind would walk away from.[17]

An Uncommon Banker Shares His Office with Rufus T. Klail

Doing things "under [his] own steam and terms" (**RAFE**:56) is what takes priority with Jehú. This becomes particularly apparent in **PARTNERS** where we learn that in 1965, at age twenty-nine, Jehú goes back to the Bank after realizing that dedicating three years to grad school was a "half-baked idea" (156). In chapter 24, a singularly introspective Jehú replays in his mind the events from **RAFA/RAFE**. We are now in 1972, Jehú is thirty-six years old, and he reminds himself and the reader how much the career expectations of Mexican Americans have changed when he declares that his job as vice president "sure beats picking citrus" (**PARTNERS**:98). He also remembers how turning his back on the Bank, and on his priceless connections to the almighty KBC, separated the wheat from the chaff as far as friends go.

The narrative of the *KCDTS* skips over most of the events during the ten years between 1962 and 1972. We do learn that Jehú gave up womanizing when he got formally engaged to Olivia San Esteban and that part of the reason he gave up studying for his Ph.D. in Austin had to do with supporting Olivia while she was in medical school in Galveston (see her brother's testimony in **FRIENDS** [78]). Then, Olivia gets in a car accident during her third year at the university (details in **FRIENDS**:18, 42). She lies in a coma for "ten days, two weeks" (18), during which Jehú does not leave her bedside. While these events are not expanded upon, **FRIENDS** makes several subtle references to Jehú's grief, such as Martín San Esteban's remarks about Jehú's impeccable comportment towards Olivia's parents, behaving "as if they'd been married" (79). Becky Escobar mentions that he went calling at the San Estebans' house long after Olivia's death (157). And, on an even subtler note, the text intimates that Jehú could not possibly have felt more grief and obligation if he had been properly married to Olivia. The mortuary where Olivia is prepared for the burial is called "Witwer's Mortuary" (German for widower's mortuary), thus leaving no doubt as to the severity of Jehú's loss.

While most of these details emerge in the duo texts **FRIENDS/AMIGOS**, the narrative of **PARTNERS** concentrates on Jehú's role as a minor character in the *Rafe Buenrostro Mystery*. Jehú is a banker with a conscience who goes out of his way to make his own special contribution to the improvement of race relations in the Valley. He makes sure more Mexicans are hired by the Bank, and he gives loans to small, promising Mexican American and Anglo businesses without showing favoritism. His strategy pays off, as some of the testimonies from satisfied customers indicate (see, for example, Vicente de la Cerda [**RAFA**:99–100], Eugenio Peralta [**RAFA**:93], Edwin Dickman [**RITES**:102], and Martín San Esteban [**FRIENDS**:77]).

Hinojosa incorporates Jehú in the crime-mystery plot by having him participate in the uncovering of a drug-money laundering operation involving bank tellers at several Valley branches. The author also seizes the occasion to insert small references to the Valley's past history of Anglo landgrabbing, as described above with respect to the King Ranch. For example, in chapter 24 Jehú looks at the painted portrait of General Rufus T. Klail on the wall of his office and states: "As fine a man as ever robbed the helpless" (**PARTNERS**:155).[18] None of the KBCers with offices at the Bank wanted the General looking down on them. Jehú, though, keeps him there as "a private joke between himself and his sense of humor," and as a constant reminder of what the combination of power, greed, and lack of humor can turn a man into.[19]

Jehú is further linked to the activities of the Valley's law enforcement agencies through his romantic involvement with Irene Paredes, an assistant with the Belken County Homicide Lab. Though their relationship is not fleshed out much in the novel, Irene deserves to be mentioned as part of the ever-increasing cast of strong, emancipated women characters in the Series.

The Rogue Is Roped

While the assertive, nontraditional Chicanas were prominent in the previous texts of the *KCDTS*, the text of **FRIENDS/AMIGOS** takes up the theme of *la mujer nueva* with unprecedented vehemence. And naturally, it takes a male who is somewhat of a maverick to take up Becky's cause in a notoriously patriarchal Mexican society. In the *KCDTS*, Jehú is the unbowed nonconformist personage, the self-sufficient orphan who answers to no one, and hence he is the logical choice as Becky's male champion. From the moment Becky sends Ira Escobar packing in the opening of the story, we can almost be sure of Jehú's involvement in the controversial affair.

The story line of **FRIENDS/AMIGOS**, and the details divulged by the various informants, hardly contribute anything new to what we already know about Jehú Malacara, except that he started dating Becky seriously when she decided to get a divorce from Ira Escobar (see Isidro Peralta's interview in **AMIGOS** [30]), that they got married, and that Jehú lovingly cares for Becky's two children. Apparently, he thought it awkward to work at the Bank together with Becky's ex-husband and asked to be transferred to another branch. However, Noddy Perkins and E. B. Cooke considered him too valuable in his present position and insisted that he stay at the Bank (**FRIENDS**:84–85).

Perhaps one of the most thrilling episodes in the text puts a new slant on the previously discussed confrontation between Noddy and Jehú with respect to Jehú's affair with Sammie Jo. It is included in the interview with the Bank's secretary Esther Lucille Bewley, which appears exclusively in **AMIGOS** (63–65). Esther, who is deeply infatuated with Jehú, and therefore very much interested in everything concerning Jehú's person, overhears two crucial conversations in which Sammie Jo reveals her involvement with Jehú, first to her father, Noddy, and then to Becky Escobar.

These details are of a particularly trivial and gossipy nature, and it is precisely for that reason that they provide a new angle not only on Jehú as one of the principal narrators of the Series but also on the code that governs the transfer of information in an oral society. Unlike Galindo, or his nameless successor "the listener," Jehú is not a neutral, impartial observer. Jehú is personally involved in all of the events concerning the Chicano community's dealings with the KBC, and as a consequence, a lot of information that pertains to him personally is kept from him. Thus we find Jehú in his office much later, in the 1970s, thinking back on how he deceived Noddy, still believing that "[e]verybody should have one secret for himself, and that one was his" (**PARTNERS**:156).

The text of the *KCDTS* suggests that in the oral community of Belken County scandalous secrets are virtually impossible to keep. Paradoxically, though, the keeper is not necessarily aware that his/her secret has been uncovered. Jehú's adulterous relationship with Sammie Jo is a perfect example of this paradox. Perhaps for the sake of peace, perhaps in order to let the adulterer save face, or for the community's prolonged entertainment, the perpetrator is permitted to either smirk or be contrite—depending on her/his disposition—while thinking her/his covert transgression an intimate secret. Jehú's remorse affirms that he is not the smirking rogue anymore: "Jehú thought, and thought long and sadly too: he'd betrayed Noddy Perkins. Not his trust; his daughter. Sammie Jo Perkins. *That* had stopped in '62, and *that* secret was ten years old" (**PARTNERS**:156, original italics). However, aside from Sammie Jo and Jehú's eternal confidant, Rafa, at least six other people (the *listener*, the Peralta twins, Esther Louise Bewley, Noddy, and even Jehú's own wife Becky) know about Jehú's secret. Apparently, a number of key persons in Jehú's life have recognized that Jehú has changed his wicked ways and have chosen to leave well enough alone. The reader, who participates in the completion of the oral ritual, is placed in the same position as the affected individuals in the story; he knows that Jehú is unaware of the uncovering of his secret. Illustrated in one of Bruce-Novoa's topological paradigms, the deep structure of the ordering experience in the text presents itself as follows:

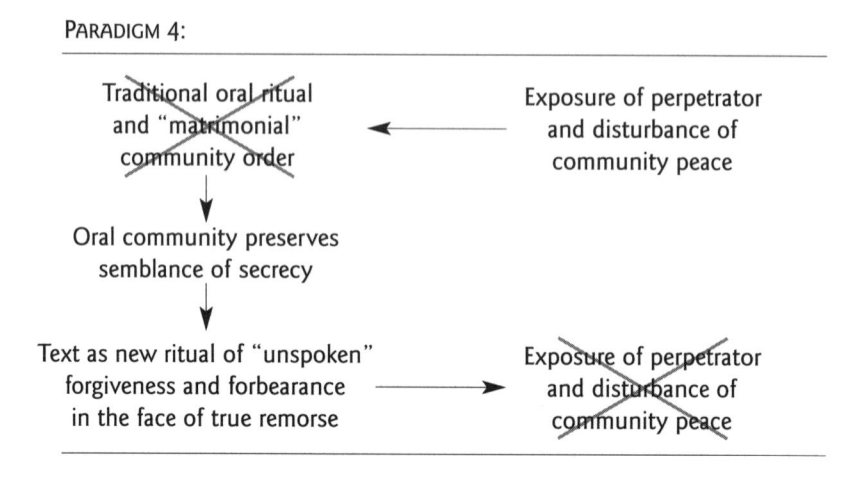

PARADIGM 4:

~~Traditional oral ritual and "matrimonial" community order~~ ← Exposure of perpetrator and disturbance of community peace

↓

Oral community preserves semblance of secrecy

↓

Text as new ritual of "unspoken" forgiveness and forbearance in the face of true remorse → ~~Exposure of perpetrator and disturbance of community peace~~

It is Rolando Hinojosa's secret if, or when, Jehú Malacara will make another appearance in the *KCDTS*. Unfortunately, Jehú's only genuinely new contributions to the *dénouement* of the Series since his eccentric behavior in **RAFA/RAFE** are limited to his cameo in **PARTNERS** and his male supporting act to Becky's female lead in **FRIENDS/AMIGOS**. Apart from this uncharacteristically amiable impersonation of "the husband," eighteen years of rapid *KCDTS* progression have gone by without bringing Jehú back into the limelight he deserves.

In light of the fact that both Jehú's roles as narrator and protagonist made for some of the true highlights in the *KCDTS*, it is to be hoped that Rolando Hinojosa is planning an encore for his most engaging male character whose biography, as the following remarks will show, is in part modeled on that of a biblical king.

In the 1978 installment, *Korean Love Songs,* Hinojosa rings in his narrative poem with this portentous quote from 2 Kings 9:19, "And Jehu said, What hast Thou to do with peace?" In the foregoing chapter, the discussion has revolved around a troubled period in Jehú's life in which he is seen writing ominous letters, purging false friends, rebelling against the mighty KBC, turning his back on the worshippers of worldly riches, and struggling to walk the straight-and-narrow, but eventually being drawn back to the business of money-making at the Klail First.

Incidentally, the biography of the biblical Jehu (son of Jehosh´aphat, King of Israel) is very similar. Jehu kills the licentious Jezebel, rebels against King Ahab's worshipping of Baal, and writes letters issuing the death sentences for Ahab's seventy sons. He also pretends to pray to the false god, Baal, gathers all the priests and disciples together and has them slain by his guard, annihilating the House of Ahab and its idolatrous cult.

> And the Lord said to Jehu, "Because you have done well in carrying out what is right in my eyes, and have done to the house of Ahab according to all that was in my heart, your sons of the fourth generation shall sit on the throne of Israel." But Jehu was not careful to walk in the law of the Lord the God of Israel with all his heart; he did not turn from the sins of Jerobo´am, which he made Israel to sin. (2 Kings 10:28)

Just as Jehú Malacara struggles to find the right direction in his life, denounces his job at the Bank, stops womanizing, and goes back to school, the biblical Jehu tries to do well in the eyes of the Lord. And yet, both will eventually return to the golden calves. Still, in spite of his less than perfect faith, God permitted that "Jehu reigned" for "twenty eight years." Jehú Malacara, too, rises quickly and consolidates his position in the Bank's hierarchy after his return. Are we, then, to read this metatext as an augury that predicts the rise of this and other Texas Mexicans to the top of the

Belken County corporate world? There is reason to believe that Jehú will eventually move into the upper echelons of the KBC management. Perhaps, the *KCDTS* suggests that changes in the Belken County race and power structure are expected to be momentous. For now, though, we must close the book on Jehú with the same unanswered question that closes Jehu's story in the Bible:

> Now the rest of the acts of Jehu, and all that he did, and all his might, are they not written in the Book of the Chronicles . . . ? (2 Kings 10:34)

22

ESTEBAN ECHEVARRÍA

Memories of Arcadia

IN his trailblazing, sociohistorical and literary study *With His Pistol in His Hand* (1958), Américo Paredes characterizes the first one hundred years in the history of Nuevo Santander as one of Arcadian isolation, simplicity, and prosperity:

> Most of the Border people did not live in the towns. The typical community was the ranch or the ranching village. Here lived small, tightly knit groups whose basic social structure was the family or the clan. The early settlements had begun as great ranches, but succeeding generations multiplied the number of owners of each of the original land grants. . . . Thus the Río Grande people lived in tight groups—usually straddling the river—surrounded by an alien world. . . . It was the Treaty of Guadalupe Hidalgo that added the final element to Río Grande society, a border. The river, which had been a focal point, became a dividing line. Men were expected to consider their relatives and closest neighbors, the people just across the river, as foreigners in a foreign land. A restless and acquisitive people, exercising the rights of conquest, disturbed the old ways. (Paredes 1958:9, 13, 15)

The history of displacement and resistance experienced by the descendants of the first Escandón colonists begins at the end of this period, in 1835, with Anglo American expansionism in the American Southwest. Esteban Echevarría, the oldest of the four chroniclers of the *KCDTS,* is a representative of the first generation of Texas Mexicans who were born as U.S. citizens after the Republic of Texas joined the Union of the United States of America in 1845. Even though Echevarría was not born until the 1860s, his life is almost entirely marked by the legacy of the Spanish-Mexican hacienda culture that dominated the Valley for decades after the War. As Montejano has pointed out, the construction of a railroad from Corpus Christi to Laredo in 1880 left the Lower Río Grande Valley completely isolated from trade and progress:

> The remoteness . . . together with its Mexican influence had retarded its growth and the development of its natural advantages. . . . The politics of the Lower Valley retained a distinctive insular character. In Brownsville, the Anglos who had settled in the immediate postwar years had intermarried with each other and the elite Mexicans and for *the next fifty years* ran "the county, the city, and the Mexicans almost as a feudal family system." (Chatfield quoted in Montejano 1987:98, my emphasis)

As a consequence of this isolation, the tenure of this quasi-feudal ranch society was perpetuated into the first decade of the twentieth century. It is precisely this period that I will foreground in the passages narrated by Echevarría. In order to avoid unnecessary repetition, the present chapter was written with a relatively narrow focus on Esteban Echevarría as the narrational link to the anachronistic societal conditions in the Valley that spanned almost the entire nineteenth century. The discussion, then, will serve as a prelude to subsequent chapter in which we will explore the role of the Buenrostro family in the making of Texas during the troublesome period after the onrush of Anglo farmers from the Midwest and the South in the early nineteenth century.

Echevarría, who does not take center stage more than a few times in **CONDADO/KLAIL** and **VARONES**, is deftly introduced in **ESTAMPAS/ VALLEY** as a frequent visitor to the *Aquí me quedo* bar, where Rafa, the bartender, has been instructed by Lucas Barrón not to serve beer to Don Esteban when he is over his limit because "you know how he gets after a while" (**VALLEY**:52). By that, Lucas means that once Echevarría gets started on Anglos, sellout Mexicans, Texas Rangers, and politics, there is no stopping him. We get a first sample of that in "Echevarría Has the Floor" in **KLAIL** (16–19), where the old man has been treated to drinks by the regulars of the *Aquí me quedo* and promptly starts in on his favorite subjects.

There is a curious ideological dichotomy that reveals itself in the passages narrated by Esteban Echevarría. Though of rudimentary education, he is a man obsessed with the rights of the individual in a democratic society. He passionately urges Texas Mexicans to participate in politics as constituents and officeholders, pointing out that for generations the Anglo minority has governed the county by buying the Texas Mexican vote (see **VARONES**: 199–205). On the other hand, he yearns for an earlier world of isolated, self-sufficient ranches with an antiquated patriarchal structure. The contradiction can perhaps be reconciled by considering the following passage from Paredes:

> The simple pastoral life led by most Border people fostered a natural equality among men. Much has been written about the democratizing influence of a horse culture. More important was the fact that on the Border the landowner lived and worked upon his land. There was almost no gap between the owner and his cowhand, who often was related to him anyway. The simplicity of the life led by both employer and employee also helped make them feel that they were not different kinds of men, even if one was richer than the other. (Paredes 1958:10)

The society that Paredes extols (perhaps a little too enthusiastically in view of its feudal nature) and that explains why Echevarría would remember it as a free quasi-democratic brotherhood, is in fact the horse culture Echevarría and Jesús Buenrostro were born into. The fact that Echevarría feels no need to stress the social gap between the Buenrostros and himself bespeaks Paredes's largely correct evaluation of this society. Montejano agrees that "[h]ere the class distinctions between ranch owner and worker were clearly drawn, but these actors were bound to each other in a manner that tended to produce a sentiment of kinship" (Montejano 1987:88). The treatment of the subject in the *KCDTS* is, as always, covert and underhanded; two fairly conspicuous passages mention Jesús's horsemanship at an early age (**VARONES**:181, 221), and in another passage, Echevarría laments the fencing in of the prairies, a procedure that is generally considered the principal cause of the demise of the cowboy culture (207).

Hinojosa elaborates on the kinship between rancher and worker in the fragment "The Dogs Are Howling" (**KLAIL**:27, 28). Echevarría is back in the cantina ranting against the Leguizamóns. The subject inevitably leads him to the murder of Don Jesús, and suddenly he falls silent and turns toward the door, overcome with emotion. The telling of the incident has evoked the memory of the night of the killing when Echevarría was alerted by the howling dogs that guarded the tents in the Buenrostros' camp (another reference to the Buenrostros being cattle men). Echevarría's obligation toward his landlords compels him to pick up his rifle and stand by them in their fight against the aggressors, the Leguizamóns.

The passage in which the flashback occurs heralds the transformation of Echevarría's disposition from anger to nostalgia, which will become more noticeable in his monologues in **VARONES**. Moreover, the oddly poetic quality of the passage, inserted into an otherwise vernacular piece, anticipates Echevarría's heightening glorification of the Valley enclave as an erstwhile Eden:

> It'd been a hot spring, the orange blossoms were trying their best to bloom out-a the buds, and it was on an April evening that someone sneaked up and murdered don Jesús. (**KLAIL**:27)

The sketch "Galindo VIII," and the last three pieces in **VARONES** embrace this sentiment and represent Echevarría's farewell. The key passage is narrated by Galindo:

> Echevarría se dirige al mezquite que le plantó su padre en su honor el día de su nacimiento allá en el último tercio del siglo diecinueve, recién acabada la guerra que los americanos sostuvieron entre sí. No es el mezquite más viejo ni es Echevarría miembro de las Cuatro Familias que lograron sostener parte, tampoco mucha, de esta tierra que acapararon en los tiempos de las mercedes cuando Escandón.
>   Echevarría no necesita ser miembro de las Cuatro Familias; ha sobrevivido a todos los de su edad y ahora es el único que todavía se acuerda de cómo era el Valle. De cómo fue y de cómo era el Valle antes de que vinieran los bolillos a montón, y "todo el desmadre que arrambló con tierras y familias; con el desprendimiento personal y el honor de haber sido lo que fuimos . . ." Sí; piensa morir. Quizá dure dos, tres días, de ahí no pasa. (**VARONES**:129)
> [Echevarría heads for the mesquite tree his father planted in his honor the day he was born way back during the last third of the nineteenth century; right after the war the Americans had between themselves. This isn't the oldest mesquite on this land which they were given

during Escandón's land grant period, nor is Echevarría a member of the Four Families who managed to take part, though not much, in that enterprise.

Echevarría does not need to belong to the Four Families, he has survived everyone from his generation and now he is the only one who still remembers how the Valley used to be. How the Valley had been and how it used to be before the Anglos came in herds, before the army, the state government and its rangers, all the bureaucratic paperwork and "all the excesses that swept away lands and families; along with personal generosity and the honor of having been whom we'd been. . . ." Yes; he's planning to die. He'll die in two, three days, no more than that. (**VARONES**:128)]

How the Valley and its people used to be when Echevarría was young is the principal theme of Echevarría's last monologues that have attracted much critical attention. This is partly due to the delayed publication of **VARONES**, which prompted Hinojosa to submit the pieces independently to periodicals and anthologies. They stand out for their stream-of-consciousness style that is borne forward by a lyrical rhythm, enhancing the nostalgia that emanates from Echevarría's words. I quote the following passage from "Con el pie en el estribo" in order to underscore the *anciano's* transfigured vision of this South Texas Arcadia:

Me acuerdo, Rafa. . . . Carne seca colgada en los alambres de la lavada y cabritos que se mataban en los solares, árboles llenos de higos y de miel de abejas que chupaban la flor de naranjos . . . ruidos de animales que ya no se oyen ni se ven . . . bailes con gente invitada y ahora me cuentan que se tiene que pagar la entrada, pero, ¿te das cuenta, Rafa? Y allí están las palmeras . . . Las palmeras que daban en el Valle y que crecían como Dios quería hasta que la bolillada vino con sus hachas y las cortaron como si tal cosa . . . (**VARONES**:209)
[But I remember, Rafe. Meat hung out to dry on the wire clothes line and goats slaughtered in our backyards, trees loaded with figs, and honey from bees that drank the nectar from the orange blossoms. Sounds from animals that one no longer sees or hears. Dances open to the public and, now, I hear you even have to pay to get in, can you imagine, Rafe? And what about our palm trees? Palm trees that grew as God wanted them to until the Anglos came with those axes o' theirs and then cut them down as if they were nothing. (**VARONES**:208)]

Echevarría adds credibility to his panegyric of the early days by emphasizing that the early Anglo settlers that came to the Valley in the late nineteenth century adapted readily to the idyllic Mexican pastoral society, a phenomenon that manifests itself in the complete acculturation and Mexicanization of some Anglos right down to the spelling of their last names ("don Benjamín Mackintaya" **VARONES**:221). We will come back to this issue later on in the Rafa section, where the historical setting of the *KCDTS* will be discussed against the background of Hinojosa's family history. Suffice it to say for the moment that Hinojosa's Anglo mother came to the Valley "at the age of six weeks in the year 1887 along with one of the first Anglo American settlers enticed to the Valley by Jim Wells" (Hinojosa 1984a:18). In contrast, with the second onrush of Anglos from the north in the 1910s and 1920s, relations between Anglos and Mexicans deteriorated to a point akin to slave-master relationships, where the laborers even took on their masters' names ("Esos eran unos Cano—nada parientes de estos de acá—a cada uno le decían 'la Brady' porque trabajaban con un ranchero de ese nombre . . . Ah, raza . . . ni que fuéramos negros, tú . . ." [213] ["Those were from the Cano family—no relation with the Canos from around here—everybody called them 'the Bradys' because they worked for a rancher by that name . . . Ah, raza . . . as if we were Negro slaves" (my translation)]).

Thus, Echevarría has endured the erosion of the Valley culture from a feudal but essentially harmonious Spanish-Mexican hacienda society to an Anglo-Mexican ranch society, and finally to a segregated farm society. As the text states, Echevarría is the last person in the Valley to have seen all these stages in one lifetime. His collection of memorabilia is entrusted to Rafa for safekeeping:

> Valle, Valle, ¿quién te ha visto y quién te ve? . . . y yo soy el Valle, tengo el honor, como decía la vieja canción. . . . ¿Y ahora? Nada. . . . Me voy, Rafa, tú te quedas . . . muchacho joven que vives entre los viejos y con sus viejos recuerdos . . . (**VARONES**:209)
> [Valley, oh Valley . . . those who beheld you then, will they recognize you now? . . . and I am the Valley, I have the honor, as the old song goes. And, now? Nothing. I'm leaving, Rafa, but you are staying . . . a youth who lives among the old with their old memories. (my translation)]

The previous paragraph has already indicated that the transformations suffered by the Valley's Texas Mexican population during the period between Texas independence and present times are best explained as a succession of societies, each new one undermining the previous one in an attempt to adapt to new economic conditions. The societies model as a sociohistorical framework designed to explain race relations in South Texas has been mapped out compellingly by David Montejano in his study *Anglos and Mexicans in the Making of Texas: 1836–1986* (1987). In the subsequent Rafa section, I appropriate Montejano's model for my own charting of the race relations in Belken County against the background of economic transition.

23

RAFA BUENROSTRO

The Making of Texas

THE history of the Buenrostro family is the history of South Texas. It would be unthinkable to chart Rafa's personal history without drawing on the richness of his family background, which in turn is modeled on the 250-year presence of Rolando Hinojosa's own family in the Lower Río Grande Valley.

Generations of Anglo historiographers have recorded the chronicles of Texas as a history of Anglo American colonization. In their view, the Lone Star State did not enter the crucial stage of its history until Moses and Stephen Austin brought the first American settlers to the province of Texas, which in the early 1800s still belonged to the Mexican State of Coahuila. In his analysis of the *KCDTS* as a revisionist literary history of Texas, Manuel M. Martín Rodríguez underscores the flagrant brazenness with which white-supremacist historiographers like Walter Prescott Webb claimed that "the first permanent settlers" in the Río Grande Valley were "Anglo-Americans from the United States" (Webb quoted in Martín Rodríguez 1993b:92). As we know today, it was the unchecked tide of Anglo American settlers into Texas, their rebellion against the troubled Mexican government, and the subsequent secession from Mexico that led to the foundation of the Republic of Texas in 1836. The undebated high point of this strictly Anglo history is the gloriously heroic, mythologized defense and fall of the Alamo in 1836, of which David J. Weber writes:

> It seems safe to suggest that the events of March 6, 1836 at the Alamo have contributed more to Mexican American school children's loss of self-esteem than any other historical episode. Children learn that thousands of Mexicans needlessly and wantonly slaughtered some 175 Americans who courageously chose to die.
> The story of the Alamo was never so simple. (Weber 1973:109)

Tourists visiting San Antonio today, as well as many American school children in history classes, are presented with a simple story of good versus bad, making heroes of Davy Crockett, Jim Bowie, and Colonel Travis, while making villains of the Mexican attackers. This version is symptomatic of the slanted, Anglo-centric documentation of the role played by both Mexicans and Anglos in the making of the Lone Star State.

In contrast, Rolando Hinojosa's history of Texas starts in 1747, when the Spanish explorer, Captain General José de Escandón, arrived in the Valley in order to prepare for its colonization. Escandón came back in 1749 to found the province of Nuevo Santander (named after his native Santander on the Spanish peninsula) and to establish several settlements along the Río Grande, starting with Camargo on March 5, followed in close order by Reynosa, Revilla, and Mier. Among the first colonists whom Escandón brought to the Valley on that second trip was the Hinojosa family. In his Los Caminos del Rio Heritage Project, entitled *A Shared Experience,* Mario L. Sánchez writes:

> Most of the land was owned by prominent families. At Reynosa, for example, the Cano, Hinojosa, Garza, Garza Falcón, Cavazos, and Ballí families became cattle barons. In Laredo, it was the Sánchez, García, Benavides, and Farías families. In most of the *villas,* the notable families intermarried, producing even greater cattle empires. One of the largest dynasties was that created by Juan José de Hinojosa, chief justice of Reynosa. (Sánchez 1996:8)

In a personal letter to me dated April 28, 1998, Rolando Hinojosa confirms that

> nosotros provenimos de José Maria Hinojosa, uno de los hijos de Juan José de Hinojosa; los Falcón y Garza Falcón son parientes porque

doña Rosa Maria Falcón se casó con uno de los Hinojosa; allí también entran los Ballí, por ejemplo, Padre Island se llama, en español, la isla del padre Ballí Hinojosa.

[we are descended from José María Hinojosa, one of the sons of Juan José Hinojosa; the Falcóns and the Garza Falcóns are relatives because Doña Rosa María Falcón married one of the Hinojosas; this is also where the Ballís come in, for example, Padre Island is called, in Spanish, Father Ballí Hinojosa's Island. (my translation)]

He goes on to describe that every possible combination of the names listed above can be found in the Valley due to the long history of intermarriage. The writer wryly adds, "[q]ue yo sepa, ningún Hinojosa salió idiota, imbecilico, debido, creo, a que nunca se casaron primos hermanos" ["as far as I know, no Hinojosa was ever retarded or backward, because, I believe, there were never any marriages between first cousins" (my translation)]. The Garcías, relatives of his, still live on the original land-grant "la merced del Llano Grande," east of Hinojosa's hometown, Mercedes. Mario L. Sánchez provides a detailed historical account of the procedure and the circumstances surrounding the distribution of land by the Spanish crown among the early colonists:

> Largely because of the reports of José de Escandón in 1755 and Tienda de Cuervo in 1757, the Spanish government considered the question of giving the citizens of Nuevo Santander individual land grants. The Viceroy, in recognition of the desire for land ownership by the Rio Grande settlers, appointed a Royal Commission in 1767. This commission selected Juan Fernando de Palacios to head a "General Visit of the Royal Commission to the Colonies of Nuevo Santander." It has been properly observed that the only other events in the history of the Lower Rio Grande to compare to the importance of the visit by the Royal Commission were the Mexican-American War and the coming of the railroads, both in the nineteenth century.
>
> The process used for distributing the land in most of the Rio Grande settlements was similar. At the completion of mass, all the citizens of the community gathered together. The Commissioners then informed the citizens of the purpose of their visit and the procedure by which the land would be surveyed and divided. Experts and surveyors were sworn in as "agents of the Royal Government," and three kinds of land were designated: that which could be irrigated, that which could be used for grazing, and that which could comprise the town proper.

Next, six leagues were marked off in the area around the town, in four directions. These plots became the jurisdictions. Within each jurisdiction, the land would be partitioned into individual plots that were given to the individual settlers. The amount of land the settlers received was determined by several criteria, including the number of years a person had served the crown in either a military or civilian capacity, and the number of years the person had lived in the village. (Sánchez 1996:7)

In his 1997 comparative cultural study *Border Matters,* José David Saldívar (1997:18) describes his attempts to fully comprehend the plight of the Escandón settlers holding the line "against English, French, and Anglo-American encroachment," and how hard it is today to imagine these borderlands as a onetime "ecological whole." Can gazing at a map, Saldívar wonders, awaken a true understanding of how Mexico, in the turmoil of its own struggle for independence, had "to fight off the United States in its quest to fulfill its manifest destiny?" And what did it truly mean for the inhabitants of this contested territory to have a border drawn through their very lives? "For years," Saldívar states "I have tried to piece together what it must have been like for Reyes and Carmelita Saldívar, my great-great-grandparents, to have been almost overnight 'incorporated into the Union of the United States' (Treaty of Guadalupe Hidalgo, article 9)."

In the same way that José David Saldívar conjures up the images of his distant forebears as a kind of visual stimulation in order to comprehend their predicament, Hinojosa invigorates his fiction by instilling it with the memories passed on across generations of Hinojosas. The graves of the eighteenth century Hinojosa-Ramirezes, Hinojosa-Garzas, Hinojosa-Hinojosas, can be visited in the cemetery in Ciudad Mier on the Río Grande today. Likewise, in Belken County all the Buenrostros are buried "in the Old Families cemetery by the Carmen Ranch" (**POLICEMAN**:19). Therefore, when compared to other Chicano narratives, one cannot overstate the fact that Hinojosa's literary production does not predominantly focus on his protagonists' struggle for identity in a bicultural world. Héctor Calderón (1991:14) confirms that "because of historical circumstances—the conflict of cultures in Texas and the institutionalized racism toward Mexicans—these characters already knew who they were." Juan Bruce-Novoa goes further still in his appraisal of the particular significance of the Buenrostro family history in his 1989 review of **VARONES**, in which he explores the book as a history of struggle and resistance:

the series' protagonists are descendants of a Texas-Mexican landed aristocracy of sorts, albeit with all the rusticity the area calls to mind. The Buenrostro family owned enough land so that they could distribute it to others (**VARONES**:23). They themselves base their sense of clan on property ownership, distinguishing themselves from other Buenrostros by the fact that they are "Los del Carmen" (175). We should not dismiss the ramifications of these revelations. While on the one hand, they affirm a continued struggle over land recuperation, a theme dear to the Chicano political movement, they also distinguish Hinojosa's writing and his story from that of other Chicanos who write from the perspective of immigrants, of landless poor, whose ideal of property ownership is not based on the actual fact of previous, legal possession, but on the promise of eventual acquisition. Hinojosa's tone is unique in Chicano literature, closer perhaps, to that of the fallen Southern plantation owners in post-Civil War fiction (166). (Bruce-Novoa 1989)

There is little doubt that David Montejano's 1987 *Anglos and Mexicans in the Making of Texas, 1836–1986* spearheads revisionist Texas historiography. The particular mode in which "Montejano's self-conscious revisionist history" and Hinojosa's "creative interpretation of a native son" can mutually inform one another has previously been pointed out by Erlinda Gonzalez-Berry in her introduction to **CONDADO** (5). Sketching out a précis of Montejano's social history of South Texas, she points to a number of passages from the *KCDTS* that highlight the common thrust of Hinojosa's and Montejano's writings. Thus, Gonzalez-Berry has staked out the theoretical territory that this study will appropriate and expand. Taking up the thread where Gonzalez-Berry left off, I will chart the past and present history of Hinojosa's Belken County community by implementing the patterns that David Montejano has "teased from an entangled web" of border history. The organization of Montejano's book, as summarized below, corresponds to a sequence of four class societies that each had distinct ethnic constellations and relations. Also, each society was undermined by the one succeeding it (see Montejano 1987:8):

1. Incorporation (1836–1900): "a Spanish-Mexican *hacienda* society undermined by the Mexican War in the mid-nineteenth century."

2. Reconstruction (1900–1920): "an Anglo-Mexican ranch society undermined by an agricultural revolution at the turn of the century."

3. Segregation (1920–1940): "a segregated farm society undermined

by world war and an urban-industrial revolution in the mid-twentieth century."

4. Integration (1940–1986): "a pluralistic urban-industrial society for the latter half of the twentieth century."

Accordingly, the present chapter will read the history of the Buenrostro family as a succession of the four societies. Montejano's book, despite its towering academic standard and its 350 pages, is an engaging read that does not deserve to be dismembered and abridged. Still, even as I urge readers to turn to Montejano's original, I consider it indispensable for our present purposes to provide brief outlines of the book's principal sections. After each of these outlines, I will portray Rafa's history, past and present, against the backdrop of Montejano's succession of four societies, placing special emphasis on the fact that even within South Texas the Valley is consistently portrayed as a world apart.

The history of displacement and resistance in this enclave as experienced by Rafa Buenrostro and his forbears begins in the mid-nineteenth century with Anglo American expansionism in the American Southwest. Growing up "entre los viejos y con sus viejos recuerdos" (**VARONES**:209) ["among the old and with their old memories," (my translation)], Rafa Buenrostro becomes the chronicler of an oral history that counters the official textbook version of Anglo Texan historiography. At the same time, he never loses sight of the struggle and strife that embroils Texas Mexicans today, while extending his prophetic vision into the Valley's near future.

INCORPORATION (1836–1900)

The Land

In this first section, Montejano focuses on the mercantile and territorial interests that gave Texas its present geographical shape. In the aftermath of the Mexican War, the new Republic of Texas sought to acquire as much of the Río Grande Valley as possible in order to gain control of El Paso del Norte as well as the access to the Gulf Coast. Thus, with the panhandle in the west and the Río Grande Valley forming the southern apex, Texas acquired its characteristic star-shaped contours.

One of the obstacles the emerging commerce-oriented upper class had to deal with was the concept of "entailment." Under the old Spanish law, "entailed" land titles could not be divided up and sold because they were to be the inheritance of a specific line of heirs. In United States jurisprudence, however, entailment was an unknown concept. Suddenly, land could be divided up and sold in small parts, a measure many of the Mexican land holders were forced to take in order to pay their tax arrears and private debts. These so-called Sheriff's sales were land auctions imposed on the landowners with bidders agreeing to bid low beforehand. As an example of these "legal" procedures, Montejano cites the Hinajosa grant [not Hinojosa] in Hinojosa's native Hidalgo County, of which eight thousand acres were sold for $32.15 in 1877 (Montejano 1987:52).

"Ownership of land," writes David J. Weber (1973:154) "the basic unit of wealth and social status in the agrarian and pastoral economies of Mexico's far northern frontier, came under fire after the United States took control of the area." In Texas, the shift of land from Mexican to Anglo hands had started as early as the revolution days. Only people who had fought against Mexico in the Texas Revolution were entitled to land in Texas, and, predictably, Mexicans were not given the benefit of the doubt. Consequently, lower-class Mexicans were easily bullied off their lands. Upper-class Mexicans in Texas, as well as in the other states, found their old claims called into question by Anglo lawyers who based their litigations on new laws that demanded that all pre-war land grants be confirmed. The Mexican *hacendados* saw themselves confronted with unfamiliar legal procedures in a foreign language. Since the federal government was faced with a flood of title claims, the procedures became almost interminable, and increasingly expensive. The consequence was not only the loss of property and the traditional way of life that went with it, but also for decades Mexican Americans were kept too busy to focus their energy on rallying a political force within the Mexican community.

Early Subjugation and Insurrection

While in many parts of Texas the Mexican population was soon outnumbered by Anglos and rapidly began to suffer the consequences of racial subjugation, in the Valley the population and customs remained overwhelmingly Mexican. In 1850, according to Montejano's sources, the society that Esteban Echevarría would soon be born into consisted of "approximately 2,500 Anglos and probably 18,000 Mexicans" (Montejano 1987:31). This demographic mix did not make for harmonious coexistence and was therefore not conducive to mercantile enterprises. As an example of the precarious stability of peace in the region, Montejano cites Cortina's War, a historical episode that merits closer inspection because it has a significant bearing on the Buenrostro family history.

Like Hinojosa's family, Juan Nepomuceno Cortina's predecessors had come to the Valley with the first Escandón colonists and had founded the actual Rancho del Carmen. On July 13, 1859, Juan Nepomuceno protested the beating of a Mexican at the hands of the Brownsville Marshall, Bob Shears. In the ensuing fight, Cortina shot and wounded the Marshall in self-defense, and escaped across the border. He came back with a small force of friends, attacked Brownsville, freed twelve imprisoned Mexicans, and "killed three Anglos whom he regarded as corrupt" (Weber 1973:231–32).[1] Returning to the Rancho del Carmen, he issued a proclamation to the people of Brownsville, calling for a defense against the Anglo oppressors. With a force of some 500 men, Cortina defeated several Anglo militias and was not brought under control until the U.S. Army was called in. Even though he lost his war, he went on to become governor of the Mexican state of Tamaulipas and would later be known as the "Robin Hood of the Río Grande."

Peace through Acculturation from the Top

This and other incidents demonstrate that the Texas Mexicans were not as docile as many historical accounts would have us believe. Nonetheless, the new South Texas upper class—consisting of merchants, lawyers, officers, and office holders—finally achieved a "[f]abric of peace" through affixing themselves "atop the Mexican hierarchy" (Montejano 1987:34). Thus, the Mexican hacienda culture with its hierarchical system of landed elite, rancheros, and *peones* was perpetuated as the basis of the new "peaceful order." Generally, most Mexican *hacendados* adjusted well to the new situation. In times such as the Cortina War, however, when loyalties were put to the test, responses to the shifted power centers varied from tactical marriages with Anglos and unwavering support for the Anglo military forces to quiet approval of the rebels (see Montejano 1987:36).

On the other hand, many of the Anglos—both Americans and Europeans—were eager to acculturate in the interest of peace. Where intermarriage was not a possibility, *compadrazgo* (sponsorship of marriages, baptisms, confirmations) became a way "of securing political and economic alliances through kinship" (Montejano 1987:37). When it came to the right to vote, though, kinship simply meant that Mexicans had to support their Anglo allies. Although attempts to formally disenfranchise nonwhites failed, Mexican voters were continually intimidated or "organized." Active political involvement had to be authorized by the Anglo bosses.

A New Racial Order

At the turn of the century, when the economic structure changed from a pastoral world of subsistence farming to a commercialized, open-market cattle industry, few of the older upper-class Mexican families succeeded in making the transition. Montejano provides ample data to show how Mexicans had to sell because they were caught short financially during bust times. The prime example of unchecked territorial expansion on the part of some Anglo Ranchers is Richard King, who bought up most of the Mexican ranchos within his reach between 1875 and 1913. See chapter 21 on Jehú for a description of the King Ranch as the historical model for the Belken County KBC ranch and Bank empire.

The subsequent disappearance of the Mexican landed elite and the rising influx of Anglo settlers led to a gradual Americanization of society. The practice of intermarriage decreased, the Spanish language suffered displacement, separate neighborhoods were formed; the "race issue" in the former integrated enclave could no longer be ignored. Predictably, this development hit the cities and small towns early on, while life at the large, self-sufficient ranches in the Lower Valley went on essentially as before. Gradually, however, the paternalistic structure at the hacienda was organized along racial hierarchical lines and finally penetrated all aspects of daily life. Ironically, the existence of upper-class Mexicans who managed to hold on to their land and wealth somehow presented a hitch in the new racial order. The slight dilemma was solved by romanticizing these good citizens as European Spaniards who had little or nothing in common with the poor landless Mexicans.

For our following exploration of these aspects in the text of the *KCDTS*, it is vital to remember that many of the circumstances discussed by Montejano in the South Texas context of the late 1800s arrived in the Valley with a considerable lag. South Texans today are forever pointing out the separateness of the Valley from the area closer to the two Laredos farther north, not just for the differences in landscape and vegetation but especially for the distinct historical and cultural backgrounds that mainly stem from the area's isolation during much of the nineteenth century. Hence, the bulk of the historical evidence that emerges in the *KCDTS* regarding the period of Incorporation circles around occurrences during the first two decades of the twentieth century, only a decade away from Rafa's birth in 1929. Since the railroad bypassed the Río Grande region below Laredo, the Valley "was spared the trauma of railway-related modernization for another two decades" (Montejano 1987:96). As astonishing as it may seem, the old order of the Mexicanized, Anglo pioneer aristocracy maintained its quasi-feudal system far into the twentieth century. The conflict involving the Buenrostros, the KBC, and the Leguizamóns constitutes a case in point.

*Incorporation in Belken County: Land Loss,
Anglo Acculturation, and the Racial Order*

Seldom does the *KCDTS* allude to the historic events and conditions described above in an overt fashion; rather, "Hinojosa's strategy is to reproduce the semblance of the oral tradition in its style of fragmentary recounting" (Bruce-Novoa 1989:166). As a consequence, references to the radical transformations that took place in the Valley during most of the lifetime of Rafa's father, Don Jesús Buenrostro (1887–1946), are usually indirect, oblique, and may occur in removed contexts. Perhaps the earliest examples of this technique present themselves in **ESTAMPAS** (99–101), in an *estampa* entitled "Los Leguizamón" ["A Leguizamón Family Portrait"] (**VALLEY**:86–88). With deceptive casualness, the sketch broaches the crucial issues that shaped the Valley during the period of incorporation: landgrabbing, political alliances, intermarriage, and Mexican resistance. The Buenrostro family is given only parenthetical mention, but by drawing the portrait of their arch-enemies, a seminal picture of the Buenrostros' predicament emerges that will have to be completed by the reader with information from remote parts of the Series.

Unlike Rafa's family, the Leguizamóns came to South Texas in 1865, "después de atole" [after the pudding], which, I understand, is a Valley-way of saying that they arrived after the major repercussions of the war and the Texas revolution had abated. All the important details relative to the Leguizamóns' alliances with the Anglo political power holders in Belken are divulged in the sketch. They sided with the Texas Rangers during all the major waves of ethnic conflict in 1901, 1915, and 1923. Their earliest engagement with the old families took place during "one of the first shootouts against the Vilches and Malacara families" (**VALLEY**:87). Typical of Hinojosa's narrative technique, the Buenrostros' crucial role in these early cases of Mexican armed resistance is revealed in a separate sketch. In **ESTAMPAS/VALLEY** (92/80), we learn that the skirmish between the old families and the Rangers-Leguizamón faction later turned into a week-long siege of the Rancho del Carmen during which the Buenrostros proved worthy of the Cortina legacy and repulsed the attackers:

> Los Vilches, los Garrido, y los Malacara viejos se aliaron para sostener las tierras contra los rinches, primero en el rancho Toluca de los Vilches, cerca de Relámpago, y luego, durante toda una semana santa, en el rancho del Carmen, en las tierras de don Jesús Buenrostro, "El Quieto." Después de estos dos encontronazos los rinches se dejaron de estar molestando. (**ESTAMPAS**:93)

[The first run-in against the Rangers—*los rinches*—was at the old Toluca Ranch, a Vilches family holding, hard by Relámpago, but closer to the old burned church. The second engagement took place at the Carmen Ranch held by don Jesús Buenrostro, who was also called *El quieto*. The fighting started on a Palm Sunday and ended the following Easter Sunday. *Los rinches* stopped their harassment at that end of the Valley when the mexicano ranch hands started firing back at them. (**VALLEY**:80)]

The Leguizamón family portrait makes another tacit allusion to the Buenrostros in a short characterization of Alejandro Leguizamón, the man who had ordered Jesús Buenrostro's death:

Alejandro, the tallest, a gambler and a womanizer but no coward, also sided with the Anglo Texans; his reward was not an insignificant one: some eight thousand blackdirt acres in Ruffing. Alejandro was found dead by the early crowd on its way to mass at the Our Lady of Mercy Church. Alejandro's head had been bashed in and his brains scrambled somewhat with a tire iron found lying across his chest. (**VALLEY**:87)

From subsequent references to this incident across the entire Series, readers find out that this was Julián Buenrostro's retribution for the death of his brother Jesús. *El Quieto* had to die because he stayed ahead of the Leguizamón clan and the Texas Ranger, Charles Markham, in the struggle over El Carmen. It is E. B. Cooke, of all people, who reveals one of the most intriguing aspects of the mystery surrounding the Buenrostro ranch, and curiously this key passage is only included in the Spanish-language **AMIGOS**. In his interview, the KBC lawyer is expressing his surprise at how well Jehú has turned out as a banker for the KBC, considering that he is a relative of the Buenrostros. With the mention of that name comes the association with the land, and suddenly he makes an unexpected disclosure about El Carmen:

El Carmen. Rancho pequeño pero decididamente el lugar más precioso del Valle. Y no lo vamos a comprar. No podemos. Se dividió en tantas parcelas que no hay bastantes abogados y papeles para llegar a un acuerdo.... Otra cosa ese Quieto, ¿eh? (**AMIGOS**:62)

[El Carmen. A small ranch but positively the most beautiful place in the Valley. And we're never going to buy it. We just can't. It was divided up into so many little parcels that there will never be enough lawyers and documents to reach an agreement.... He was something else, that Quieto, wasn't he? (my translation)]

The passage, which to my knowledge is the only instance in the *KCDTS* where the physical beauty of the Carmen Ranch is praised, is significant in that it makes an oblique reference to the practice of entailment and it sheds some light on the periodic—and sometimes quite cryptic—allusions to the Buenrostros' custom of giving away their land. The descendants of the early settlers did not regard the land granted by the King of Spain as a commodity to be sold when the necessity arose; rather, the haciendas were small independent worlds that represented tradition, heritage, and homestead. After U.S. annexation, division of land grants became common practice and usually worked to the landowners' disadvantage, for example in the case of the before-mentioned Sheriff's sales. Very likely then, when E. B. Cooke says that Jesús Buenrostro was "otra cosa" ["something else"][2] he is expressing his admiration of the patriarch's ability to beat the land grabbers at their own game. Instead of trying futilely to preserve the patrimony in one piece, Jesús—and later his sons Aaron, Israel, and Rafa—distribute the land among their relatives, friends, allies, and confidants. As we have noted in the Jehú section, the Dellis County Chicanos use the same method when Noddy Perkins steps forward to buy the Landín property. Below, we will see that Rafa, too, uses his father's strategy to makes sure that the land he has inherited is safe from the Leguizamóns' insatiable greed.

Hinojosa demonstrates anew his technique of staggering the data across several separate fragments. In an altogether underhanded fashion, the *KCDTS* narrators repeatedly make remarks about people who have received land from both Don Jesús and Rafa. References to the distribution of land appear, for example, in **VARONES** (23, 51), **RITES** (109), and **CONDADO/KLAIL** (42/28). Then, in his letters in **RAFE**, Jehú makes several obscure references, in his abridged style, about a man named Acosta. The statements are unrelated to the immediate context of the letters, but they reveal their significance when considered consecutively, which is why I document them here in full:

As per your request, I did go see Acosta about your farm land; he'll be out of town for a while, but I left word for him to call me at the Bank. Israel and Aaron have been alerted. (**RAFE:**24)

I finally got Acosta as per your inst. and took him over to the Court

House. Everything's in order there: taxes all paid up, the property lines well-marked and defined, and no changes whatsoever. Of course, he'll still have the Leguizamóns as his next door neighbors, as did our grandfathers and before. I then called Israel and Aaron on this and mailed copies of the deeds, etc. by special deliv. (**RAFE**:28)

Just wait for the gnashing of teeth when the word gets out that you *gave* Acosta that land for $10. total. They'll call you a fool, our friends will. (**RAFE**:48, original italics)

Evidently, Rafa continues his father's practice of selling the land for purely symbolic payments, making double sure that all the paperwork is in perfect order. If we transpose the information given here to the situation at the turn of the century, when the Leguizamóns showed up at the Carmen Ranch with lawyers and the local sheriff (**CONDADO**:41), we can infer that the state of affairs they found looked something like this: there were no tax arrears, the property was clearly demarcated, the papers were in order, and—most importantly—legal land ownership had been distributed among a host of titleholders.

In accordance with Hinojosa's aesthetic agenda, it is the reader's job to draw the direct links between these various incidents after having successfully completed the detective work of assembling the evidence. Visualized in one of Bruce-Novoa's topological paradigms, the dynamics of the land loss theme present themselves in the following way:

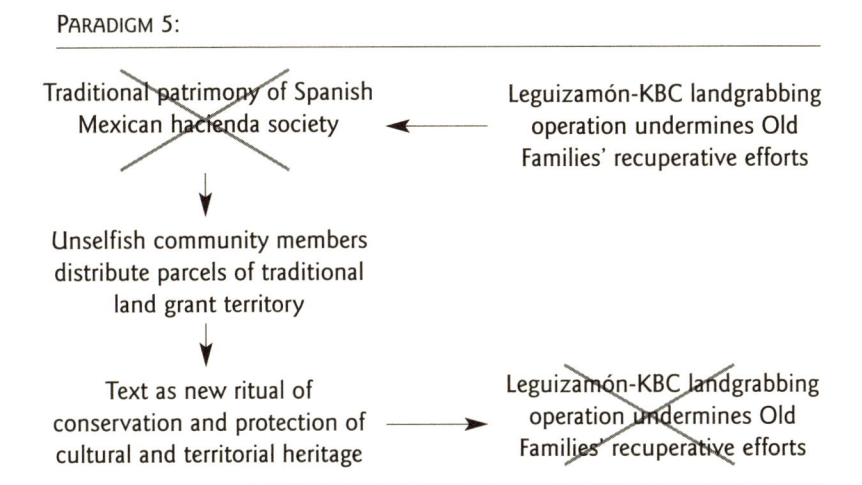

PARADIGM 5:

Traditional patrimony of Spanish Mexican hacienda society [crossed out] ← Leguizamón-KBC landgrabbing operation undermines Old Families' recuperative efforts

↓

Unselfish community members distribute parcels of traditional land grant territory

↓

Text as new ritual of conservation and protection of cultural and territorial heritage → Leguizamón-KBC landgrabbing operation undermines Old Families' recuperative efforts [crossed out]

Although the Leguizamóns failed in their attempts to take over the Buenrostros' land grant, they managed to form profitable kinships through intermarriage with the KBC clan. Antonia Leguizamón married one of the "rich Blanchards, and her sons and daughters, one by one, made Anglo Texans of themselves" (**VALLEY**:87).

It is a telling feature in this community, where everybody knows everybody else's lineage, that the exact origin of the Leguizamóns remains obscure. This will later facilitate their smooth merger into the new racial order as "Old Spanish" (**RITES**:67), as O. E. Patterson's testimony in **RITES** confirms:

> Yessir, people can talk all they want to, but there's no escaping the fact that the Leguizamóns are fine, upstanding Christian Americans; and they are patriotic, to boot, and they're not afraid to show it.
>
> They came to the Valley like a lot of people did right after the Civil War; they're Old Spanish, you know: directly from Metsico. (**RITES**:67)

> When Antonia Leguizamón married to the first Jimmy Cooke way back there, it was a matter of money to me, but there was a lot of love, too. And they was proud of their Spanish blood, and now Jimmy Three's got a quarter of Spanish in him. That's why he's got that temper, see. (**RITES**:68)

The curious artificial dichotomy of things Spanish and things Mexican initially stems from the sophistication and the splendor of the old Southwestern families many Americans were rather taken with at the time. It was later put to use in order to justify the separate treatment received by the landed Mexican gentry and the poor landless Mexicans at the hands of the new Anglo masters. However, David Weber has pointed out in his discussion of ethnicity in late eighteenth century California, that to associate the glorious "Days of the Dons" with pure Spanish heritage proves fallacious. A census conducted in California as early as 1781 includes accurate information on the *mestizaje* [the racial mixture of the population] and destroys the illusion that the American Southwest was settled by pure-blooded Spaniards (Weber 1973:33).

In Belken, the old families strongly resented political turncoats such as the Leguizamóns, who profited from the new discriminatory ethnic structure and didn't think twice about shedding their Mexican identity and declaring themselves Spaniards. Remembering well which of the families were the collaborators and opportunists, steadfast Valleyites continuously scoff at those Mexicans who claim to descend directly from "Peninsular Spanish" ancestors. Frequently, their contempt even extends to recent immigrants from Spain and their way of pronouncing the Spanish language. Ridiculing both authentic and would-be "*gachupines*" is almost a leitmotif, which can be traced across the entire *KCDTS*. Viola Barragán exemplifies those Valley Mexicans who have come to hate the *gachupín*. In **AMIGOS** (23–24) she launches into a longish rebuke of "ideas gachupinas de su-pe-ri-o-ri-dad . . . y ese ceceo casi insultante" ["Spanish notions of superiority . . . and that downright impertinent Spanish lisp" (my translation)]. And she mentions a conceited Spaniard who married a Buenrostro woman and soon "se le quitaron los humos" ["he stopped putting on airs" (my translation)]. In **FRIENDS**, she explains:

> I'm saying all of this because of the Navarrete family. They were old Mexicans, mexicanos viejos, but at one time they thought of themselves as Spaniards; can you beat that? Just like the Leguizamóns. Oh sure. The Leguizamóns considered themselves Spanish for a while there. They're a bunch of obliging shits, they are. And they're the first to spot which way the wind is blowing, too. (**FRIENDS**:24)[3]

On a similar note, Otila Macías Rosales is outraged when the Catholic Church sends "one of those" Spanish priests to the Valley; "uno de ésos que hablan como si la lengua les fuera demasiado grande para la boca" (**AMIGOS**:116) ["one of those who talk as if their tongues were too big for their mouths" (my translation)]. And even in distant Korea, Rafa and his tejano buddies make fun of a Chicano from Colorado who claims that "his people came from Spain, and then Charlie and Joey asked him if those were the Spaniards that landed in Virginia and then trekked across the South until delivered safely and soundly to the Promised Land" (**SERVANTS**:41).

In addition to the subject of Mexicans forming political kinships with Anglo bosses, there are also numerous examples of Anglo acculturation in this early Texas period. Some of the names that come up time and again in this context are Martin Holland and Catarino Caldwell. The former is mentioned by John Goodman in **RITES** (86–89) as the prime example of an Anglo gone native ("Anyway, Martin Holland's the one to ask . . . if you can get him to speak English. Ha! Oh, he ain't forgot none . . . he just likes the Spanish"). Goodman himself is married to a Mexican woman and lists a number of instances of intermarriage. One such case is that of Becky's father, Catarino Caldwell, who even spared his wife, Elvira Navarrete, the trouble of learning proper English by Mexicanizing himself (**FRIENDS:** 119).

The Valley, then, is a place where even in the 1950s and 1960s the old customs, alliances, and political conditions that date back to the previous century still survive in remnants. In order to maintain one's land, tradition, and patrimony, one must distinguish between those who are to be trusted and those who are not. The early attacks on old land by the Anglo-Mexican alliance of Johnny-come-latelies at the turn of the century, were only a first sample of the battles that would be fought once the land became a highly prized commodity. With the advent of thousands of Anglo American farmers in the Valley, a new period of social, economic, and cultural transformation set in. For the Anglo old-timers in the region, the changes were a godsend in the shape of a general reconstruction of the Valley's infrastructure. For the tejanos, it meant an era of unprecedented heights of racism and subjugation.

Reconstruction (1900–1920)

In the isolated, remote, and still very Mexican Lower Río Grande Valley, the pastoral Spanish-Mexican hacienda society had gradually been replaced by a commercial—though equally patriarchal—Anglo-Mexican ranch society. The great transformation did not occur until the completion of the St. Louis, Brownsville, and Mexico Railway on July 4, 1904. The Texas cattle industry had been in a slump for some time, prices for farmland were dropping, and the landowners had started to experiment with new irrigation techniques, hoping to make the transition from ranching to farming. When the new railroad took up its service, it brought Midwestern farmers, land developers, irrigation engineers, and produce brokers to the Valley (see Montejano 1987:107). Prices for land soared, the population tripled, and the ranchers saw their opportunity to shed the thousands of acres of land they had amassed, which had become unproductive. While most of them quickly adapted to farming, their old feudal order soon clashed with the new farmers' ideas of progress and competition. And once again things in the Valley did not quite take the same course as elsewhere in Texas. Among the tide of farm workers and day laborers were numerous Mexican nationals from across the border. As a result, the Valley remained predominantly Mexican, and along the Río Grande border, the struggle between old-timers and newcomers took on a racial character.

For the farmers from the North, Mexicans were Mexicans, and the differences between Mexican landowners, independent vaqueros, and laborers—a hierarchy understood by the old-timers—meant nothing to them. Suddenly, the peace structure that had made compadres of old American and even older Mexican families broke apart and left the Valley with only two major classes: Anglo farmers and Mexican laborers. The consequences for the Mexican population were disastrous.

The Second Wave of Subjugation and Insurrection

Mexicans now found themselves treated as an inferior race, segregated into their own town quarters and refused admittance at restaurants, picture shows, bathing beaches, and so on. (Montejano 1987:114)

While the old-time Anglos were initially embarrassed by the treatment that many of the Mexican gentry received at the hands of the newcomers, they were soon "swept up by the racial hysteria" (117). The Texas Mexicans, however, were not ready to give up their rights and dignity without a fight, and confrontations between Anglos and Mexicans became more frequent and more violent. The era of the famous—or infamous—Texas Rangers had arrived. Initially brought to the Lower Valley in order to prevent violence, the Rangers soon turned out to be a major source of conflict, which, in Montejano's view, only led to a more determined Mexican resistance. While the years between 1909 and 1912 saw an upsurge of violent incidents, the open insurrection that lasted from 1915 to 1917, and its brutal suppression by Texas Rangers, "turned the Valley into a virtual war zone" (117).

On February 20, 1915, an irredentist movement called "El Plan de San Diego," comprised mainly of Texas Mexicans but also of members from other segregated ethnic groups, proclaimed independence from the Yankee Tyranny and called for the foundation of an independent republic in the former Mexican territories. During most of 1915, small groups of rebels were organized into raiding parties that attacked countless Anglo establishments and installations all over the Valley. In traditional historiography, the surprisingly purposeful and methodical actions of the seditionists are generally explained away by attributing them to an alleged international conflict that had its origins in Revolutionary Mexico. In contrast, Montejano credibly argues that although the conflict did have an international background, it stemmed overwhelmingly from the unbearable racial situation in the Valley (Montejano 1987:118).

Those old-time Anglos who had not yet embraced the new segregated society hurried to do so upon learning that many of the former Mexican elite engaged in seditious activities, and thus the floodgates of savagery against Mexicans were opened. Montejano reports that finding dead Mexicans became so common that it ceased to be newsworthy (Montejano 1987:122). The individual circumstances he describes are accurately reflected in Hinojosa's fictional accounts discussed below. Also, the fact that many Texas Mexicans, like the Kiñenos (the King Ranch Mexicans), fought against *los sediciosos* is frequent narrative material in the *KCDTS*. Eventually, the arrival of U.S. Army troops and the continued bullying and brutality by the Rangers made the frontier safe for farming. Of the few Mexican families that had been able to hold on to their land, the great majority gave up in the face of death threats followed by outright slaughtering of entire Mexican villages (see 127). Ironically, the Texas Rangers' activities were eventually curbed not for the atrocities they committed, but rather because they began to side with the new farmers against the old order. Legendary Texas lawyer/politicians like Jim Wells and Archie Parr used their political clout to have the Rangers "reorganized." This new development was symptomatic of the continued struggle between new order and old order in the Valley, which would leave the Texas Mexicans once more caught squarely in the middle between a progressive commercial agricultural society and a reactionary ranch world.

Politics

The two institutions that customarily represented these factions were the Good Government League (GGL) and the established local political machines. In the 1910s and 1920s, these diametrically opposed contestants locked horns in the county political arena, and it was the Texas-Mexican vote they fought over. Both parties soon understood that the Mexican voters were the key to power in the Valley, and since they would most certainly side with the old Anglo bosses who had at least a semblance of respect for them, the opposite party did its utmost to disenfranchise the Mexican voters. The poll tax, whites-only primaries, and legislation against assistance to Spanish speakers and nonnaturalized citizens were some of the "legal" measures used to keep Mexicans from casting their votes. An incident that illustrates the extremes the two factions would go to is the 1928 Hidalgo County Rebellion, where the battle over political control between the GGL and the political machine was fought on the backs of the Mexican American population. Apparently, GGL supporters had successfully intimidated Mexican voters, and three to four thousand people actually picketed at the polling places to keep Mexicans out. The opposite party was no less determined to hold their grip on the county. An official investigation found that Hidalgo County boss A. Y. Baker, Sheriff and ex-Ranger, had tampered with the ballot boxes and had disappeared before he could be prosecuted. The newcomers were coming out on top and "the decline of machine politics was evident" (Montejano 1987:148). The struggle, however, resulted in the division of several counties and the creation of new local governments. Thus, the thirteen counties that exist in South Texas today still resonate the clash between ranchers and farmers, during which the Texas Mexicans were used and abused by both.

Reconstruction in Belken County: Farmers, Seditionists, Rangers, and Politicians

There is an almost uncanny correlation between Montejano's classification of Texas history and Hinojosa's fictional treatment of the same data. In the previous section on incorporation, the same central issues that Montejano had foregrounded in his sociohistorical study could all be found grouped together in Hinojosa's *estampa* "Los Leguizamón." Likewise, we can single out Abel Manzano's testimony in **RITES** (109) as a point of departure for our reading of the *KCDTS* as a novelistic portrayal of reconstruction in the Valley. And just as in "Los Leguizamón," the allusions are extremely tenuous and seemingly insignificant. That, however, is an intrinsic element of Hinojosa's tactics; below we will see that the evidence is all there.

Abel Manzano was born in 1882, and he is seventy-seven years old. He grew up on one of the original land grants, but now he lives with his daughter and son-in-law in Klail City. In keeping with the Belken custom of establishing one's loyalties, he is quick to point out that his son-in-law is not a "[KBC-]Ranch Buentello" but from the "old Malacara property by El Carmen Ranch near where the old Klail City pumping plant used to be" (**RITES**:109). In a string of associations, Manzano alludes obliquely to farming, the seditionists rebellion of 1915, and the Texas Rangers' sinister role in it:

Don Hilarión [Echevarría's father] received forty acres of his own from the Buenrostro family. This land was from the grants.

That property is near the pumping station by El Carmen Ranch where the Texas Rangers shot the three Naranjo brothers in 1915. In cold blood. At night. And in the back. I was the same age as Jesus Christ then, and I found them where they were left: on the Buenrostro property; the Buenrostros were blameless, and they had nothing to do with that. They were left there until I cut them down. With this. Look.

It was the Rangers who took them from the deputies, and it was the Rangers who executed them. I have heard *now* for the last twenty years, that Choche Markham had nothing to do with the shooting; I remember that from then, the year Fifteen, until yesterday, as we say, he always claimed credit for that.... That it is now inconvenient, is something else. (**RITES**:109–10, original italics)

At first glance, the "old pumping station/plant" near the Carmen Ranch, mentioned twice on page 109 by Manzano, seems to be no more than an old landmark. But against the backdrop of Montejano's account of the Valley's transformation from a ranching to a farming society, the existence of a plant for pumping water near El Carmen is charged with meaning, especially when considered in conjunction with other passages in the *KCDTS* such as this one:

Luego, porque el Río no tenía agua para todos, la raza empezó el sistema de norias para regar. Las resacas servían, sirvieron y sirven como tanques de agua y de ahí que el Valle, en gran parte, se convirtiera en lo que es.

Después vinieron los bolillos y ellos impusieron las leyes y sus sistemas de regar. (**VARONES**:115)

[Then, because the river didn't have enough water for everybody, the Mexican-Americans started the well irrigation system. The ox bow lakes—resacas—are used as water tanks, and that's how the Valley, for the most part, has become as fertile as it is.

Later, when the Anglos came, they imposed the laws and adopted the irrigation system: To this day, the state courts don't know what to do with so many water district suits, but that's another matter. (**VARONES**:114)]

Irrigation techniques in South Texas changed with the arrival of Anglo farmers. While the *norias*, the water wheel pumps, were sufficient for subsistence farming, the Anglos' market-oriented idea of farming called for irrigation on a larger scale. Montejano reports that the turn of the century saw the implementation of deep wells that tapped into huge underground lakes, and the so-called artesian wells made use of underground water without pumping (Montejano 1987:106). He also reports that only very few of the former Mexican landowners made a successful transition to farming and that as a consequence the great majority lost their land to aggressive land developers who were eager to make the land profitable. From the existence of a pumping plant near the Carmen Ranch and from other references thinly scattered across the *KCDTS,* we know for a fact that the Buenrostros belonged to the fortunate few Mexican landowners who became successful farmers. In **POLICEMAN** (35), Israel Buenrostro plants sugarcane; in **FRIENDS** (152), Ira Escobar wonders if it is legal that the Buenrostros farm 200 hectares in Soliseño/Mexico "right across from the El Carmen Ranch" on the original Llano Grande grant. And in **RITES** (15), Rafa expertly discusses the various crops grown on El Carmen with a Louisiana farm boy. From this combined information, we can gather that in the midst of the 1915 rebellion, the Buenrostros had water and were farming competitively; also, they were once again implicated in insurrectionist activities. Before exploring their involvement with the irredentist Ejército Liberador México Texano, a brief digression is called for in order to illustrate the import of the Buenrostros' successful conversion to irrigation farming.

Hinojosa never loses sight of his main objective, his *axis mundi,* which, in Bruce-Novoa's words is "the praxis of the discovery" (Bruce-Novoa 1990b:154). The books themselves hold out to the reader the possibility of discovering the Chicano community in a synthesis of tradition and adaptation in a modern American reality. Rafa and his brothers personify this synthesis on the one hand by preserving their familial Mexican heritage and on the other by realizing that certain allowances to the new order must be made. Consequently, they carry on their father's legacy of farming and distributing land. Synthesis between the new and the old is also reflected in the brothers' career choices. Israel and Aaron uphold the pastoral patrimony, while Rafa becomes an English teacher, a lawyer, and a policeman.

This synthesis of the new and old is laid out in a vast network in the *KCDTS,* waiting for the reader to discover its interlacements. Such is the case even in a seemingly removed installment like **SERVANTS**, where the reappearance of the old "Pumping Station" (**SERVANTS**:186) draws attention to the surrounding passage. The reference occurs in a letter addressed to Rafa from another Valley boy and Korean vet named Rudy Hernández. I quote the respective passage below faithfully, i.e., with Rudy's own grammar and spelling:

> one of he reasons I am also writing to you is to please take time off to go see my folks, Mr. And Mrs. Rodolfo and Paula Hernandez. They don't live right in Bascom, but over by your families cemetery. Right

close to the Pumping Station and that old Church that was burn to the ground before you or me was born. Well its right there where they live. He farms for himself and he rents land from your cousin Rufino F. G. [Fischer Gutiérrez, in whose cotton field Tomás Imás was attacked by a rattlesnake] And he goes on thirds, fourths, or halves with him. Anyway, everybody knows my Dad and my Mom there, you just ask for them. (**SERVANTS**:186)[4]

The interlacements in this passage reach out in several directions. Fischer Gutiérrez is another rancher-turned-farmer; he is part of the old families network in the Valley; he is directly involved in Jehú's scheming against the KBC-Leguizamón landgrabbing pact (**RAFA**:34); and he rents out land to smaller Mexican farmers such as the Hernández family. Once again, the network's connecting tendrils are slight and sometimes far between. It is the reader's experience of discovering them that lends them strength, thereby evoking a successful synthesis of the ancestral rural Chicano culture with a market-oriented agricultural structure:

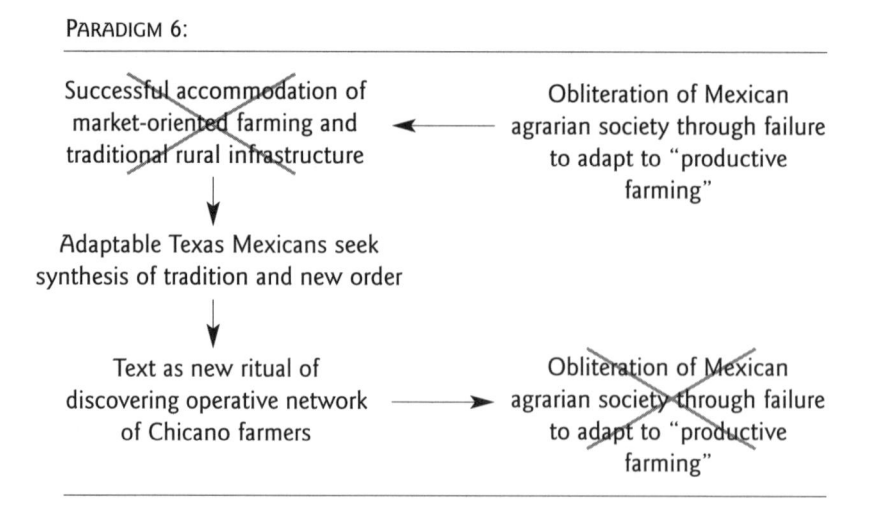

PARADIGM 6:

~~Successful accommodation of market-oriented farming and traditional rural infrastructure~~ ← Obliteration of Mexican agrarian society through failure to adapt to "productive farming"

↓

Adaptable Texas Mexicans seek synthesis of tradition and new order

↓

Text as new ritual of discovering operative network of Chicano farmers → ~~Obliteration of Mexican agrarian society through failure to adapt to "productive farming"~~

When the Ejército Liberador México Texano fought for the secession of Texas, lynchings of Texas Mexicans became so frequent, Montejano notes, that the newspapers ceased to mention them. However, the lynchings of the innocent Naranjo brothers on Buenrostro land, which is recalled here by Abel Manzano, did stir up both the Mexican and Anglo communities. John Goodman (**RITES**:88–89), an ex-soldier and acquaintance of the notorious Charles Markham, remembers it vividly, and he actually blames the Rangers for unnecessarily exacerbating the conflict. The fact that the Texas Mexican ranch hands were executed clandestinely on Buenrostro land[5]—perhaps as a threat or a challenge—is critical considering that in 1915 the Buenrostros hosted and fed a seditionist war party on their land. The passage that narrates the episode occurs in one of Rafa's miniatures in **VARONES** (35), and Hinojosa directly mentions the "Liberating Texas-Mexican Army" in **VALLEY** (79). Echevarría recalls that he saw a party of thirty-five seditionists riding down Klail's main street, and that they had camped in the park that divided Anglo Town from Mexican Town. The next day, according to Echevarría, they saddled up and rode on to Julián Buenrostro's land; "éste los recibió y les dio un becerro para la barbacoa" ["my uncle welcomed them and gave them a calf for the barbecue" (my translation)].

Hereafter, the passage assumes even greater import as it makes reference to the multiethnic make-up of the Ejército Liberador México Texano and to a Texas Ranger named Baker. Both elements emphasize the authenticity and accuracy with which Hinojosa incorporates historical data into his fiction. The seditionist army indeed consisted of a mix of various segregated ethnic groups and dissenting Anglos, and "Baker" is the actual last name of a corrupt Hidalgo County boss, an ex-Ranger, who played a sinister part in a 1928 attempt to disenfranchise Mexican voters in the Hidalgo County Rebellion. Incidentally, the nonfictional Baker was a bit of a coward who backed out as soon as his scheme was discovered, and the fictional Baker in Hinojosa's sketch is not exactly the epitome of the legendary Texas Ranger dare-devil either, as Echevarría tells Rafa:

Este mismo día, ya tarde, llegó Ned Baker con sesenta o más; policías, marciales, condestables, gente del condado, y los mirones de regla.

Al preguntarle Baker a Esteban que qué se sabía, éste le dijo: "Entre ellos iban los Montoya, el Negro Brown, Charlie Perkins y pura gente conocida. ¿Ves aquel humo? Es de ellos; seguro que mataron algo del ganado del 'Quieto' o de Julián."

Baker dijo que los seguiría el día siguiente.

El día siguiente, tú. (**VARONES**:35)

[That same day, later on, Ned Baker arrived in Klail with sixty deputies or so: policemen, marshalls, constables, county officers, rangers, and the usual hangers-on.

When Baker asked Esteban what he knew, Echevarría said, "They went through here, the Montoyas; Brown, the black man; Charlie

Perkins; well-known people. You see that smoke over there? It's theirs; they're probably cooking some of *Quieto's* or Julian's stock."

Baker said he would follow them the next day.

The next day, yeah! (**VARONES**:34)]

Esteban's words forebode the Rangers' frustrated attempts to curb the activities of the seditionists. Instead, they wreaked such havoc among the civilian population that the State of Texas finally decided to reorganize the Rangers. John Goodman remembers that "there *was* that State hearing with that Mex legislator from Jonesville . . . that legislator was not afraid to speak up, but that was one voice. . . . One thing, though, they *did* cut the number of Texas Rangers; . . . they was busted down to four companies for the whole state, and I think each company had something like seventeen men. Yeah, they were broken" (**RITES**:87, original italics).

The truth about the Rangers' less than glorious role during the 1915 irredentist movement had long been ignored by Texas historiographers. Américo Paredes writes: "If all the books written about the Rangers were put one on top of the other, the resulting pile would be almost as tall as some of the tales that they contain" (1958:23). Chicano scholarship, meanwhile, is revising this Anglo-centric history, and Hinojosa as an artist has created a befitting metaphor to couch the momentous impact of this process. Abel Manzano, in his account at the end of **RITES**, explains that the Anglos, at one time, had changed the course of the Río Grande where it borders on the Carmen Ranch. In **KLAIL** (27), Echevarría also mentions that "the Carmen Ranch was almost cut off from some good Rio Grande River water." After the 1915 clash with the Rangers,

> the Buenrostros put dynamite on that bend of the Río Grande and the Río changed course for half a mile. The Anglos had changed the old channel years ago, and the Buenrostros just put it back to where it was. (**RITES**:110)

The passage will gather additional import if the word "channel" in the last sentence is replaced by "history." Indeed, it would seem that Hinojosa's complete authorial agenda appears emblazoned on the page.

With the Rangers unable to complete the task, the U.S. Army had to step in to bring the seditionists under control and to make the Valley safe for the Anglo farmers and their new order, which did not make any provisions for the Texas Mexican as a citizen, voter, or landowner. One such Anglo farmer, who had come to the Valley from the north in 1920, was Rebecca Ruth Verser's father. Mrs. Verser's statements in **RITES** (97–98) are symptomatic of the newcomers' reaction upon finding South Texas populated by Mexicans who had not yet grown accustomed to their "inferior status":

> The main thing I don't like about Mexicans—young or old, it doesn't matter—is the way they look at you. Brazen. I warned you that I am a frank person. They see you coming: they look at you. You walk past them: they look at you. I know *what* they're looking at, they are looking at my legs! I'd pull their eyes out, if I could. They're horrible; I wouldn't have them working for me for anything. And inside the house? Are you kidding? Never. No sir. The way they look at you. . . .
>
> My father came to the Valley in the Twenties, and he said they were worse then. Worse than niggers, he said. Worse is what he said because they didn't know their place. . . . They weren't uppity, you know . . . they just wouldn't go away . . . they were *always* around. And speaking Spanish; all the time. It's enough to . . . oh, I don't know. (**RITES**:97–98, original italics)

As Mrs. Verser's testimony indicates, the unprecedented segregational rigor that would reign in the Valley throughout much of the following decades arose from the inflow of Anglo settlers like Mr. Verser, who brought his preconceived ideas of "inferior races" to the Valley. Evidently, white supremacist convictions had not diminished notably in the 1960s when Mrs. Verser makes the above comments. Mrs. Verser's ardent indignation about Mexicans' strengthened self-confidence in the 1960s must ultimately be explained by her growing up at a time when both Mexican Americans and Anglo Americans were impregnated with the culture of segregation.

SEGREGATION (1920–1940)

In the previous section it was noted that the conflict between recently arrived farmers and old-order ranchers resulted in the establishment of separate Mexican ranch counties and Anglo farm counties. The necessity to adequately depict this dissimilarity of conditions in South Texas during the 1930s and 1940s is one of the reasons why the chapter on segregation is by far the most voluminous in Montejano's *Anglos and Mexicans in the Making of Texas*. Inevitably, the nutshell account that I am about to provide of Montejano's acute, exhaustive sociological analysis, must omit scores of details that speak eloquently of race relations in South Texas during Rafa Buenrostro's early childhood. I have therefore taken care to select those aspects that I consider particularly beneficial to the understanding of Hinojosa's text.

> Having cleared the area of chaparral, mesquite, and conservative ranchers, the newcomer farmers were essentially free to build a new society. The trappings of development were dramatic signs of the new order. Introduced rapidly in the 1920s, automobiles, highways, libraries, movie houses, drugstores, and so on soon distinguished modern farm areas from the horse and cow country of the ranch counties. So impressive were the changes that many newcomers saw themselves as the "first settlers" of the region. (Montejano 1987:159)

At the same time that these "first settlers" delighted in the new benefits that came with the agricultural revolution, urbanization, and manufacturing, the Mexicans who literally lived across the tracks felt the full brunt of a complete and absolute residential, educational, social, political, and occupational segregation. Racial discrimination and subjugation as a repercussion of the war, or as an outgrowth of struggle over land, was not exactly new to Valley Chicanos. Yet the unsettling proportions and intensity of this new surge of racism, as Montejano compellingly illustrates, can only be explained within the framework of the restructured labor force in a completely modified economy.

Montejano isolates three major areas where the new commercial agriculture had had a momentous impact on Mexican-Anglo relations in the Valley. First, the farmers needed an abundant work force that had to be "tied to the land through non-market means—through violence, coercion, and law" (Montejano 1987:160). Second, in contrast to the paternalistic ranch society, the new society was structured along the lines of a strictly formal boss-laborer relationship that fomented anonymity and mistrust on both sides. The third point focuses on the notion that even before the advent of the new order, Texas had had a long record of racial division. The new labor situation suddenly made the division of ethnicities appear reasonable and natural, which led to a revival of old ideas of Mexican inferiority and the creation of new ones.

Whereas in the past segregational practices more or less arose as responses to conflict between the ethnic groups, the new racial order resulted in the coherent planning of two separate societies with cities divided into a Mexican Town and an Anglo Town. The occasional, inevitable crossing of the line between the two was regulated by a strict code of behavior that clearly reflected the racial hierarchy. As examples of separate schooling, Montejano cites the farm communities along highway 83—among them Hinojosa's native Mercedes—with their unbroken policy of Mexican school segregation (Montejano 1987:168). Predictably, segregated schooling meant substandard education for Mexican children, who were frequently taught by grudging, badly paid Anglo teachers who openly considered their Mexican students academically inferior, unclean, and linguistically inadequate. Most teachers, principals, and educational administrators admitted that these were excuses for a general lack of interest in educating Mexicans. As one superintendent of a segregated school district put it: "So you see it is up to the white population to keep the Mexican on his knees in an onion patch or in new ground. This does not mix very well with education" (quoted in Montejano 1987:193).

"This Migrant Earth"

With the increasingly market-oriented structuring of commercial agriculture in Texas, the older system of tenants and sharecroppers became economically unsound due the higher overhead costs.[6] While there was an abundance of cheap labor, there were always shortages during harvest times. Soon it occurred to the Anglo farmers that the ideal way to get good use out of this work force was a system of labor controls that would assure the availability of cheap labor at the proper time. Meanwhile, it was necessary for the workers to be mobile but not so mobile as to go and look for higher wages. The practices implemented by the Anglo farmers to achieve these contradictory objectives covered a wide range of institutionalized, borderline-legal, and outright criminal measures. Montejano shows how the procedures to immobilize Mexican labor changed depending on which level in the administrative hierarchy they were implemented. The element of cruelty, though, was inherent in all of them.

Individual farmers often used personal violence (Montejano cites shotguns, horsewhips, and chains, 1987:201), various forms of debt peonage, and the "shotgun settlements" of labor contracts where workers were dismissed without pay under some pretext. This last practice did not exactly immobilize workers, but it certainly was an effective measure to render their services profitable. Agricultural companies sent out contractors who lured laborers to farms with false offers and made them work off advance payments under slave-labor conditions. County governments would start enforcing vagrancy laws during picking times. Hired laborers, who protested against unacceptable working conditions upon arrival at the farm, were found guilty of vagrancy, fined, and then forced to work off the fines. When these "convicts" were needed elsewhere in the county, they were given passes that permitted them to travel only to the designated areas.

It is ironic that these practices were eventually counteracted in the interests of agribusinesses from northern states who blamed the immobilization of migrant workers in Texas for their own labor shortages during periods of restricted immigration from Europe. Texas, however, responded with legislation at state level: in 1934, the Texas Farm Placement Service was officially established, highways were manned, and workers systematically distributed to farms (see Montejano 1987:213). Below we will see that Hinojosa makes frequent references to the plight of the migrant workers and their annual migration north, driving at night and using back roads in order not to be "immobilized" by the local authorities. In fact, Montejano emphasizes that Mexicans were not just suffering impassively. The underground railroad along the back roads to the sugar beet fields in Michigan were only one of the countermeasures Mexican farm workers employed in order to exercise their right to sell their labor to the highest bidder. Resistance commenced with workers creating an information network that helped avoid highway controls, bad contractors, and mean employers, and it frequently resulted in strikes, political protest, and even violent opposition. As a final resort in the face of unrelenting racism in Texas, many Chicanos emigrated to the northern United States. They were quickly replaced by immigrants from across the border, which had been coming in great numbers since the Mexican Revolution and have kept up their steady flow into the United States ever since.

The Rationale of Segregation

Segregation in Texas, as we have seen, must ultimately be understood in the context of economic interests and political control. While most of the Anglos were perfectly aware of the pragmatics, justification was commonly sought elsewhere and grew into a fabrication of theories about "inferiority of the Mexicans." Scientific, religious, and historical arguments abounded. Farmers took anthropology courses that not only furnished scientific "evidence," but also taught them how to pick workers with the correct pigmentation for working in the Texas heat (Montejano 1987:222–25). Dark skin and typical poverty-related diseases quickly gave rise to the conviction that Mexicans were dirty and infested with germs. But in order to preserve the stability of the situation it was not enough that only the Anglos were convinced of these truths. Rather, it was imperative that the Mexican children recognize the supremacy of the white race and their own inferiority. This was transmitted through the sheer inferiority of Mexican schools, hand-me-down textbooks, segregated athletic leagues, and the perpetuation of the myths of the Alamo. In high schools that were not segregated, strong antagonisms and mutual hostility often made the Mexican children wish they had a separate school.

Responses from the Mexican community were diverse. Some accepted and internalized the teachings of Anglo superiority and Mexican inferiority. Others suppressed their hate and frustration, and again others accepted Anglo standards as a challenge and tried to rise to them. Such was the case with the League of United Latin American Citizens (LULAC), whose protest, however, was directed only against discrimination of clean and educated Mexicans, thus creating an ambience of racism and class-consciousness within their own ethnic group. What is more, they soon found out that education and cleanliness were not enough to move Anglos in their racist intransigence.

Clearly, Texas Mexicans fared worst in the economically progressive, rigorously segregated farm counties. Yet in some parts of Texas, for instance in the Winter Garden part of the state, the urgency to hold the labor force in place worked in the Mexicans' favor. In pursuit of their particular interests, Anglo farmers, and particularly the Anglo merchants, were perfectly capable of going out of their way to coddle and protect the Texas Mexicans, who in turn, seized these opportunities to improve their situation, mostly through legal threats combined with boycotts of local Anglo businesses.

On the same score, Montejano stresses the existence of a world apart in the still vigorous Anglo-Mexican ranch society. Here, the paternalistic, though rather more congenial, racial order was largely intact, and created considerable confusion when individuals crossed the county lines that separated them from the farming districts. Ranch Mexicans coming to farming communities flared at discriminatory treatment, and Anglos who moved from segregated farm counties to ranch counties were disgusted by the way "they mix here like one race" (Montejano 1987:245).

Segregation in Belken County: Immobilization, Barrioization, Separate Schooling, and the Logic of Supremacy

If Belken County is faithfully modeled on Hidalgo, Texas in the 1930s, then Rafa Buenrostro is born into a truly antagonistic environment at the height of the segregationist period. Montejano repeatedly describes Hidalgo as one of the farm counties where separation was particularly rigorous. It seems that initially Rafa was not afflicted by these antagonisms, because he spent his early childhood in the sheltered world of El Carmen. Potential clashes with Anglos constantly overshadow life in the Chicano community, but they never really take center stage. This is due to the fact that the early books, which are set during the period of segregation, were expressly created as literary portraits that predominantly depict the Belken County Chicano community from within. In the opening of **CONDADO**, the narrator announces:

> El número de bolillos que se ve en estos escritos es bien poco. Los bolillos están, como quien dice, al margen de estos sucesos. A la raza de Belken, la gringada le viene ancha; por su parte, la gringada, claro es, como está en el poder, hace caso a la raza cuando le conviene: elecciones, guerra, susto economico, etc. (Las cosas más vale decirse como son si no, no.) (**CONDADO**:29)
> [The number of Anglos to be seen on these pages is rather scant. The Anglos are, in a manner of speaking, on the margin of these events. The Belken County Texas Mexicans, though, think that there are more than enough Anglos; it goes without saying that the Anglos, for their part, take notice of the Mexicans only when there is a reason: elections, wars, economic recessions, etc. (It's better to tell it like it is, or else to shut up.) (my translation)]

The passage—albeit a disclaimer for the scarce presence of Anglos in the book—accurately pinpoints the nucleus of the conflict. The Anglo power holders ignored the Chicanos unless they needed them as voters, soldiers, and laborers or as scapegoats during economic crises. Outside of these conditions, the two societies lived alongside each other pretending that the other did not exist.

Again, Anglo historiography reflects these circumstances by simply passing over Mexican presence in the Valley. We noted earlier that all three books belonging to that first generation of *KCDTS* installments pay tribute to medieval Spanish portraiture.[7] In accordance with his revisionist agenda, Hinojosa's literary portraits place his Belken County Chicanos at their center, focusing on individual, isolated characters and incidents, and leaving it to readers to experience the discovery of a complete social fabric. Rosaura Sánchez has pointed out that the early books "decontextualize events so that the impact of history or social change on individual lives and on particular social classes is not evident" (Sánchez 1984:76). At this juncture of my presentation, it is perhaps necessary to reiterate that the first chapter of this study portrayed the books in their individuality and in their decontextualized narrative. Conversely, the present chapter's objective is to contextualize the sketches of individual lives and events with the combined help of Montejano's sociohistorical analysis and the evidence spread across the entire length of the *KCDTS*.

A first example of Rafa's shock upon experiencing the harshness of city segregation emerges as a portrait of the racial hierarchy in the Valley in which the Mexicans did not even occupy the bottom rung:

> Aside from a library and a stopped-up swimming pool, there were two cafés on Ruffing's main street along with some beat up buildings. One of the cafés didn't allow Texas mexicanos in while the other one did; now, it could be that the first would allow us entry but no service which comes to the very same thing. My father and I were in the second one when I spotted a black family, man, wife, and two boys just about or a little over my own age. Dad turned to me and said that black folks would only be served in the kitchen, if there. I didn't understand that part of it, and he repeated once and then again.
>
> On the way home, I wondered how the black man had first explained it to his kids when they entered the kitchen for service. (**VALLEY**:46)

From a child's perspective, Rafa wonders about the nature of segregation, not grasping its impact on others even though he himself is a direct victim. Certainly, on an immediately visible plane, young Rafa is expressing his empathy for the humiliating condition of the black children, who he suspects are just as puzzled as, and even worse off, than he is. Additionally, when contextualized in the Buenrostro family history, the passage captures for the first time the notion that will resound time and again in the Series: the Valley has been the Buenrostros' home for centuries, and Rafa has grown up with the certainty of who and what he is. Therefore—and contrary to what one would expect—the effect of being made to feel inferior does not fully register until Rafa sees it reflected in other segregated individuals.

While the scarcity of data on this kind of experience suggests that it was not very frequent during Rafa's early childhood, we do know that Rafa and his cousin Jehú attended the segregated, 100 percent Mexican North Ward Elementary School. There, they were taught by Miss Moy and Miss Bunn, two Anglo women who were clearly unhappy about teaching Mexican children. Rafa remembers Miss Moy particularly for her red hair and freckles, and because "she was forever washing and soaking her hands in alcohol and then drying them off with disposable napkins" (**VALLEY**:43). One of the major themes in race thinking identified by Montejano is the hygiene-germ theory (Montejano 1987:225). Apart from the purely pragmatic reasons for segregation, a number of "scientific" justifications were given. One of them claimed that Mexicans were dirty, and had germs and lice; segregation was therefore considered a kind of quarantine. Apart from the lamentable fact that Mexican children did suffer from poverty-related diseases, there was never actually any proof of Mexican uncleanliness. Miss Moy, though, was probably convinced that she was taking the necessary precautions for one who enters a quarantined area.

Rafa puts a more humorous slant on the encroachment of Anglo culture in a purely Mexican classroom in the following sketch, in which he alludes to a phenomenon that Elaine Dorough-Johnson has labeled "dietary ethnocentrism" (Dorough-Johnson 1978:47). The children in Miss Bunn's class are taught "What Every Young Child Should Eat for Breakfast" (**VALLEY**: 43). Lucy Ramírez—her name alone suggests an advanced degree of assimilation—tries to satisfy her teacher's curiosity as to her eating habits by checking off the list of All-American breakfast items:

> Un día se le ocurrió a Miss Bunn preguntarle a Lucy Ramírez que qué se había desayunado esa mañana. La muy mentiretas dijo que había tomado un vaso de orange juice y dos scrambled eggs con toast y jelly. (**ESTAMPAS**:114, also see **VALLEY**:43)
> [One day it occurred to Miss Bunn to ask Lucy Ramírez what she'd had for breakfast that morning. Lucy, the little fibber, said she'd had a glass of orange juice, and two scrambled eggs with toast and jelly. (my translation)]

When she puts the same question to Leo Pumarejo, "el cabrón de Leo" lays bare the pitfalls of dietary ethnocentrism. He looks at Lucy and tells the truth: "one tortilla de harina WITH PLENTY OF PEANUT BUTTER!"

And yet, while the purely Mexican schools were badly equipped and staffed with grudging teachers, they did nurture sentiments of solidarity and self. Attending a mixed but discriminatory school, where they were hazed and cuffed, made many Mexican children wish they had their own schools (Montejano 1987:231). Rebecca Verser tells Galindo in **RITES**, "in *my* day, the Mexicans didn't go to school with us; in Ruffing [where restaurants were segregated!], for example, they went only as far as the fifth . . . any higher, and they had to come here to Klail" (**RITES**:97, original italics). This coincides with Montejano's findings, according to which Mexican school children in most parts of South Texas during the 1930s and 1940s did not attend beyond elementary school, and if they did, they had to find a high school that would accept Mexican students. In those mixed schools, Mexican students were frequently antagonized to such a point that they felt humiliated and disheartened. Such a case is reported in **CONDADO/KLAIL** (74/70), where Rafa spells out the difference between the South Ward mexicanos who had gone to a mixed elementary school, and himself and his friends who came from the exclusively Mexican North Ward. When the two groups of Chicanos meet in high school, it becomes obvious what attending school with Anglo children had done to the South Warders:

they were different from us, somehow. Jehú Malacara, a cousin of mine, called them "The Dispossessed." Now, these mexicanos were one hell of a lot more fluent in English than we were, but they came up short on other things; on the uptake, for one, out on the playground for another.

Example. When it came to handing out athletic equipment, we pushed and shoved as well as anyone; the American way, right? But these mexicanos hung back. (**KLAIL**:70)

Territorial turf meant nothing at North Ward since most of us came from the same neighborhoods. It was different at Memorial Junior High and at the [Klail] High, too. We noticed that the North Warders who'd made it to high school always sat on the gym steps; our legacy, then.

The South Ward mexicanos had no place to go; in limbo, as it were. To add to this, we made it a point to speak Spanish on the school grounds, even if it meant licks from the principal and detention hall, to boot. (**KLAIL**:73)

In this section in **CONDADO/KLAIL** Rafa's miniature sketches capture a number of brief scenes that attest to the separate treatment of Anglos and Mexicans by teachers, football coaches, school officials, library staff, and fellow students. Rafa makes it clear, though, that the North Warders never accepted, were resigned to, or internalized these discriminatory practices. The point cannot be emphasized enough, for, clearly, educational segregation served as much to teach Anglo children superiority as to teach Mexican children "their place." Early on, Rafa and his friends oppose the system through skillfully undermining Anglo tactics. They boycott intramural athletic competitions to blackmail the coach (**KLAIL**:72); they demonstrate outright obstinacy and resistance, defying teachers to punish them physically for speaking Spanish (73); or they actually come to blows with Anglo students ("Mexican haters") who make sure the Mexicans get the worst athletic equipment (71).

Several minor hints in the text suggest that while Rafa is attending school, he is not living at the ranch. After class he goes to his "own house" (**VALLEY**:47), in their "neighborhood" in a "section of Klail City" (44). This is fairly relevant, because it enables Rafa to draw a credible picture of residential segregation from a personal point of view. Klail, like most Valley towns in those days, had a Mexican town and an Anglo town that were separated by the railroad tracks and a park that lay "close to the railroad depot. The trains run once in a while and when they do it's to ship out the agricultural products grown in the region" (**KLAIL**:105). Here, in one paragraph, Rafa demarcates Klail City as a new order farming community that he links directly to the theme of residential segregation. With separate living quarters come anonymity, paranoia about what the power holders may do or think, and the unspoken rules of etiquette when dealing with the Anglos. Rafa's observations below concur with those of Montejano's informants in that the rules of contact with Anglos required Mexicans to assume "a deferential body posture and respectful tone of voice" (Montejano 1987:168):

1. Behave yourself; 2. Keep it down; 3. Don't do anything that'll draw the Anglo Texans' attention; 4. Etc.

The bald truth is that our fellow Texans across the tracks could hardly care about what we think, say, or do.

Here's something of what the A. T.s usually say: Oh, it's nothing, really; just one of your usual Mexican cantina fan-dan-goes, 's all. They drink a little beer, they play them rancheras on the juke box, don't you know; and then one o' them let's out a big squeal, and the first thing you know, why, they's having theirselves a fight.

See what I mean? (**VALLEY**:51)

Also, doing business during the period of segregation was no small feat for Mexican entrepreneurs, as Johnny Pike's account in **RITES** (77–78) illustrates. He tells the story of Vicente Vizcarra, who bought a new car during the Depression and rented an office "right smack in the middle of Anglo town." This aroused the suspicion of the local sheriff, Walt Dembro, who went to see Vicente and asked him where and how he got the money. Pike, born and raised in a segregated Klail, tries to justify "Walt's point of view" seeing that Vicente "couldn't, I mean didn't-a, didn't have a bank account. . . . Know what I mean?"

The Sheriff found out that Vicente had been working for a Houston insurance company for some time and "had all Mexican town sewn up." When the company representative from Houston came down to Klail, he complained about Vicente's office located by the before-mentioned park in the Mexican quarter. Thus, it was actually the company that then rented "a nicer office" for Vicente in Anglo town. Most revealingly, Pike peppers his account with remarks such as "first Mex in that part of town," "the Company did the paper work," "caused a slight commotion," and "did have a leetle trouble getting himself a phone."

The passage is charged with layers of meaning as to the culture, pragmatics, geography, and power structure of segregation. It was all right for Vicente to be successful in Mexican town until he violated the rule of not arousing the Anglos' attention. The small town authorities tried to interfere with his entrepreneurial activities but balked at opposing the big company from Houston. The company man from Houston objected to Vicente's office very probably not for its size or condition but because of its location in Mexican town. And for all his business acumen and hard work, Vicente could just barely get a telephone, while a bank account was entirely out of the question. From whichever angle we look at Vicente's success story, it always has the earmarks of a purely paternalistic, patronizing, and pragmatic racial order. Luckily, Vicente knew how to play one segment of the power structure against another.

A very similar picture emerges in an interview with Thelma Ann Watling (**RITES**:90), who seems to be genuinely fond of Rosendo, a worker in her husband's produce packing shed, whose daughters work as maids in Thelma's home. Her interview reveals, though, that Mrs. Watling is not beyond hiring a thirteen-year-old to work as a full-time maid while her own daughters go to high school and college. The Watlings clearly appreciate the Mexicans' tractability (in Thelma's own careless words: hard-working, long suffering, loyal, grateful, and appreciative), and they honor it by giving them presents: they would "drive out to deliver citrus baskets to them," and Thelma's husband did not even expect Rosendo to carry the baskets. Thelma herself would "stay in the car and wave at the girls; prettiest things you've ever seen." Hinojosa's true-to-life picture of this different, more insidious nuance of the discriminatory racial order comes complete with a small allusion to in- and out-migration of Mexican nationals. While Rosendo Macías, who had come to the Valley from "across" in the 1920s, chose to stay, the second generation of the Macías family left for a better life up north. With the benign treatment they received from her, Thelma Watling is genuinely perplexed that the Macías girls would have moved to Chicago "of all places."

The fluctuation in the Mexican labor force, of both Texas Mexican and Mexican citizens, was a constant source of concern for the growers in the Valley, as Montejano has exhaustively documented. Thelma Watling's statements confirm that many Mexican nationals moved on before they had properly taken roots in the Valley, and the exodus of old-time Valleyites was continuous as well. The need to immobilize this work force, especially during harvest times, created one of the worst episodes of institutionalized civil rights violations in modern U.S. history. In his 1976 *Klail City y sus alrededores* (**CONDADO**), Hinojosa devotes a series of *estampas* to the migrant farm workers, whose plight was not just limited to the hardships of the trip and the less-than-human work conditions at some of the farms. Even before leaving Texas territory, they had to use all their ingenuity to elude local sheriffs, corrupt *contratistas,* brutal farmers, and the Texas Farm Placement Service. When Hinojosa rewrote **CONDADO** in 1987 as **KLAIL**, he grouped the scattered sketches of itinerant workers together in one chapter that he called "The Searchers."

The topic of the itinerant workers is included here in the chapter on Rafa in spite of the fact that the singular status of the Buenrostros as successful farmers and landowners seems sufficiently documented in the text. In fact, the text underscores that the legendary Don Jesús, owner of El Carmen, farmer and distributor of land, also gets in the truck with the migrant workers to go and pick cherries in Michigan year after year. According to a sketch in **ESTAMPAS/VALLEY** (119/57), Rafa has made the trip with his father six times at a fairly young age. Why the Buenrostros leave their farm during the summer is not documented in the text (presumably even landowners had to make up for a poor crop by going north) but their participation in the annual migration lends credibility to Rafa's concern with the migrant workers' plight.

The five pieces that make up "The Searchers" (**KLAIL**:46–69) stand out as an isolated segment in the *KCDTS* chronicles, which generally circle around the theme of early Valley history, property disputes, resistance against illicit land claims, family allegiance, and the oral tradition in the community. In "The Searchers," Hinojosa charts a segment of Texas history that has its roots and origins in the social conditions of the Valley, but which, by nature, propels the narrative outside of the Valley and into the United States at large. The individual pieces of "The Searchers" comprise an extremely fragmented, disjointed collection of short dramatic scenes, some of which are narrated by Galindo and some by Rafa. They are given unity through their common subject matter and through references to a number of familiar characters. Above all, they are replete with suggestive, yet obscure passages that can only be properly interpreted in the context of workers' immobilization in the interest of growers in Texas and other states.

The first series of those ominous passages occurs in "The Searchers II" (**KLAIL**:51), where we eavesdrop on a conversation between two men about to embark on the long trip north. They lament that many of the northern states have poor, narrow roads unlike the wide, smooth Texas roads. Curiously, they make it clear that these wide Texas roads are not for them: "Made just for *us*, right? Shoot. . . . we got mighty fine roads made in Texas, all right, but this here state a-ours is a skin-flintish son-of-a-bitch." Only two pages further on, in another anonymous conversation, the following information is exchanged: "And you *got* to watch them, otherwise they'll keep you up there till January or February, even. . . . Remember what happened *last* year?" (53, original italics). The series of portentous allusions is continued on pages 57 and 58, where Leocadio Gavira tells Galindo about a town in Illinois that appears on the map "just south of Peoria, but I'd say it's probably closer to Hell'n anything else." When Galindo inquires further, all he learns is that something very bad "happened to a truck load of us there one picking season." On page 58, we observe a Leocadio Gavira who is evidently worried about the Texas officials' practice of pulling over the migrants' trucks. Dead-tired, he insists on staying at the wheel of his truck until they have crossed the state line. Then, and only then, he explains to Galindo, "I can let you take over again; the cops ain't as picky there, see?"

Evidently, they are traveling on the underground railroad along the back roads to the sugar beet fields in Michigan. Always on the lookout for attempts at immobilization, they exchange information about ruthless employers who think nothing of keeping the workers against their will if that's what the market calls for. Based on the text alone, with imagination filling in the gaps, a picture of abuse, of staying out of sight, of constant fear and watchfulness begins to emerge. Primed by Montejano's account of horsewhips, chains, and shotguns, we catch a glimpse of an even bleaker image, approximating Gavira's gloomy recollections of a place in Illinois that deserves to be named "Hell."

INTEGRATION (1940–1986)

When the state government established the Texas Farm Placement Service in 1934, it was essentially an attempt of a would-be sovereign state to institutionalize a formal system of labor control. These imperial pretensions of the former Republic of Texas could not go uncontested. Midwestern and northern agricultural and industrial lobbies were too influential for Texas to keep their hold on the Mexican labor force. The advent of great farming corporations such as Del Monte and the growing preference of consumer stability over segregation gradually eroded the racial order in Texas. Montejano, nevertheless, places great importance on the fact that the gradual changes in the economic and commercial infrastructure were "by themselves insufficient to upset the segregationist order. The demise was not predestined; rather, the system persisted, until finally worn down by the trauma of two major crises—World War II and the civil rights movement of the 1960s" (Montejano 1987:259).

Even though in Texas during the 1940s Mexicans were legally Caucasians, and there were no actual Jim Crow laws, factual segregation in many counties was no different from that of blacks in the South. Texas Mexicans were gradually learning to use their leverage as workers, consumers, and voters when World War II provided a sudden catalyst for change:

> The need for soldiers and workers, and for positive international relations with Latin America, meant that the counterproductive and embarrassing customs of Jim Crow had to be shelved, at least for the duration of the emergency. In more lasting terms, the war created a generation of Mexican American veterans prepared to press for their rights and privileges. The cracks in the segregated order proved to be irreparable.
>
> The cracks did not rupture, however, until blacks in the South, and Mexican Americans in the Southwest mobilized to present a sharp challenge from below in the 1960s. In Texas the protest activity among all segments of the Mexican American community—farm workers, factory workers, students, professionals, businessmen—was unprecedented. (Montejano 1987:264)

Up until the late 1930s, Mexicans in many counties were refused service in restaurants, could buy real estate only in Mexican neighborhoods, suffered frequent police brutality, and were only allowed into certain professions. Even in industrial labor and the railroad industry, they had lower wages for equal work, separate eating and washing facilities, and could not join the unions. It was only the combined impact of World War II, mechanization of farm labor, urban political power, and the civil rights struggle that caused dramatic changes in the racial and social landscape.

Change was not accomplished, Montejano reiterates, through a common liberal climate, for even as the United States fought a war against Hitler and his race supremacy, the country suffered a new upsurge of racism. Also, little change occurred on the political front. The big farmers controlled the Democratic Party, which controlled Texas politics and had anti-labor laws, oppression of blacks and Mexican Americans, and states' rights (to immobilize labor!) high on their political agenda. Conservatism in Texas was reinforced by the emergence of McCarthyism in the 1950s and didn't begin to lose its force until the end of the decade when the liberal wing in the Democratic Party once more "began to challenge the conservatives aggressively" (Montejano 1987:276). But it was Kennedy who finally managed to rally Mexican Americans, blacks, liberals, and labor, and his narrow victory in Texas in 1960 proved that things had finally turned around.

The first major changes resulted from the incorporation of middle-class Mexican Americans into city governments. Veterans from World War II and the Korean War used their GI Bill money to get college degrees, joined the growing Mexican American middle class and became politically active. While the status of Mexican Americans in the cities improved steadily, they were still second-class citizens in most of the rural South Texas areas. Then, in 1962, PASSO, a coalition of several Mexican American political associations, formed an alliance with the teamsters and won their first political campaign in Crystal City. At the height of the conflict, the largest employer, Del Monte, tried to keep the Mexican American workers from going to the polls by forcing them to work overtime. Jimmy Hoffa personally threatened union action against the company. The workers were allowed to vote, and the election turned the entire political structure of Crystal City upside down.

> The mobilized Mexican American majority defeated—"overthrew" is not an excessive term—the long-established rule of the Anglo minority. As a symbol of what was possible in South Texas, the event far outweighed the takeover of a community of 9,000. It symbolized the overthrow of Jim Crow. (Montejano 1987:284)

Encouraged by the consequential strikes organized by César Chávez and his National Farm Workers Association in California, the Chicano civil rights movement grew more militant and organized countless activities all over the South Texas countryside during the 1960s. The formation of El Partido Raza Unida and its crucial role in the electoral takeover of several Anglo dominated counties "stunned the state, frightened the Anglo residents of South Texas, and prompted Gov. Dolph Briscoe to denounce Zavala County as 'little Cuba'" (Montejano 1987:285).

In the 1970s, as Montejano cynically remarks, the political activists achieved some of their goals—one being the expansion of ethnic limits in college education—and saw the middle-class Mexican-American dream fulfilled, which LULAC had so fervently espoused in the 1920s. The rebels, once they were victorious, vanished.

For the 1980s, Montejano offers preliminary observations that illustrate an incipient new order. Increased use of English, intermarriage, and upward mobility speak for a rising degree of integration, yet they cannot conceal the fact that "the Texas Mexican community lags far behind on all mainstream indicators in the areas of education, health, income, and political influence" (Montejano 1987:288). One of the critical consequences of the Mexican American electorate gaining power in the liberal wing of the Democratic Party was the flight of conservative Democrats to the Republican Party, which made Texas a two-party state; a development that is a recurrent theme in Hinojosa's recent books. Other crucial aspects of progress were the battles for reapportionment (each legislator representing an equal number of constituents) and against annexation and expansion of voting districts, measures that resulted in electoral victories by Mexican Americans first in San Antonio and later in numerous communities. The successes soon snowballed because of higher voter turnouts. In 1984, Mexican Americans had influential membership in thirty-six and controlling membership in nine of the forty-five counties with Texas Mexican commissioners—a distribution, then, that puts Belken County's lonely 1960s puppet-on-a-string, Ira Escobar, into the historical perspective of a transitory phenomenon. (See **FRIENDS** (128) for a direct reference on how reapportionment affects Ira Escobar.)

Montejano's account ends in 1986, the year of the sesquicentennial celebration of the battle of the Alamo, the cradle of Texas independence, hosted for the first time by a Texas Mexican mayor. "In his public address before the Alamo," writes Montejano, "it is not surprising to hear [Henry] Cisneros emphasize the American identity of Texas Mexicans, for Cisneros himself represents the reconciliation that has taken place between Anglo and Mexican in Texas" (Montejano 1987:306). Montejano does not conclude without cautioning that this new and fragile climate of negotiation and compromise is once again coming under fire from exclusionist movements against bilingualism, affirmative action, and immigration. Twelve years have passed since the publication of *Anglos and Mexicans in the Making of Texas,* and more recent publications such as José David Saldívar's 1997 *Border Matters* prove Montejano's premonitions right. Saving tax payers' money through denying undocumented workers public education, health services, and other benefits (Proposition 187) stands vis-à-vis amply-funded programs for increased militarization of the border. Crassly prohibitive, reactionary legislatures, combined with English-only laws in almost half of the states of the Union, clearly corroborate Montejano's suspicions. And again, Rolando Hinojosa demonstrates how close a surveillance he keeps on events in his Valley and how skillfully he incorporates recent developments in his fictional—albeit highly accurate—South Texas history, as we shall see presently.

Integration in South Texas: Corporation Farming, Texas Mexican Politics, and the Spoils of War

This final segment in the social history of Texas is where Montejano and Hinojosa part ways for a short stretch of their expedition through the Texas Mexican landscape. The contentious issue is the isolated, but nevertheless crucial, matter of militant, political activism. Although politics as such is a frequent concern in the *KCDTS*, it is always explored in the context of the feud between the old-families and the KBC-Leguizamón alliance. Hence, as we had occasion to observe in the previous sections, Hinojosa's authorial agenda is a far cry from the antiestablishment attitudes of a minority protest literature with a specific political ideology. Characters in the *KCDTS* do *not* question the U.S. political system as a whole, and neither do they scoff at middle-class ambitions, the free market, corporate America, and Puritan work ethics. On the contrary, the portraits of Viola Barragán, Becky Escobar, and a host of characters in **FRIENDS/AMIGOS** applaud private entrepreneurship, hard work, and family values. This absence of a contentious political agenda has been lamented by critics such as Rosaura Sánchez who denounces the Belken County Chicano entrepreneurs as exploitative and paternalistic (Sánchez 1992:82). Similarly, Montejano regrets that the young Chicano rebels of the 1960s blended into the middle class and adopted its tenets as soon as they had won a few decisive battles in their fight for equality. In Hinojosa's work, however, a literary treatment of the civil rights movement and the militant activism that was so widespread in rural Texas in the 1960s is conspicuously absent. Nevertheless, there is no doubt about the fact that the young upwardly mobile characters in the *KCDTS* have strong political convictions and embrace all the beliefs that characterize the average U.S. liberal. And while there exists an isolated passage that actually suggests that Jehú harbored sympathies for the communists in the midst of the McCarthy era (**RAFE**:69), it seems fairly safe to put that down to Jehú's notorious predilection for everything forbidden. But apart from Hinojosa's—perhaps not purposeful—exclusion of the civil rights movement, he and Montejano agree on the same mix of causes for change during the period of Integration.

The gradual transformation from a network of private farms to an industrialized world of agricultural corporations is hinted at in the early books. In **ESTAMPAS** (79), Baldemar Cordero and Gilberto Castañeda work in the Royce-Fedders tomato packing shed. The passage occurs in a section that revolves around the fatal stabbing of Ernesto Tamez, and it tells a story about the indifference of Anglo jurisprudence towards Texas Mexicans ("Por esas cosas que pasan" [69–82]). At the same time, the story prophesies a change for the better by forecasting the current civil rights conditions in the big northern produce companies on the future of Texas. Marta Cordero reports that her father Don Albino Cordero died in an accident in a big pickle factory in Michigan. This is the same "Big Buddy Cucumber" that lures "The Searchers" to Michigan with promises of decent housing in **KLAIL** (51). Apparently, the big company wasn't such a decent employer after all. Marta's account implies that the company was responsible for Don Albino's fatal accident in the factory. The management, however, refused to pay damages to the Mexicans until the Corderos sued and, much to their own surprise, won. The episode anticipates a time when the advent of big produce corporations in the Valley will eventually make labor protection more practical than labor repression. There is also a reference to the famous Del Monte corporation (50), which is hiring laborers from the Valley for their plantations in Indiana. This is the same Del Monte whose plant in Crystal City, Texas will succumb to the consequential 1962 Crystal City Uprising, a momentous affair that actually initiated a series of Texas Mexican political takeovers in Texas. Admittedly, evidence of these developments is scant in the *KCDTS*, but luckily Montejano's study provides the necessary data to complement Hinojosa's sparse treatment of the subject.

The gradual increase of Texas Mexican apportionment in county politics is amply documented in both Hinojosa's and Montejano's writings. Previously, we have Jehú Malacara's close encounter with Valley politics during the 1960s in **RITES** and **RAFA/RAFE**. The woeful role that the KBCers have assigned to Ira Escobar in their jockeying for power leaves no room for doubt that, in Belken County during the 1960s, Texas Mexican politicians were used as bait by the Anglo bosses in order to capture the substantial Texas Mexican vote. Considering that Texas has a democratic system of free and secret elections, the logical question arises of why the Texas Mexican majority does not simply take over the political power in their home state. This question has already been answered in part in the Jehú section where we have seen that Texas was basically a one-party state at the time. Although this is never expressly said in any of the books, it can be inferred from the constant intonation of the significance of primaries.[8] Generally, the person who was elected as candidate did not have any competition in a state where the only party that ruled was the Jim Crow Democrats.

That the times are changing becomes evident in **VARONES** (199–205). In a sketch narrated by Rafa Buenrostro, Echevarría explains that in order for the party (obviously the Democrats) to win the elections, the Anglos have to offer a bigger bait to the Mexican electorate. Therefore, "Morris Frawley y Gene Brown y todos los demás, salieron conque en vez de uno iba haber dos raza como comisionados de Belken después de las últimas elecciones cuando el partido por poco perdía."[9] ["after the last elections, which the party almost threw away, those Anglos like, you know, Morris Frawley and Gene Brown, and all the rest, well, they decided that instead of just one Mexicano as commissioner of Belken, they'd go for two of 'em." (**VARONES**:198)] Unfortunately, the Texas Mexicans themselves forfeit the chance to have two representatives in the commissioners court on account of their internal bickering and quarreling. When one of the two original tejano candidates suddenly dies, several contending groups—each with their particular agenda—start pushing their own nominees. Nobody in the Valley wants the Leguizamóns' candidate, of course, and the Mexicans from Edgerton are not beyond nominating an Anglo ("Miren, h'mbre: dándole la soga al que te ahorca. ¡Qué bonito, chingao!" [**VARONES**:199]) ["Can you imagine? Handing over the hanging rope to your own executioner? Isn't that the damndest thing you've ever seen?" (**VARONES**:198)]. Literally as a by-the-way, Rafa mentions that his name was submitted with a list of candidates that could be expected to act in the interests of the Chicano community at large. The internal bickering, however, leaves the matter undecided for the time being, and *la raza* may end up with only one representative even though by now the Mexicans have enough leverage to send at least three Chicanos to the commissioners court, as Echevarría claims (205).

The episode touches on at least five different areas of significance, the first but not the least of which is Rafa's willingness to actually seek political office, an absolutely unique occurrence in the *KCDTS*, though apparently a passing fancy. Second, the passage takes up once more the theme of loyalties and factions. As always, the blame goes to the Mexican sellouts who prevent the Chicano community from closing ranks against the Anglos. The third area of significance pertains to the reform of electoral structures in South Texas, an issue that is closely analyzed by Montejano. He explains that the difference between two or three seats in the commissioners court is equivalent to the difference between swing influence and controlling influence in the five-member central government body (Montejano 1987:294). Echevarría and Rafa, understandably, prefer the latter, and Montejano's prognosis gives them every reason to hope for an expansion of Texas Mexican apportionment in county politics.

Education is the fourth issue, and its importance is stressed by Echevarría. All four men on Rafa's list are college educated, and Rafa stands out for his graduate law degree ("¡Fíjense! ¡Cuatro muchachos con colegio y hasta un licenciado!" [**VARONES**:201] ["Look at that! Four college men, and one o' them an attorney!" (**VARONES**:200)]). Presumably, these four men belong to Rafa's generation, which was the first to get university degrees thanks to the GI Bill. In addition, many World War II and Korean vets came back from the Army with a heightened sense of self and dignity. In Rafa's Korean stories in **SONGS** and **SERVANTS**, discrimination is seen predominantly as a problem that exists between the common soldiers, rather than a problem of hierarchy. The intrinsic laws of the strictly pragmatic military rank-system do not leave much room for overt discriminatory practices. In his journal, Rafa repeatedly reports racial friction, mainly for speaking Spanish in the presence of other Anglo soldiers, but there is never any mistreatment at the hands of superiors that would be attributable to racism. After many months spent together either in utter boredom or life-threatening combat, bonding occurs totally independent of ethnic backgrounds. As a result, these young men return to the still largely segregated Valley after risking their lives on the front line for the principles of democracy and after having savored a taste of what it means to be American citizens with all the corresponding rights and privileges. After college, many, like Rafa, are prepared academically and ideologically to stand up to the Anglo bosses in the political and professional arenas.

A fifth and final aspect that can be extrapolated from the passage in **VARONES** is the impending demise of the one-party rule in Texas, which is implied in Echevarría's statement about the last elections that the party almost lost (**VARONES**:199). Through the rising influence of Texas Mexicans in county politics in the 1960s and 1970s, the liberal wing of the Democratic party was strengthened substantially. This led to a flight of conservative Democrats to the Republican party. We can see now why the Belken County Anglo bosses regard the politician Morse (or "Roger") Terry as such a threat and therefore try to strong-arm him into the fold of the KBC. In **RAFE**, according to Jehú, Terry is a liberal Democrat ("Do you recall MT? He was up at Austin with us; speaks Spanish (natch), and he's a friend of the mexicano. Sure he is." [**RAFE**:17]). Also, Jehú mentions that Noddy made a statement to the effect that "he [Noddy] contributes to both sides of the Demo. [Democratic] factions" (**RAFE**:27). This indicates that the Democratic party in Belken County has to face the competition of the Republicans, which has sparked an internal struggle between Jim Crow Democrats and liberal Democrats over the future direction of county politics and the Texas Mexican role in them.

In short, politics in Belken County are at a turning point that bespeaks a rapidly rising measure of integration. While this concurs with numerous signs of the swift corrosion of segregation in the text, it must be stated in the strongest terms that the picture of integration that Hinojosa paints does *not* accentuate Mexican assimilation and acculturation into the Anglo mainstream. Most of the characters that are interviewed in the Becky books, for example, are middle-class Chicanos who come across as firmly rooted in their ethnicity. Characters like Otila Macías Rosales and Reina Campoy (**FRIENDS**:103, 107) actually display a new variety of Chicano ethnocentrism. Astonishingly, Anglo interviewees like Sammie Jo, E. B. Cooke, and Edith Timmens are at pains to assert their bilingual/bicultural identities. Intermarriage seems to be the order of the day and *compadrazgo* as a form of interracial bonding is rediscovered: E. B. Cooke is a witness at Becky and Jehú's wedding (84). How far the pendulum of this reversed assimilatory tendency has swung in Belken can be gauged from the fact that Ira Escobar is the only one among the borderers—Mexican and Anglo!—who stands out for not being competent in Spanish. That's a drastic change from the days when Noddy Perkins called Jehú a "Mexican son-of-a-bitch" (**RAFE**:54) and Rebecca Ruth Verser made no bones about Spanish-speaking Mexicans making her nauseous (**RITES**:29).

Whereas in **FRIENDS/AMIGOS**, Hinojosa weaves a fabric of a society marked by diversity in which the true borderers are bicultural and bilingual, regardless of their ethnicities, **POLICEMAN** takes the evolution of ethnic relations in the Valley still one step further. In the 1990s, Belken County has reached a perhaps not entirely desirable stage of integration, where some of the formerly excluded advocate exclusion and where the recent immigrants, once they are naturalized, become the staunchest defenders of tight anti-immigration measures.

In the preface of his 1997 *Border Matters*, José David Saldívar cites the case of Ariana Huffington who appeared together with the conservative journalist William F. Buckley in a PBS debate program, called *Firing Line*, opposite the former New York mayor Ed Koch. Saldívar recalls that he was "riveted to the screen" as

> Buckley and Huffington called for new enforcement measures against the "hordes" of illegal immigrants flooding across our nation's borders. Huffington, a recent immigrant herself (from Greece), called, without irony, for more guards, more border fences, and the use of sophisticated military vehicles and technologies left over from Desert Storm to patrol the U.S.-Mexico border. Koch rebutted Huffington's position by reminding her that had the national borders been closed and more draconian restrictions placed on immigrants by the U.S. government in the 1960s, she would never have had the chance to become a hyphenated ethnic-American herself. This debate about immigration laws and border crossings highlights, I think, how the mass media are constructing a popular narrative of national crisis. (Saldívar 1997:x)

The construction—and deconstruction—of a border-crisis narrative is exactly what is at the center of the conflict between Chief Inspector Buenrostro and the D.A. Florencio Valencia in **POLICEMAN**. Hinojosa is taking the pulse of the nation when he portrays Valencia as an up-and-coming hyphenated ethnic-American who, when speaking about border crime, produces prepared speeches such as: "They're just part of the package of the systematic violence that some of the undesirable element from across the river has been visiting upon us" (**POLICEMAN**:158), and who also wants to buy sophisticated military technologies to protect the border.[10] The media, with the help of the Huffingtons and Valencias, are constructing their particular kind of a border narrative where the lines between good and bad, haves and have-nots, ins and outs, desirables and undesirables are sharply drawn. The concept of reality in this narrative resembles a postmodern Baudrillardian simulacrum in that it is always programmatic and deliberate and contains insufficient substance. At the opposite end, we observe Rafa Buenrostro's efforts to deconstruct this simplistic narrative by creating a public forum for a debate on border issues by actually trying to get at the motives for border crime, by de-escalating and appeasing the antagonisms, and by scrutinizing the evidence for the elusive truth. What he finds is that the undesirable element that is responsible for the violence "from across" are not the wetbacks and the undocumented workers. In **POLICEMAN**, organized border crime is in the hands of a few, traditionally moneyed families who own houses on

Padre Island on the Texas side where their money is always welcome. They have impressive bank accounts in Klail City, buy their expensive cars from Klail car dealers, send their children to American schools, seek treatment in U.S. hospitals, and sell their cocaine to the interracial Belken County jet-set.

The deconstruction of simplistic border narratives through a refusal to give his readers a unitary, unilateral, and programmatic text is at the heart of Hinojosa's agenda as a writer, which in the *KCDTS* is epitomized in the figure of P. Galindo. A chapter on Galindo's vision of how a *cronicón* ought to be written presents a perfect opportunity to recapitulate the argumentational steps of this study and will therefore conclude the discussion. Before we move on to this final chapter, I will chart one last topological paradigm in order to demonstrate that the seemingly conventional crime-mystery narrative of **POLICEMAN** rightfully occupies a place in Rolando Hinojosa's portrait of the traditional South Texas community. As we will see, even in the nineties the well-being of the community may depend on the soundness of its oral memory and the familiarity with local cultural idiosyncrasies on both sides of the river.

Going back to the conclusion of **PARTNERS**, we recall how Rafa begins to suspect that Lisandro Gómez Solís might be the mastermind behind the killings and the drug smuggling. When his colleague, Culley Donovan, asks him what had aroused his suspicion, Rafa explains,

> The phone calls here, I guess. The calls came from Soliseño; it's there on the clerks record.... Who owns the village of Soliseño? The ranch? The *municipio*, practically? They do, the Solíses. (**PARTNERS**:242)

All the other detectives had seen the telephone records, but Rafa is the only one who makes the connection, evidently because of his familiarity with the village of Soliseño. It isn't until **FRIENDS** (152) that we learn that Soliseño is across the river from the Carmen Ranch on the original Llano Grande grant (where Hinojosa's relatives, the Garcías, still live), and where Rafa himself actually "owns and farms 200 hectares." Subsequently, the advantages of belonging to an old Valley family that is steeped in border culture and history is evidenced in a passage of **POLICEMAN** (114). The detectives are investigating the details of the sordid Gómez Solís family history in which the birthright of the twins Juan Carlos and José Antonio is an important clue. Oral memory and genealogy come into play once more when Rafa calls his aunt Agnes Rincón-Buenrostro, an eighty-five-year-old nun who used to be in charge of the pediatrics ward at Klail's Villa

María and Mercy Hospital. Agnes, who is here taking over the legacy of Echevarría as a storehouse of the Valley's collective memory, remembers the Gómez family history and even knows the lineage of Lisandro Gómez's wife Blanca Gallardo ("of the up river Gallardos. They're not related to us, you understand" [**POLICEMAN**:114–15). Agnes's account of Blanca's insanity and the annulment of the marriage by the Mexican bishop is important for the detectives since it helps them understand the dimensions of Felipe Segundo's twisted mind, inducing him to raise his brother's sons and subsequently driving them to commit patricide.

The table below charts the dynamic tension between potential threats to the Belken community and the restorative powers of an operative oral culture. Hinojosa spreads clues across the course of three recent texts in the *KCDTS* that show how Rafa can tap into the oral culture's resources at will, giving him an edge in the solving of homicide cases in both **PARTNERS** and **POLICEMAN**. Hinojosa convincingly incorporates his fictional recreation of an oral culture into a book that follows the conventional formula of the popular crime-mystery genre, thus linking traditional values with sociopolitical commentary. The text seeks to destroy the illusion that undocumented workers, illegal maids, and the small-time drug smugglers pose a threat to the U.S. economy and social stability, as politicians and the media would have us believe. Rather, the real source of border strife may be located in the greed and decadence of such families as the Gómez Solíses. They already own and control a whole town that presumably has been the family's traditional homestead for generations—and yet they crave more. Opposite the Gómezes, Hinojosa places the small-time gangsters like Packy Estudillo and Daniel Varela, who get caught between the big players and end up either dead or in prison (**POLICEMAN**:25). Whether Hinojosa's reading of the border situation is entirely accurate or not is a moot point. What matters is that it forces readers to rethink their ideas on cultural identities and the homogeneity of the nation state. Hence, it is infinitely more discerning, authentic, and equitable than the media's narrative about hordes of illegal immigrants invading the U.S. like "an illegal outside force, an alien nation 'polluting' U.S. culture" (Saldívar 1997:x). Therefore, in certain ways, the chart below epitomizes the dynamics of the entire *KCDTS* in which Hinojosa charts his own version of the border narrative. Hinojosa's strategy aims to rebut both the new exclusionary tendencies that once more seek to stigmatize people of color living on or across the border, as well as to revise the familiar Anglo-centric historiography that managed to exclude and belittle the contributions of Texas Mexicans in the making of Texas.

193 : Rafa Buenrostro

PARADIGM 7:

~~Multi-cultural inclusivist border society with common commitments to solidarity and coalition~~ ←——— Criminal activity and corruption along border fosters "narrative of national crisis"

↓

Recuperation of oral knowledge helps uncover wealthy string pullers in contemporary border crime

↓

Text as new ritual of gathering and transmitting of crucial genealogical and cultural data ———➤ ~~Criminal activity and corruption along border creates "narrative of national crisis"~~

24

P. GALINDO AND THE LITERARY QUEST

A Conclusion

IN the previous chapters on Echevarría, Jehú, and Rafa, we have noted that Hinojosa places them at strategic positions in his narrative, enabling them to highlight certain facets of the South Texas history and social fabric. While their narratives overlap, each has a unique agenda around which his story gravitates. Echevarría personifies the collective memory that provides a nostalgic view of the Valley. Jehú Malacara sets out on his wanderings as an orphaned *pícaro* through an exclusively Chicano world and ends up as a banker with the KBC, a position that affords him privileged knowledge on politics, business, and private affairs. Rafa Buenrostro's family background represents the Valley's history of land loss, the transformational stages of its various economies, and their repercussions on the Chicano community. Eventually, he becomes a policeman and gains insight of a scope similar to that of his cousin, the banker.

While the distinctive narrational agendas of these three are shaped by who they are, or what they have become, Galindo's program is different because his personal affairs have little bearing on his status as a narrator in the Belken County chronicles. This becomes manifest in the scarcity and inconsistency of the information he gives about himself. We meet him as a skinny man of twenty-six who travels in the truck with Leocadio Gavira to Michigan. His parents were killed in an accident, he says, and he was raised by a foster family. By the time he starts investigating Jehú's disappearance from the Bank in **RAFA**, he is already terminally ill and an anonymous successor takes over the investigation in **RITES**. Deliberately making his personal life an enigma, he gives out contradictory information about his marital status. In **RAFA** (90), he states he is "soltero" while in **RAFE** (103) he is "married, widowed; married, widowed; married, divorced. Bachelor." Outside sources later claim they saw him shortly before his death, driving around with his wife of many years making his good-byes (**FRIENDS:145**).

Unlike the other characters, he hardly participates in the plot. Instead, he sees that gaps left by others are somehow filled. In **CONDADO/KLAIL**, he provides short sketches of the migrant workers' plight, and in **VARONES**, he relates incidents with a slightly ethical, moralistic slant while in **RAFA/RAFE** he goes to the extreme of impartial narration by means of a reportage-style depiction of the events. On the whole, his contributions make up a seemingly random, decentered conglomeration of stories, research notes, interviews, and overheard conversations. In the words of José David Saldívar, Galindo personifies the author's idea of "text-making and rhetoric-making" that "highlights the constructed nature of cultural accounts" (Saldívar 1990:260). In Galindo's own laconic words, everything is worth recording, and the truth will eventually trickle down to the bottom:

> mejor es oír y escuchar todo (y con cuidado) para así seguir tratando de asirse de la verdad que se venga destilando por la coladera. (**RAFA**:100)
> [Thing to do, then, is to listen, to hear, to assess, and to see what truths drip out from time to time. (**RAFE**:115)]

When Hinojosa returns to the reportage genre in order to explore the theme of *la mujer nueva* in **FRIENDS/AMIGOS**, Galindo is virtually reincarnated in the person of the radically neutral (and neuter) *listener*. This is a new narrator who is a relative of Galindo with much the same agenda for providing unprocessed samples of oral statements that will invariably contain pieces of the irrepressible truth.

> Belken County, Klail City, the Valley. This world where people talk, and talk, and talk. And despite much of the foolishness which is said, sputtered out and, at times hissed out, the truth comes spilling out. (**FRIENDS**:9)

Galindo's (and the listener's) secret of success is that he does not take sides, does not express opinions, never coaxes, coerces, or manipulates his informants. Based on Galindo's solid reputation as a neutral listener, even characters such as Polín Tapia, Ira Escobar, or Bowly Ponder talk freely and candidly, and between the lines they divulge the shameful details of the KBC-Leguizamón conspiracy.

When the nameless relative, the listener, takes over Galindo's legacy and his notes, he/she is initiated to the oral history of the Valley as a reader. He/she reads, edits, compares, and points out contradictions and discrepancies (see, e.g., **FRIENDS**:45). Like the ideal reader of the Series he/she is put through a hard test that makes him/her re-enact the rituals of the oral community by sifting through the copious information, evaluating, approving and rejecting.

The question as to why Hinojosa wished to do away with such a useful narrator is answered by Galindo himself:

The wri has spent the last two weeks in bed or near it. His insides, or what's left of them, served notice that he needed a rest, some time-off. The running around after this act or that one is not conducive to rest, peace, and tranquillity.

The ups and downs, and the comings and goings, cannot but be detrimental to one's health, to one's peace of mind. *Being back in the Valley has helped the writer to recover some of his good spirits, if not his health.*

The X-ray machine, unfortunately doesn't lie. The wri himself saw the telltale pictures when he was going over his notes and first drafts. The wri, or so he thinks, is on the verge of arriving at the end of his work. It's merely a matter of a few more conversations. (**RAFE**:103, my italics)

Written by the moribund Galindo, the passage is making a roundabout, though consequential, commentary on Hinojosa's aesthetic concept of his Belken county chronicles. "Rest, peace, and tranquillity" is what the writer craves but instead, his life is filled with a hustle and bustle that is "detrimental to one's health, to one's peace of mind." Evidently, the Valley provides a sanctuary to which Galindo can return in order to "recover some of his good spirit."

As readers know, Hinojosa, too, lives outside of the Valley and he, too, is compelled time and again to return to the setting of his Belken County chronicles. Hence, it is more probable than not that Galindo's musings really contain Hinojosa's tongue-in-cheek innuendo about the need to rediscover and reinvent himself whenever he feels the urge to seek shelter in the therapeutical, albeit fictional, space called "the Valley."

Galindo's health, however, is precarious and the recovery, he feels, is only temporary because he knows that his existence as *the writer* has all but come to a close. It is the telltale writing itself that provides the evidence. Its mercilessly revelatory powers are likened to those of an X-ray machine. What the notes and drafts reveal is that Galindo has served his purpose in the *KCDTS* and that he must be sacrificed to Hinojosa's compulsive quest for new modes of narration. Galindo knows it's for a good cause: "The wri acknowledges that this may be his last contribution to the Klail City entries; there is no need to wear sack cloth, brothers" (**RAFE**:8).

The passage shows that Galindo has an uncanny degree of awareness of his condition as a functional—and disposable—element of the Series. What is more, he is aware of the evolution of the *cronicón* in which he appears as a fictional character (**RAFA**:8). He also associates with Octavio Romano (**CONDADO**:98), Américo Paredes (**VARONES**:76), and José Limón (**RAFA**:8), all prominent, accomplished men in Chicano-studies; real-life poets, writers, and researchers. The unusual strategy places Galindo in a metafictional space that functions as a pivotal intersection between readers, the Belken County community, and the real life world of Chicano letters. At the same time, it is illustrative of Hinojosa's peculiar aesthetic concept that Galindo falls terminally ill at a time when he is at his most prolific. Galindo's death represents a sacrifice to the constant generic evolution and to the continual, impassioned quest of the Series for new ways of distilling the truth about the history of South Texas.

In short, the Galindo section exhibits the central ideas of Hinojosa's literary project. Galindo's gathering of unadulterated oral samples typifies the heteroglossic nature of the Series; his death stands for the continual renewal of its generic make-up, and his reiteration of the irrepressible nature of truth points the way to an adequate response on the part of the reader.

This study has organized its discussion according to these three principles: first, the texts of the *KCDTS* aim at a representation of a traditional oral culture that is deliberately constructed as a decentered, fragmented heteroglossic text. Second, the experiments in literary genres bespeak the author's quest for an adequate literary capturing of the changing conditions of the Belken County community. And third, owing to the narrators' strategy of making only partial disclosures, a close reading of the text, if it is intended to be meaningful, will inevitably lead to the reader's participation in the text's oral rites.

The discussion has passed through a series of steps that began in part one with the broad perspective of the *KCDTS* as an artfully constructed cultural account, a multifaceted border narrative. Focusing in on each fascicle, it has demonstrated how the form purposefully adapts to content and ideology. For instance, the author inserts dispassionate legal documents in order to expose the indifference of the judicial system, he sketches family portraits in order to capture the themes of loyalty and alliance, he dispatches a *pícaro* on a trip around the county to take the pulse of the community, he recurs to mixed-code writing in order to introduce a phase of transition in ethnic relations, he writes a soap-opera script to expose triviality and decadence, he chooses the epistle where he needs to convey the harshest inside criticism, and conversely he sets out on a reportage-style documentary in order to show the community divided over the gender issue. The latest maneuver includes the implementation of the murder-mystery genre ("the procedural" to be precise) that is perfectly geared to the transportation of issues such as revenge, border crime, militarization, and exclusionary tendencies, but also integration and reconciliation between the ethnicities. These are only a few examples of an interminable list, confirming that the constant generic renewal is a deliberate and calculated undertaking that strives for complete and utter writerly penetration of the Valley's true story.

Naturally, the singular fragmented, heteroglossic constitution of Hinojosa's work invites critics to discuss a possible classification within the framework of literary currents. The application of postmodernist aesthetic and ideological concepts suggests itself, yet upon closer inspection, part two confirms the suspicion that the *KCDTS* defies classification within the known typologies. At best, we can affirm a recent wariness of essentialist discourses with respect to gender, language, and ethnicity that correlates with the latest postmodernist critique of ethnic essentialism as propounded, for instance, by the critic bell hooks. Instead of a postmodern vision of the border culture, everything seems to point to an attempt at a mimetic representation of its oral culture by way of including the reader as a player in the game of decoding the diverse, encoded interlocutions.

Part three of this project has examined the position of such a reader/player through performing an analysis of how the encoding works. The intricate process of completing oral rituals (which were left uncompleted in the text) is made visible through the implementation of Bruce-Novoa's topological theory of constant properties and with the help of his charted paradigms. They reveal that the author staggers strings of data over several textual fragments and volumes. The reader's job consists of linking the data and processing the information. The completed transaction generally reveals a collapse of an important element of the community's operative culture, such as the recuperation of the lost land titles, a necessary synthesis of tradition and the new order, the traditional network of foster parents, or even the pardoning of a repentant adulterer. The reader collaborates in the quest for the traditional elements and experiences their recuperation in the text.

A second area of investigation is interested in a reader-friendly presentation of these processes. The assumption that there are four scattered sections (which point to a strong Faulknerian legacy in Hinojosa's text) proved to be a useful stratagem on which to base a complex literary analysis of a large disjointed, multigeneric body of fiction. Hinojosa comes close to the Faulknerian model by ostensibly instrumentalizing his four narrators as structural guides in the narrative.

Part four actually carries out the reconstruction of the four sections and assumes the position of the reader who partakes in the completion of oral rituals. Charted against the background of theories on the picaresque novel, Jehú's life emerges as a kind of moralistic tale as it evolves from moral delinquency to a conscientious banking career, with Jehú eventually turning into a reformed womanizer, faithful husband, and loving foster father. Echevarría, generally seen as a good man and a staunch supporter of the Buenrostros, grows out of his habit of getting drunk and giving speeches in bars that are like rehearsed pieces about the good old days, the despicable Texas Rangers, and the heroic Buenrostros versus the cowardly Leguizamóns. With time, Echevarría's drunken raging against the injustices inflicted on *la raza* is replaced by pensive nostalgia over the gradual disappearance of the Valley culture. He is the last person in the Valley who has witnessed this culture in its authentic state and he hands the storehouse of his memories over to Rafa.

Rafa's family history reveals itself as a deconstruction of simplistic border narratives, both the familiar historical ones and the new programmatic ones. Rafa, a lifetime-borderer, a detective, a lawyer, a close reader, and a man at peace with himself (though not with the Chip Valencias of this world), enjoys a privileged insight into the border's past, present, and near future. How well he knows his Texas history and how closely he monitors recent tendencies on the border has been documented beyond a doubt in my reading of Rafa's family history combined with David Montejano's sociohistorical analysis *Anglos and Mexicans in the Making of Texas* (1987).

The *KCDTS* is a singular artistic project in American Literature. Hinojosa endeavors nothing less than a representation of an American experience that adjusts the exterior pattern of his literary project every step of the way to the new conditions his protagonists are confronted with. The result is a work with an extraordinary scope, flexibility, and an evolutionary force that is unprecedented in American Literature.

In the face of the overwhelming evidence of Hinojosa's concern for a faithful portrayal of Mexican-Anglo relations in the Valley, it seems astonishing that a recently published book would claim that "not until *Dear Rafe* . . . does Hinojosa introduce a serious concern with the racial issue." This quote from Joyce Glover Lee's *Rolando Hinojosa and the American Dream* (1997:87) is consistent with her overall assessment of the *KCDTS*. Thus, she regards **PARTNERS** and **FRIENDS** (the Spanish-language titles are neglected) as across-the-board failures since they were written, in her opinion, in an "upbeat and cheerful mood" in order to "gloss over" the "gloomy" installments of the Series (167). The gloomy installments are the remaining ones that "depict a world that is either dead or dying; this is the world that Hinojosa and his characters have left behind, both literally and figuratively. It is only a memory, a sketch, a portrait. Yet we come to see that no alternative exists."

Lee's reading represents a literary criticism that fails to distinguish the *KCDTS* as a project that goes beyond the formula novel. Hence, she disregards the dynamics of disintegration and integration in Hinojosa's work and neglects to address the reader's crucial role in the completion of oral ritual. As a consequence, she comes to questionable conclusions, declaring that Hinojosa's heroes have found "a new identity" (Lee 1997:204) and censuring Hinojosa's work for its alleged failure to address the racial issue, as well as for its absence of overt social criticism. Admittedly, Hinojosa's strategy, like Faulkner's, is uncommonly taxing. Yet it is particularly rewarding for those readers who are willing to match their perceptiveness against the author's uncanny skill of planting a seed at one point in the text and letting it sprout at an unexpected juncture elsewhere. The last word on the subject I give to P. Galindo *(pega poco, pero pega lindo)* who, as his name implies, is not always on target but when he hits it, he is dead center:

> As is usually the case, that which was thought to be a simple matter of research turns out not to be that at all. And, in spite of what has been said, by those who would know, and by the rest, those who know less but clamor the more, everything hinders and everything helps that which the wri would like to present and make known. A paradox, but here it is. (**RAFE**:103)

NOTES

INTRODUCTION

1. The author's complete name is Rolando R. Hinojosa-Smith. In keeping with Spanish and Mexican tradition, he keeps the surnames of his Texas Mexican father and his Anglo Texan mother. As an author of fiction, though, he is generally known as Rolando Hinojosa.
2. The political success story ends here. In 1996, Cisneros stepped down following an FBI investigation into his extramarital relationship with political fund-raiser Linda Medlar. During a routine background check, he had lied to FBI agents "about payments he had made to Medlar" (Martin 1996:3). On January 23, 1997, Cisneros accepted the post of president and chief operating officer of the Spanish-language television network Univision.
3. For more information on Belken County and its citizens see Wolfgang Karrer's Website at <http://www.lili.uni-osnabrueck.de/hinojosa_census.html>. Karrer, a professor at the University of Osnabrück/Germany, has gone to the trouble of indexing all characters that appear in the first thirteen novels of the *KCDTS*. The index is posted on the web page along with a map of Belken County and a short vita of Rolando Hinojosa.

PART ONE

1. Adding to the general confusion, the term "bilingual" is also applied to some editions of Hinojosa's novels that contain translations furnished by other authors such as the facing page bilingual edition of *Claros Varones de Belken/Fair Gentlemen of Belken County* (translated by Julia Cruz), or the early editions of *Estampas del Valle y otras obras* (translated by Gustavo Valadez and José Reyna). Here, of course, "bilingual" is not used at all to describe the linguistic behavior of the characters in the books.

2. For an analysis of the concepts of "domestication" and "foreignization" as classifiers for the modifications made in the process of self-translation see Angie López, "Transfer Strategies in Rolando Hinojosa's Self-translation of *Mi querido Rafa*" (2000:203–9).

CHAPTER 1

1. The installments of the *KCDTS* will subsequently be referred to in abbreviated form. These abbreviations will appear in bold uppercase type. I will always quote from the latest editions, which, in some cases, have been given new titles. Here, for example, the first edition was published in 1973 as *Estampas del Valle y otras obras*. I will cite from the 1994 critical edition *Estampas del Valle* and refer to it hereafter as **ESTAMPAS**.
2. The dialogue with medieval peninsular writings is relevant and revealing in connection with the first three prose works of the *KCDTS*. I will therefore revisit this subject in the opening paragraphs of the exposition on *Claros Varones de Belken*, the fourth installment and the third one in prose.
3. In *Dear Rafe* we learn about an alleged romantic entanglement of Jovita de Anda, sister-in-law of Ernesto Tamez, with Jehú Malacara. Much later, in *Becky and Her Friends*, the landlord of the bar, Lucas Barrón, actually puts Jehú at the scene of the crime ("It's too goddam bad to be a kid and to have seen that kind-a shit" [**FRIENDS**:101]).
4. Please see my subsequent discussion of Hinojosa's 1983 English rendition *The Valley* for a description of how the author broke up and rearranged the sections of the book, one of the goals presumably being a proper exposition of his two main characters.

CHAPTER 3

1. The abbreviated title **CONDADO** refers to the latest edition of the second *KCDTS* book with the new title *El condado de Belken: Klail City* (1994b) Thereby, I also hope to avoid confusion with the English rendition *Klail City* (1987a), which I will refer to as **KLAIL**. Earlier Spanish-language editions were entitled *Klail City y sus alrededores* (1976) and *Generaciones y semblanzas* (1977).
2. For more details about this literary competition, the jurors, and other aspects of this novel's publishing history, please see Erlinda Gonzalez-Berry's introduction to *El condado de Belken* and the author's own account in the prologue of that same edition (Hinojosa 1994b:10).
3. Guzmán's *Generaciones y semblanzas* was published in 1512 and is generally considered the first of its kind in the genre of literary character portraits in Spain.
4. Hinojosa himself patiently explains in his prologue to *El condado de Belken: Klail City* (25) how he suggested to the publishers three different titles, which were all rejected. The publishers feared that there might be a mix-up with the English-language version *Klail City*. Finally, the editor came up with the new, commonly acceptable title for an award-winning novel that had enjoyed readership and scholarly interest perfectly well under its original title for twenty years. It is nowhere satisfactorily documented just why readers, libraries, retailers, etc. cannot be trusted to identify *Klail City y sus alrededores* as a book in Spanish or why *Generaciones y semblanzas* was not even considered a possible choice.

5. See Yolanda Julia Broyles's article "Oral Culture and Print Culture" (1984) for an account of the tradition of Mexican DJs on both sides of the Río Grande. She illustrates the status of the *locutor* by citing a nomenclature of famous, even legendary, Chicano radio announcers across the southwest, thus placing this particular sketch in the context of Hinojosa's portrait of Chicano oral culture.

CHAPTER 4

1. In the corresponding Spanish passage in **CONDADO**, the creative process of writing is likened to the inevitable, uncontrollable course taken by such illnesses as the measles and later to a devilish rabbit bolting out of unexpected places (74).
2. My attic image actually mirrors rather neatly something Hinojosa later said in an interview. When I asked him about the structural changes in *The Valley*, he said among other things: "In every house I used to live when the family lived together I had a large room and I would put stuff on the floor. So I could walk around in it and I just decided, this is gonna go here, this is gonna go here.... And I think it works—the way *The Valley* is laid out."
3. The topic of the migrant harvest workers has been compellingly thematized in Tomás Rivera's Chicano classic . . . *y no se lo tragó la tierra* (1971) and Rolando Hinojosa's inspired 1987 translation entitled *This Migrant Earth*.

CHAPTER 5

1. I quote from the 1991 German/English edition edited by Wolfgang Karrer. The book was first published in 1978 with the title *Korean Love Songs*. For a brief summary of the course of events during the Korean War and Rafa Buenrostro's involvement in it as an artillery man, skip ahead to my discussion of Rafa's war journal in Hinojosa's 1993 entry *The Useless Servants*.

CHAPTER 6

1. The author confirms that his 1986 installment *Claros varones de Belken* is his fourth book and explains the delayed publication in his interview with José Saldívar (1984b:182): "It was accepted for publication by Justa, but not published. The contracts were signed, but Justa Publications suffered some reversals . . . y allí se quedó. Nothing was done with it." The English subtitle *Fair Gentlemen of Belken County* refers to Julia Cruz's translation published in the same volume. Unless otherwise noted, all translations from **VARONES** follow Julia Cruz's translation printed in the same volume on facing pages.

    Generaciones y semblanzas by Fernán Pérez de Guzmán (1378?–1460) was not published until 1512, yet it was explicitly mentioned by Hernando del Pulgar (1430?–1493) as one of the models for his *Libro de los Claros Varones de Castilla* (1486).
2. In an interview on September 17, 1996, Hinojosa told me that at some point he had decided "to have everything in both languages. I even have three quarters of Varones done, but I haven't touched it in three years."

CHAPTER 7

1. Rafa Buenrostro's first name is spelled "Rafe" in the English-language books. The 1985 English rendition of *Mi querido Rafa* is entitled *Dear Rafe* and will be referred to as **RAFE**. The spelling alternatives indicate a different pronunciation, with "Rafa" following Spanish phonetics [′rafa] while "Rafe" would be pronounced according to the English system [reif]. In this study "Rafa" will be given preference when not quoting directly from an English text. As would be expected, Jehú's name will also vary in pronunciation though not in spelling: Spanish [xe′u] ; English [′ja hu:] or perhaps [′dxi hyu:]. Typical of Hinojosa's wry humor, Jehú's name, when in the mouth of an Anglo, is sometimes phonetically spelled "Ya hoo"—incidentally reminiscent of the name of a brutish race of creatures in *Gulliver's Travels* (**VARONES**:161).
2. In "A Close Shave with Politics" in my chapter on Jehú Malacara in part four, I provide an outline of the events and discuss the details of Noddy Perkins's machinations and Jehú's attempt to foil them, against the background of politics in Texas in the 1960s.

CHAPTER 8

1. It has been pointed out to me that using both **RAFA** (*Mi querido Rafa*) and **RAFE** (*Dear Rafe*) as abbreviations for two different books may be confusing to some readers. While I recognize the problem I would like readers to bear in mind that the spelling variants indicate a different pronunciation. In the context of cultural and linguistic blending along the border, I actually consider this a telling feature, suitably significant to distinguish the two books.
2. Mejía bases these assumptions not solely on the chronological coincidence of events but also on voices in the press criticizing Hinojosa's lack of flashiness as director of a writing program endowed with a $15 million donation made by Texas writer James Michener.
3. "No hay ninguna novela escrita en spanglés; hay algún cuento y, sobre todo, poesía. Las hay muy malas, pero algunos autores son notoriamente buenos. Yo les digo a mis alumnos que si insisten en mezclar ambos idiomas van a reducir ellos mismos su público. Se convierten en intraducibles, y no los van a entender ni los anglos ni los mexicanos. Ahora, si eligen hacer eso, que lo elijan, ¡pero que no reprochen a nadie que no se les lea! Mezclar idiomas no suele llevar a ninguna parte, aunque le admito que hay algunos poemas bellísimos."

CHAPTER 9

1. In his 1993 article "Hard English and Soft Spanish: Language as a Theme in the Chicano Novel in English 1969–1985," Ernst Rudin includes **RITES** in his exploration of the "dichotomous treatment of English and Spanish" in English-language Chicano fiction (Rudin 1993:396–99). He quotes Hinojosa as one of the few writers to reject the soft-hard dichotomy that so often seems to coincide with a functional dichotomy, associating English with assertiveness in business and academics while Spanish belongs to the private, emotive domain of the family, often imbued with recollections of humble immigrant origins. Not so Hinojosa: "I was not ashamed of my parents after I received my education, for I was not ashamed of them before I acquired one; I never ran out of things to say to them

because of my education nor did they to me because of theirs. And neither of them spoke in hushed, soft-Spanish voices as some Chicano writers describe those who speak that often strident and vowel-filled language." (Hinojosa 1984b:14)
2. According to divergent information in Rafa Buenrostro's war journal, this rocket attack occurred at some point during the last days of April 1951 (see Hinojosa's thirteenth *KCDTS* installment, *The Useless Servants* 1993:166).

CHAPTER 10

1. Hinojosa's skill at creating "true" fiction when writing about his Valley can perhaps be gauged from the fact that shortly after the publication of **PARTNERS** an actual bank was caught doing exactly what the author had described in his book (see Mejía 1993a:120).

CHAPTER 12

1. From a personal conversation on September 17, 1996.
2. For an ample documentation of the characters' linguistic choices or their viewpoints on the subject please see **AMIGOS**:12, 59, 63, 66, 75, 81, 101, 121; or **FRIENDS**:16–17, 65, 81, 86, 110, 118–19.
3. To complete the picture, it should be noted that in **FRIENDS**, Edith Timmens states that her husband had no excuse for his bigotry, considering that his mother was "Mexican, and one who **didn't speak** English, and how do you like that?" (**FRIENDS**:87), whereas in **AMIGOS** (66) "*su mamá era mexicana. Mexicana que hablaba inglés*" (my emphasis).
4. "Romeo is the author's real first name used only by his immediate family. His sister and brother's nickname for Hinojosa is Romey, and he has told me that they are the only ones who ever call him by this name" (see Mejía 1993a:119).
5. Hinojosa, indeed, prepares this story for any critical contingency by thematically exploring marriage both inside (Jehú and Becky) and outside one's ethnic group (Rafa and Sammie Jo).

CHAPTER 13

1. This English-language journal is, of course, written by Sgt. Rafe Buenrostro. For the sake of consistency, I generally refer to him as "Rafa" whenever I am not quoting directly from an English-language passage.
2. Glimpses of this particularly harrowing episode are offered to us as early as **CONDADO** (77).
3. The incident has already been portrayed in **SONGS** (102). An Anglo American GI, for whom most nonwhite races seem to look the same, takes Sony Ruíz for Japanese and makes a racist slur ("Pipe the gook and them flowers there").
4. The exact date of the rocket attack is not mentioned here, but Rafa ends his account saying that he will leave for Korea on May 1. So it must have happened between April 27–29. Incidentally, according to the U.S. Army report at the end of **RITES**, which refers to the same events related here, the surprise rocket attack occurred on September 12.
5. This is not the first instance of Arte Público's editorial negligence. I have already pointed out the disappearance of several small **CONDADO** episodes plus the long

piece, "Enedino Broca Lopez" from the English rendition, **KLAIL**. Also, the first edition of **PARTNERS** appeared with two complete chapters repeated while the pagination continued. In a personal letter to Jaime Mejía, Hinojosa wrote that Arte Público's mistakes in that first edition of **SERVANTS** were not limited to the missing pages, but also included repetition of passages and changes in sentence structure and style (Mejía 1993b:57).

6. Rufino is a member of the Cano Clan, and thus, like Rafa, a direct descendant of the settlers that came to the Valley in 1749. Rufino is also at the center of the scheme that prevented the Leguizamón-KBC alliance from gobbling up more land in the Valley (see **RAFE**:95–97).

CHAPTER 14

1. In yet another of the inexplicable incongruities concerning the chronology of events in the *KCDTS*, Rafa *here* remembers that the murder of his father happened when he was only seven, which would place the year of his death somewhere around 1936 or 1937. Most other references to the incident differ significantly. In **VARONES** (11), the year of his death is 1946, and in **CONDADO** (114), Rafa himself confirms that he was fourteen when his father died.

PART TWO

CHAPTER 16

1. In his distinction of written and oral discourses, Guillermo Hernández follows Albert B. Lord's conclusions drawn from his study of Homer in *The Singer of Tales* (1971:148).
2. Saldívar's article is directed against Michael M. J. Fisher's essay "Ethnicity and the Post-Modern Arts of Memory" (1986). Saldívar resents that Fisher "appropriates 'exotic' discourses, facts, and meanings" with the purpose of "totalizing... diverse historical phenomena in terms of postmodern homogenization" (Saldívar 1990:255).
3. Taboada's distinction between the modern and the postmodern (he juxtaposes "la dimensión posmoderna" and "los proyectos radicales de la modernidad") is based on Andreas Huyssen's book *After the Great Divide: Modernism, Mass Culture, Postmodernism* (1986).

CHAPTER 17

1. For a more thorough discussion of Fiedler's ideas on democratizing the arts see Maltby (1993:524).
2. See, for example, Christopher Norris's attacks on postmodernism for effacing all sense of the difference between truth and falsehood, reality and illusion, and serious and nonserious discourse in *What's Wrong with Postmodernism* (1990).
3. The phenomenon of the androgynous narrator in the Becky books was first noted by Wolfgang Karrer in his article "Gender and the Sense of Self in the Writings of Gloria Anzaldúa and Rolando Hinojosa" (1993:243). Hinojosa himself recently commented on the issue in an interview with Barbara Strickland, which can be viewed on the Internet at
<http://weeklywire.com/ww/09-02-97/austin_books_feature1.html>.

PART THREE

CHAPTER 20

1. That struggle for the right form of expression and—more importantly—the exultation at knowing one has found it, has never been described better than in Faulkner's own introduction to *The Sound and the Fury*. The introduction, which was long believed lost, was written for a long-planned, and eventually canceled, new 1933 edition of the book (see Faulkner 1987:218–21). In it, Faulkner fervently describes how this exultation accompanied the composition of *The Sound and the Fury* and how he hoped in vain to recapture it when he was writing his subsequent books.

PART FOUR

1. In an article entitled "*La Prensa:* A Lifelong Influence of Hispanics in Texas," Hinojosa (1989:128) explains that the character, P. Galindo, is based on a poet and satirist by the name of José (Pepe) Díaz, who wrote for the Spanish-language San Antonio newspaper, *La Prensa*. Díaz hailed from Mercedes and was actually a friend of the Hinojosa family. He used the pseudonym Galindo, adding the initial "P." as a joke in a play-on-words: *pega poco, pero pega lindo*. Hinojosa explained to me: "El sobrenombre quiere decir, en el Valle, lo siguiente: tirar al blanco y no siempre pegar, pero, cuando pega, pega lindo: nicely, on target, etc." ["In the Valley, the nickname has the following meaning: to shoot at a target but not always to hit it (no siempre pegar), but if one does hit it (pero cuando pega), it's dead center (pega lindo, which is a homophone to 'P. Galindo'): nicely, on target, etc." (my translation)].

CHAPTER 21

1. The problems regarding the exact age of the two protagonists have been discussed previously (see e.g., my discussion of **PARTNERS** in part one on p. 39–40). The bulk of the evidence—including Hinojosa's own date of birth—points to their being born in 1929 (see **RITES**:38).
2. For my analysis I am reading originals and renditions side-by-side; I will quote whichever version illustrates best the particular point I am investigating at the time, without, of course, neglecting significant versional differences.
3. In **VARONES**, Jehú features as narrator of an *estampa* that once more takes up the picaresque elements of the circus-motif (149–51).
4. Again, for a brief recapitulation of the events that are narrated in loosely jointed sketches across the first two novels, please see my exposition of **KLAIL** in part one (19–20). These passages also contain my discussion of the diverse treatment of the comedy depending on whether it is written in Spanish or English.
5. Years later, in **RAFE** (16), Jehú describes Don Pedro's own funeral as an expression of the Flora Mexicanos' love-hate relationship with their belligerent, temperamental priest: "Half the world and most of Belken County showed up, and I almost broke up thinking on that grand and glorious burial we gave Bruno Cano that bright Spring morning years ago."
6. Although Jehú mentions a "good-sized crop of Mexican Protestants" in Jonesville-on-the-Río (**KLAIL**:100), we can assume that his customers on (98) are Catholics, since Jehú uses his apprenticeship with Don Pedro as a recommendation.

7. It is perhaps necessary to draw attention to Bruce-Novoa's idiosyncratic use of the term "under erasure" (fr. *sous rature*), originally coined by Martin Heidegger and made popular by the French deconstructionist Jacques Derrida to represent the instability of language by printing a word and then crossing it out. The word is inadequate and thus appears "under erasure" yet it is necessary and remains legible (see Sarup 1993:33). Bruce-Novoa explains that his use is similar to Heidegger's and Derrida's in that "the *axis mundi* is still named, but it's signifying function has been suspended" (Bruce-Novoa 1990b:153).

8. Hinojosa restructured the sequences of the sketches when he rewrote them in English, which can be confusing when reading the books side-by-side. The corresponding sections in the Spanish-language books are: **ESTAMPAS** (111–28) and **CONDADO** (74–81).

9. As evidenced in several successful initiatives to dismantle bilingual education on the state level, such as the 1998 Proposition 227 in California and the even more restrictive Proposition 203 in Arizona, which was approved by voters in November 2000.

10. See, for instance, ex-Klail High teacher Rebecca Ruth Verser's white-supremacist remarks in **RITES** (97).

11. As I have pointed out previously, the information on Jehú's latest career move was not included in the Spanish original "A Class Reunion" (**CONDADO**:143–48). It was added more than a decade later to "A Classy Reunion: the Homecoming" (**KLAIL** CITY:137–43).

12. "Texas counties are governed by a commissioners court which consists of a county judge and four county commissioners. . . . The commissioners court is really a policy and administrative body, not a judicial group. Its legally established abilities include approving the county budget and setting the tax rates. Although the other elected officials do not report to the commissioners court, the court can brandish substantial control over each official through its budgeting powers.

    "Like the commissioners court, the title of county judge is a misnomer. County judges have little or no judicial responsibility, and are not even required to be lawyers. The legislature officially removed judicial responsibilities from the county judges in counties with populations exceeding 50,000 people. County judges are elected to four year terms in a county-wide election" (Flores et al. 1997).

13. I'm quoting from a personal letter by Jaime Mejía dated February 2, 1998, in which he satisfied my curiosity about an issue he briefly touched upon in his 1993 dissertation (69). In Mejía's opinion, the principal objective of Noddy's scheme is to make sure that one Anglo Congressman is replaced by another Anglo. When Hap Bayliss suddenly steps down, Terry's write-in candidacy leaves no time for other candidates to join the race. I'm especially grateful to Jaime Mejía for clueing me in on certain aspects of South Texas electoral proceedings, e.g., the fact that in the 1960s, the Republicans did not feature in a significant way in Texas politics. Thus, the Democrat that won the primary elections in the Spring, generally had no opposition in the general elections in November.

14. Jaime Mejía (1993:70–76) provides a comprehensive account of the complex details of Noddy's ploy and of Jehú's successful effort to foil it. He also points out the omission of the word "no" in a crucial statement by Fischer Gutiérrez in **RAFA** (83) through which the entire logic of the episode is rendered incomprehensible. Mejía detected the incongruity when he was reading **RAFA** and **RAFE** side by side.

15. In **AMIGOS** (62) KBC lawyer E. B. Cooke explains that the KBC will never be able

to buy the Buenrostros' Rancho del Carmen because *El Quieto* was ahead of the game. He used the same strategy of dividing up the land into numerous titles held by members of the extended family. That way, Cooke states, "no hay bastantes abogados y papeles para llegar a un acuerdo" ["there are not enough lawyers and papers to bring us to an agreement"].

16. There are eye witnesses though; one of the Peralta twins, an electrician, tells Galindo that he actually saw Jehú and Sammie Jo in bed together at the Ranch when he was installing a security system. The hilarious interview with the identical Peralta brothers, who leave Galindo speechless with their twin routine, appears in **RAFA** (92–94) and **RAFE** (104–7).

17. Jehú mentions in letter 21 (**RAFE**:56) that he's "close to 30 yrs. of a." The statement, I believe, should be taken to mean that, after his distressing brush with Valley politics, he feels older than he actually is. After all, the addressee is Rafa, whom we can expect to know Jehú's age.

18. That same aphorism, a quote from the 1962 Pulitzer Prize-winning *Edge of Sadness*, by Edwin O'Connor is later attributed to Javier Leguizamón (**FRIENDS**:15).

19. Curiously, the General is demoted to the rank of Captain in **VARONES** (10). There is little information on the legendary Rufus T. in the *KCDTS*. Probably the most revealing passage about the patriarch's paternalistic attitude towards "his" Mexicans is revealed in Earl Bennet's account of how "the timber of the Klail voice" was sufficient to break up a fight at a Mexican dance (in **RITES**:72–73). Bennet's white supremacist rantings about lazy, cunning, shiftless, vengeful, cowardly, childlike, easy-to-please Mexicans and their "grateful" ladies leaves nothing to be desired in the way of inane stereotyping.

CHAPTER 23

1. Quoted from Weber's *Foreigners in their Native Land* (1973:231), which also contains several lengthy excerpts from Cortina's proclamations.
2. It appears that E. B. Cooke displays a prime specimen of a loan translation, a typical feature of languages in contact, when he uses the expression "otra cosa" in a direct analogy to the American colloquialism "he's something else."
3. The theme is repeated in much the same fashion in **VARONES** (145) and is linked to the Buenrostros' conflict with the Leguizamón-Texas Rangers land-grabbers in **FRIENDS** (49–50) by Andrés Malacara.
4. For a clarification of this system of tenant farming or "sharecropping on thirds, fourths, and halves" see Montejano 1987:171.
5. Goodman makes a surprising disclosure about the Ambrosio Mora shooting in this interview. Mora was a World War II veteran who was shot down by a sheriff in Flora (**CONDADO**:128). The Belken County oral history is unsure about the killer of Mora. Some say it was Van Meers, and others point at Markham. In **RITES** (76), Markham himself says he shot Mora in self-defense. The interesting new detail added by Goodman highlights the connection between the Naranjo lynchings in 1915 and the Mora shooting after World War II: rumor has it that Ambrosio Mora was a nephew of the Naranjos.
6. Hinojosa's concern for this sordid chapter in Texas Mexican history is not only reflected in his own work but also in the fact that in 1987 he took it upon himself to furnish a sensitive and captivating English rendition of Tomás Rivera's Chicano

classic. . . . *y no se lo tragó a tierra* (1971), which he entitled *This Migrant Earth*.
7. This stance is evidenced in their titles: *Estampas del Valle, Generaciones y semblanzas* (now *El condado de Belken)*, and *Claros varones de Belken* (named after *Claros varones de Castilia*).
8. "Primaries, primaries, o' when will they end?" (**RAFE**:35). "Son las primarias, sí, pero aquí éstas son las que cuentan por la seguridad que dan pa' noviembre" (**VARONES**:199).
9. When the Belken County Chicanos speak Spanish—and Echevarría is a case in point—it is represented on the page with all its phonetic and dialectal idiosyncrasies.
10. For a quick summary of recent tendencies to militarize the border, see also *Border Matters* (Saldívar 1997:x–xii). As his source, Saldívar cites historian Timothy Dunn's 1996 *The Militarization of the U.S.-Mexico Border, 1978–1992: Low-Intensity Conflict Doctrine Comes Home*.

BIBLIOGRAPHY

THE KLAIL CITY DEATH TRIP SERIES BY ROLANDO HINOJOSA

1973.	*Estampas del Valle y otras obras*. Berkeley: Quinto Sol.
1976.	*Klail City y sus alrededores*. La Habana: Casa de las Américas.
1977.	*Generaciones y semblanzas*. Berkeley: Justa Publications.
1978a.	*Korean Love Songs*. Berkeley: Justa Publications.
1981a.	*Mi querido Rafa*. Houston: Arte Público Press.
1982a.	*Rites and Witnesses*. Houston: Arte Público Press.
1983a.	*The Valley*. Tempe: Bilingual Press/Editorial Bilingüe.
1985a.	*Dear Rafe*. Houston: Arte Público Press.
1985b.	*Partners in Crime: A Rafe Buenrostro Mystery*. Houston: Arte Público Press.
1986.	*Claros varones de Belken: Fair Gentlemen of Belken County*. Translated by Julia Cruz. Tempe: Bilingual Press/Editorial Bilingüe.
1987a.	*Klail City*. Houston: Arte Público Press.
1990.	*Becky and Her Friends*. Houston: Arte Público Press.
1991a.	*Korea Liebes Lieder/Korean Love Songs*. German/English edition. Translated by Wolfgang Karrer. Osnabrück: Universität Osnabrück.
1991b.	*Los amigos de Becky*. Houston: Arte Público Press.
1993.	*The Useless Servants*. Houston: Arte Público Press.
1994a.	*Estampas del Valle*. Clásicos Chicanos/Chicano Classics 7. Tempe: Bilingual Press/Editorial Bilingüe.
1994b.	*El condado de Belken: Klail City*. Clásicos Chicanos/Chicano Classics 8. Tempe: Bilingual Press/Editorial Bilingüe.
1998.	*Ask a Policeman: A Rafe Buenrostro Mystery*. Houston: Arte Público Press.

OTHER PUBLICATIONS BY ROLANDO HINOJOSA

1972. "Por esas cosas que pasan." *El Grito: A Journal of Contemporary Mexican-American Thought* 5.3 (primavera):26–36.
1978b. *Generaciones, notas y brechas/Generations, Notes, and Trails.* San Francisco: Casa Editorial.
1979a. "Chicano Literature in Transition." In *The Identification and Analysis of Chicano Literature,* edited by Francisco Jiménez, 37–40. New York: Bilingual Press/Editorial Bilingüe.
1979b. "Literatura Chicana: Background and Present Status of a Bicultural Expression." In *The Identification and Analysis of Chicano Literature,* edited by Francisco Jiménez, 42–46. New York: Bilingual Press/Editorial Bilingüe.
1979c. "Mexican American Literature: Toward an Identification." In *The Identification and Analysis of Chicano Literature,* edited by Francisco Jiménez, 7–18. New York: Bilingual Press/Editorial Bilingüe.
1981b. "Retaguardia en noviembre. That means: The 219th isn't doing well at all." *Revista Chicano-Riqueña* 9, num. 1 (invierno):17–19.
1982b. "Conversation on a Hill." In *Hispanics in the United States: An Anthology of Creative Literature,* Francisco Jiménez and Gary D. Keller, vol. 2. Ypsilanti, Mich.: Bilingual Review Press.
1983b. "This Writer's Sense of Place." In *The Texas Literary Tradition: Fiction, Folklore, History,* edited by Don Graham, James W. Lee, and William Pilkington, 120–24. Austin: University of Texas and Texas State Historical Association.
1983c. "Out of Many Lives: One: Reflections on Fathers." *Nuestro* 7, no. 5 (June/July):61.
1984a. "The Sense of Place." In *The Rolando Hinojosa Reader: Essays Historical and Critical,* edited by José David Saldívar, 18–24. Houston: Arte Público Press.
1984b. "A Voice of One's Own." In *The Rolando Hinojosa Reader: Essays Historical and Critical,* edited by José David Saldívar, pp. 11–17. Houston: Arte Público Press.
1987b. *This Migrant Earth.* Houston: Arte Público Press.
1988. "North from the Valley." *The Americas Review* 16, no. 1 (spring):9–11.
1989. "La Prensa. A Lifelong Influence of Hispanics in Texas." *The Americas Review* 17, nos. 3–4 (fall, winter):125–29.
1991c. "Redefining American Literature." Foreword in *Criticism in the Borderlands: Studies in Chicano Literature, Culture, and Ideology,* edited by Héctor Calderón and José David Saldívar, xi–xv. Durham and London: Duke University Press.

WORKS CITED

Akers, John C.
1993. "From Translation to Rewriting: Rolando Hinojosa's *The Valley.*" *The Americas Review* 1(spring):91–102.
Anzaldúa, Gloria
1987. *Borderlands/La Frontera: The New Mestiza.* San Francisco: Aunt Lute Books.

Barry, Peter
1995.   *Beginning Theory: An Introduction to Literary and Cultural Theory.* Manchester: Manchester University Press.

Baudrillard, Jean
1981.   *Simulacres et simulations.* Paris: Galilée.
1993.   "The Precession of Simulacra." Translated by Paul Patton and Philip Beitchman. In *A Postmodern Reader,* edited by Joseph Natoli and Linda Hutcheon, 342–75. Albany: State University of New York Press.

Broyles, Yolanda Julia
1984.   "Hinojosa's *Klail City y sus alrededores:* Oral Culture and Print Culture." In *The Rolando Hinojosa Reader: Essays Historical and Critical,* edited by José David Saldívar, 109–32. Houston: Arte Público Press.

Bruce-Novoa, Juan
1978.   "Interview with Rolando Hinojosa." *Latin American Literary Review* 5, no. 10 (spring-summer):103–14.
1987.   "Who's Killing Whom in Belkin [sic] County: Rolando Hinojosa's Narrative Production." *Monographic Review* 3, no. 1–2:288–97.
1989.   "Review of *Claros varones de Belken/Fair Gentlemen of Belken County.*" *Hispania* 72, no. 1 (March):165–66.
1990a. *Retrospace: Collected Essays on Chicano Literature Theory and History.* Houston: Arte Público Press.
1990b. "The Topological Space of Chicano Literature." In *Retrospace: Collected Essays on Chicano Literature Theory and History,* 146–56. Houston: Arte Público Press.

Busby, Mark
1984.   "Faulknerian Elements in Rolando Hinojosa's *The Valley.*" MELUS 11, no. 4 (winter):103–9.

Calderón, Héctor
1984.   "On the Use of Chronicle, Biography, and Sketch in Rolando Hinojosa's *Generaciones y semblanzas.*" In *The Rolando Hinojosa Reader: Essays Historical and Critical,* edited by José David Saldívar, 133–42. Houston: Arte Público Press.
1991.   "Texas Border Literature: Cultural Transformation and Historical Reflection in the Works of Américo Paredes, Rolando Hinojosa, and Gloria Anzaldúa." *Dispositio* 16, no. 41:13–28.

Conniff, Richard
1996.   "The Tex-Mex Border." *National Geographic* (Feb.):49–69.

Dasenbrock, Reed Way, and Feroza Jussawalla, eds.
1992.   "Interview with Rolando Hinojosa." In *Interviews with Writers of the Post-Colonial World,* 256–85. Jackson and London: University Press of Mississippi.

Dorough-Johnson, Elaine
1978.   "A Thematic Study of Three Chicano Narratives: *Estampas del Valle y otras obras; Bless Me, Ultima;* and *Peregrinos de Aztlán.*" DAI, 39, 6 (Dez). Madison, Wisconsin.

Doyle, Susan
1995. "Book Review of *The Useless Servants.*" MELUS 20, no. 1 (spring):123–25.
Duke dos Santos, María I., and Patricia de la Fuente
1984. "The Elliptic Female Presence as Unifying Force in the Novels of Rolando Hinojosa." In *The Rolando Hinojosa Reader: Essays Historical and Critical,* edited by José David Saldívar, 64–75. Houston: Arte Público Press.
Dunn, Timothy
1996. *The Militarization of the U.S.-Mexico Border, 1978–1992: Low-Intensity Conflict Doctrine Comes Home.* Austin: Center for Mexican American Studies.
Faulkner, William
1960. *The Unvanquished.* Second Signet Classics Edition. New York: Signet.
1987. *The Sound and the Fury.* Norton Critical Edition, edited by David Mintner. New York, London: W. W. Norton & Company.
Fisher, Michael M. J.
1986. "Ethnicity and the Post-Modern Arts of Memory." In *Writing Culture: The Poetics and Politics of Ethnography,* edited by James Clifford and George E. Marcus, 194–233. Berkeley: University of California Press.
Flores, Gregorio, III, Michael Kelley, Roberta A. Ritvo, and Natasha Borges Sugiyama
1997. Fiscal Capacity of Texas Cities Policy Research Project Local Government Structure and Function in Texas and the United States. <http://uts.cc.utexas.edu/~rhwilson/fiscalprp/structure.html>
Goetsch, Paul, ed.
1990. *Mündliches Wissen in neuzeitlicher Literatur.* Tübingen: Script Oralia 18.
Gonzalez-Berry, Erlinda
1994. "Hinojosa's Poetics of *Aguante.*" Introduction to *El condado de Belken: Klail City,* Rolando Hinojosa, 1–20. Tempe: Bilingual Press/Editorial Bilingüe.
Habermas, Jürgen
1985. "A Philosophico-Political Profile." *New Left Review* 151:97.
1993. "Modernity versus Postmodernity." Translated by Selya Ben-Habib. In *A Postmodern Reader,* edited by Joseph Natoli and Linda Hutcheon, 91–104. Albany: State University of New York Press.
Heidenreich, Helmut, ed.
1969. *Pikarische Welt: Schriften zum Europäischen Schelmenroman.* Darmstadt: Wissenschaftliche Buchgesellschaft Darmstadt.
Hernández, Guillermo E.
1991. *Chicano Satire: A Study in Literary Culture.* Austin: University of Texas Press.
hooks, bell
1993. "Postmodern Blackness." In *A Postmodern Reader,* edited by Joseph Natoli and Linda Hutcheon, 510–18. Albany: State University of New York Press.
Huyssen, Andreas
1986. *After the Great Divide: Modernism, Mass Culture, Postmodernism.* Bloomington: Indiana University Press.
1993. "Mapping the Postmodern." In *A Postmodern Reader,* edited by Joseph Natoli and Linda Hutcheon, 105–56. Albany: State University of New York Press.

Karrer, Wolfgang
1993. "Gender and the Sense of Self in the Writings of Gloria Anzaldúa and Rolando Hinojosa." In *Gender, Self, and Society: Proceedings of the IV International Conference on the Hispanic Cultures of the United States*, edited by Renate von Bardeleben, 237–45. Berlin, Bern, New York, Paris, Wien: Peter Lang.

Keefe-Ugalde, Sharon
1985. "Two Visions of Cultural Domination: Carrero's *El hombre que no sudaba* and Hinojosa's *Mi querido Rafa*." *Bilingual Review/Revista Bilingüe* 12, nos. 1–2 (January-August):159–65.

Leal, Luís
1984. "History and Memory in *Estampas del Valle*." In *The Rolando Hinojosa Reader: Essays Historical and Critical*, edited by José David Saldívar, 101–8. Houston: Arte Público Press.

Lee, Joyce Glover
1997. *Rolando Hinojosa and the American Dream*. Texas Writers Series: no. 5. Denton: University of North Texas Press.

Lesy, Michael
2000. *Wisconsin Death Trip*. Albuquerque: University of New Mexico Press.

López, Angie
2000. "Transfer strategies in Rolando Hinojosa's self-translation of *Mi querido Rafa*." In *Literatura Chicana: Reflexiones y ensayos críticos*, edited by Rosa Morillas Sánchez and Manuel Villar Raso, 203–9. Granada: Editorial Comares.

Lyotard, Jean-François
1993. Excerpts from *The Postmodern Condition: A Report on Knowledge*. Translated by Geoff Bennington and Brian Massumi. In *A Postmodern Reader*, edited by Joseph Natoli and Linda Hutcheon, 71–90. Albany: State University of New York Press.

Maltby, Paul
1993. "Dissident Postmodernists: Barthleme, Coover, Pynchon." In *A Postmodern Reader*, edited by Joseph Natoli and Linda Hutcheon, 519–37. Albany: State University of New York Press.

Márquez, Antonio C.
1991. "Review of *Becky and Her Friends*." *World Literature Today* 65, no. 2 (spring 1991):303.

Martin, Gary
1996. "Cisneros Focused on Improving Finances, Clearing Fed Probe." *San Antonio Express News*. November 25, 1996.

Martín Rodríguez, Manuel M.
1993a. *Rolando Hinojosa y su "Cronicón" Chicano: Una novela del lector*. Sevilla: Universidad de Sevilla.
1993b. "Rolando Hinojosa y su *Klail City Death Trip Series*: Una novela del lector." *The Americas Review* 21, no. 2 (summer):89–101.

May, Herbert G., and Bruce M. Metzger, eds.
1977. *The New Oxford Annotated Bible with the Apocrypha*. Revised Standard Edition. New York: Oxford University Press.

Mejía, Jaime Armin
1993a. *Transformations in Rolando Hinojosa's Klail City Death Trip Series.* Unpublished doctoral dissertation, Ohio State University.
1993b. "Breaking the Silence: The Missing Pages in Rolando Hinojosa's *The Useless Servants.*" *Southwestern American Fiction* 19, no. 1 (fall):57–62.

Montejano, David
1987. *Anglos and Mexicans in the Making of Texas: 1836–1986.* Austin: University of Texas Press.

Morris, Richard B., ed.
1982. *Encyclopedia of American History,* 6th ed. New York: Harper and Row.

Nericcio, William Anthony
1995. "Review of *The Useless Servants.*" *World Literature Today* 69, no. 1 (winter):139–40.

Norris, Christopher
1990. *What's Wrong with Postmodernism.* Baltimore: Johns Hopkins University Press.

Paredes, Américo
1958. *With His Pistol in His Hand: A Border Ballad and Its Hero.* Austin: University of Texas Press.

Parker, Alexander
1967. *Literature and the Delinquent: The Picaresque Novel in Spain and Europe 1599–1753.* Edinburgh: Edinburgh University Press.

Peñalosa, Fernando
1980. *Chicano Sociolinguistics. A Brief Introduction.* Rowley, Mass.: Newbury House.

Riera, Miguel
1987. "El otro sur: Entrevista con Rolando Hinojosa." *Quimera* num. 70/71:112–16.

Rivera, Tomás
1971. *. . . y no se lo tragó la tierra.* Berkeley: Quinto Sol.

Rosenthal, Regine
1983. *Die Erben des Lazarillo.* Neue Studien zur Anglistik und Amerikanistik 27. Frankfurt, Bern: Verlag Peter Lang.

Rudin, Ernst
1993. "Hard English and Soft Spanish: Language as a Theme in the Chicano Novel in English, 1969–1985." In *Gender, Self, and Society: Proceedings of the IV International Conference on the Hispanic Cultures of the United States,* edited by Renate von Bardeleben, 395–410. Berlin, Bern, New York, Paris, Wien: Peter Lang.

Saldívar, José David
1984a. "Rolando Hinojosa's *Klail City Death Trip:* A Critical Introduction." In *The Rolando Hinojosa Reader: Essays Historical and Critical,* edited by José David Saldívar, 44–63. Houston: Arte Público Press.
1984b. "Our Southwest: An Interview with Rolando Hinojosa." In *The Rolando Hinojosa Reader: Essays Historical and Critical,* edited by José David Saldívar, 180–90. Houston: Arte Público Press.

1990. "The Limits of Cultural Studies." *American Literary History* 2, no. 2 (summer):251–66.
1991. "Chicano Border Narratives as Cultural Critique." In *Criticism in the Borderlands: Studies in Chicano Literature, Culture, and Ideology,* edited by Héctor Calderón and José David Saldívar, 167–80. Durham and London: Duke University Press.
1997. *Border Matters: Remapping American Cultural Studies.* Berkeley: University of California Press.

Sánchez, Mario L.
1996. "The Exploration and River Settlements of José de Escandón." In the HTML Version of *A Shared Experience,* adapted from Mario L. Sánchez's original print version at <http://www.rice.edu/armadillo/Past/Book/Part2/escandon.html>; accessed on April 4, 1998, 1–9.

Sánchez, Rosaura
1984. "From Heterogeneity to Contradiction: Hinojosa's Novel." In *The Rolando Hinojosa Reader: Essays Historical and Critical,* edited by José David Saldívar, 76–100. Houston: Arte Público Press.
1992. "Discourses of Gender, Ethnicity, and Class in Chicano Literature." *The Americas Review* 20, no. 2 (summer):72–88.
1992–1996.
        "Mapping the Spanish Language along a Multiethnic and Multilingual Border." *Átzlan* 21, nos. 1 & 2:49–104.

Sartre, Jean Paul
1987. "On *The Sound and the Fury:* Time in the Work of Faulkner." In *The Sound and the Fury,* Norton critical ed., William Faulkner, 253–59. New York, London: Norton.

Sarup, Madan
1993. *An Introductory Guide to Post-Structuralism and Postmodernism.* Athens Ga.: University of Georgia Press.

Streng, R. L.
1991. "Review of *Becky and Her Friends.*" *Western-American Literature* 26, no. 2 (August):184–86.

Strickland, Barbara
1997. "Crossing Literary Borders." *Weekly Wire Books* (an online magazine at: <http://weeklywire.com/ww/09-02-97/austin_books_feature1.Html>; accessed on December 11, 1997.

Taboada, Antonio Prieto
1991. "El caso de las pistas culturales en *Partners in Crime.*" *The Americas Review* 19, nos. 3–4 (winter):117–32.

Weber, David J., ed.
1973. *Foreigners in their Native Land: Historical Roots of the Mexican Americans.* Albuquerque: University of New Mexico Press.

Zukin, Sharon
1991. *Landscapes of Power: From Detroit to Disney World.* Berkeley: University of California Press.

INDEX

Note: Names of characters from the KCDTS are presented in italics

Der abentheuerliche Simplicissimus Teutsch (von Grimmelshausen), 107
absolution, 70
acculturation, 152
   of Anglos, 142, 159–60
   and ethnic identity, 189
   of Mexicans, 189
   vs. assimilation, 29
"A Classy Reunion: The Homecoming" (KLAIL) (Hinojosa), 21, 210n11
Acosta, 156–57
After the Great Divide: Modernism, Mass Culture, Postmodernism (Huyssen), 208(ch. 16)n3
ages, incongruities regarding *Jehú*'s and *Rafa*'s, 39–40, 109, 209(ch. 21)n1
Akers, John C., 79
the Alamo, 61, 146
Alemán, Mateo, *Guzmán de Alfarache*, 107
Los amigos de Becky (AMIGOS) (Hinojosa), 88–89, 155–56, 159
   duo text with FRIENDS, 43, 48, 51–56
   publishing history, 6
anecdotes, 27
Anglo-centric history
   revision of, xv, 62, 91, 145–46, 149–54, 168
   See also South Texas history
Anglo-Mexican communities, 46, 48, 149–50
   political kinships, 159–60
   race relations, xvi, 12, 35, 37–38, 89–90, 132
   farm society, 169–81
   hacienda society, 153–54
   ranch society, 160–61
Anglos, 70–71
   acculturation of, 142, 159–60
Anglos and Mexicans in the Making of Texas: 1963–1986 (Montejano), 125–26, 143, 149–50, 188
   Incorporation (1836–1900), 138–39, 150–54
   Integration (1940–1986), 182–85
   Reconstruction (1900–1920), 160–63
   Segregation (1920–1940), 169–73
Anglo society
   judicial system, 7
   Mexicans assimilation into, 29, 189
   rights and privileges defended by non-Anglos, 188
anti-heroes, 107

See also pícaros
Anzaldúa, Gloria, *Borderlands*, 49
Arte Público, 207–8(ch. 13)n5
"As fine a man as ever robbed the helpless," 132, 211n18
Ask a Policeman: A Rafe Buenrostro Mystery (POLICEMAN) (Hinojosa), 65–66, 89, 191–92
  dynamics of revenge subplot, 66, 68–72
  militarization of the border subplot, 66–68
  publishing history, 6
assimilation, 119
  of Mexicans, 29, 189
  vs. acculturation, 29
Austin, Moses, 145
Austin, Stephen, 145
axis mundi charted topological paradigm, 96–97, 99, 117, 210n7

Baker, A. Y., 163
Baker, Ned, 167
Barragán, Viola, 13, 21, 43–44, 159
Barrón, Lucas, 47, 138, 204(ch.1)n3
Barry, Peter, 83
Baudrillard, Jean
  "The Precession of Simulacra," 85–88
  Simulacres et simulations, 85
Bayliss, Hapgood, 127–28
Bayliss, Osgood, 128
Becky and Her Friends (FRIENDS) (Hinojosa), 44–49, 88–89, 159, 196–97
  duo text with AMIGOS, 43, 48, 51–56
  publishing history, 6, 43
Belken County, xii, 154–60, 163–69, 173–81, 185–93, 203n3
  Octavio Romano living in, 87
  and Yoknapatawpha County, 101
Belken County Police Department, 40
Bewley, Esther Lucille, 54, 133
Bibles
  sale of, 112–15
  translation of passages, 2
biculturalism, 33–34, 42, 71
  and ethnic identity, 53–54, 123

bilingualism, 33–34, 37, 42, 52–53, 71
  defined, 3, 203(pt. 1)n1
Blanchard, Fredericka (Freddie), 127
border crisis, 190
  and militarization, 66–68, 71, 185, 199, 212n10
Borderlands (Anzaldúa), 49
Border Matters: Remapping American Cultural Studies (Saldívar), 75, 148, 184, 189, 192
boss-laborer relationships, 170–71
Boynton, Sidney, 128
Briones, Chedes, 110, 121
Briones, Juan, 110
Briones family, 109
Briscoe, Dolph, 183
Broyles, Yolanda Julia, xiii
  "Oral Culture and Print Culture," 15–16
Bruce-Novoa, Juan
  "Interview with Rolando Hinojosa," 102
  "Review of *Claros varones de Belken/Fair Gentlemen of Belken County*," 148–49, 154
  "The Topological Space of Chicano Literature," xiv, 91, 95–100, 157, 165, 210n7
Buckley, William F., 189–90
Buenrostro, Albinita, 98
Buenrostro, Israel, 27, 165
Buenrostro, Jesús (El Quieto), 25, 154, 180
  death of, 8, 69–70, 89, 140, 155
Buenrostro, Julián, 69, 155
Buenrostro, Rafa, 26–28, 103–4, 187–88
  age, incongruities regarding, 39–40, 209(ch. 21)n1
  birth, xiii
  childhood, 8, 10–11, 175
  education, 26, 123–24, 175–78
  employment, 26
    as a bartender, 138
    career as policeman, 39, 42, 65–72, 190–93
  family tree, 97–98
  marriage, 27
  military service, 23–24, 29, 37–38, 57–60, 188–89

name
  spelling and pronunciation of first name, 206(ch. 7)n1, 206(ch. 8)n1
  surname, 121–23
  as a revisionist chronicler, xv, 62, 150
  Rosaura Sánchez's comments on, 122
Buenrostro family, xii, 8, 47, 154
  family history as the history of South Texas, 145, 148–51, 154–56
Buitureyra, Orfalindo, 21
Busby, Mark, "Faulknerian Elements in Rolando Hinojosa's *The Valley*", 101
"Buy land and never sell," 126

Calderón, Héctor
  "On the Use of Chronicle, Biography, and Sketch in Rolando Hinojosa's *Generaciones y semblanzas,*" xiii
  "Texas Border Literature," 25, 79, 148
Caldwell, Catarino, 159
Calvillo, Práxedes, 98
Calvillo Tapia, Sóstenes, 98
Campoy, Reina, 189
Cano, Bruno, 19, 111–12
Cano Clan, 208n6
Cantú, Ike, 66
Carmen Ranch, xii, 70, 152, 191, 210–11n15
  and irrigation, 163–65, 168
  siege of, 154–57
Casa de las Américas, 11
"El caso de las pistas culturales in *Partners in Crime*" (Taboada), 41–42, 79
Castañeda, Gilberto, 186
Cetina de Gutiérrez, Maria Luisa (Lu), 66, 69
Chapman, Elsinore, 120
charted topological paradigms, xiv, 91, 95–100, 210n7
  axis mundi, 96–97, 99, 117, 210n7
  of Chicano culture, 99–100, 116–18, 124–25, 133–34, 157, 165–66, 191–93
Chávez, César, 183
"Chicano Border Narratives as Cultural Critique" (Saldívar), 38

Chicano culture, 174
  death of, 28, 93–94
  information networks, 124–25, 129–30
  land losses, 157
  literature, 95–100
  oral traditions, 99–100, 133–34, 191–93
  paternal love, 116–18
  synthesis of tradition and modern society, 165–66
Chicano Satire: A Study in Literary Culture (Hernández), 77–78, 103
Chicano Sociolinguistics (Peñalosa), 3
chroniclers, xv, 62, 109, 150
chronicles, 57–58, 78–79, 191
Cisneros, Henry, x–xii, 184, 203n2
civil rights
  institutionalized violation of, 180–81
  movement, 183–84
Claros Varones de Belken: Fair Gentlemen of Belken County (VARONES) (Hinojosa), 25–28, 78–79, 115–16, 164, 167–68, 187–88
  Echevarría's farewell, 141–43
  publishing history, 5, 25, 104, 205 (ch. 6)n1
  translation by Julia Cruz, 26, 205 (ch. 6)n1
class conflicts, 71
"A Class Reunion" (CONDADO) (Hinojosa), 13, 21, 210n11
code-switching, 2–3
collective memory of the Valley, xv, 11–12, 26–28, 94, 103–4, 192
commercial agriculture. *See* farm society
compadrazgos (sponsorships), 152
El condado de Belken: Klail City (CONDADO) (Hinojosa), 11–13, 112–13, 174, 177
  "A Class Reunion," 13, 21, 210n11
  duo text with KLAIL, 15–22, 83
  "los desposeídos," 118
  publishing history, 5, 6, 11, 204 (ch. 3)n1
  self-translation process, 15–22
  "The Searchers," 17–18
  See also Generaciones y semblanzas

"Con el pie en el estribo" (Hinojosa), 28, 141
Conniff, Richard, "The Tex-Mex Border," 34
conversations, overheard, 13, 17
Cooke, E. B. (Ibby), 55, 127, 155, 189
Cordero, Albino, 186
Cordero, Baldemar, 7, 48, 186
Cordero, Marta, 186
Cortina's War, 151–52
creative process, 205(ch. 4)n1
criticism, literary, 35–36, 61
  in Spanish of English-language works, 41–42
cronicóns, 57–58, 78–79, 191
"Crossing Literary Borders" (Strickland), 46–47
Cruz, Julia, translation of *Claros varones de Belken: Fair Gentlemen of Belken County* (VARONES), 26, 205(ch. 6)n1
Crystal City Uprising, 1962, 183, 186

Darling, Charles, 40
de Anda, Jovita, 204(ch.1)n3
Dear Rafe (RAFE) (Hinojosa), 129, 156–57, 189, 196–98
  duo text with RAFA, 33–36
  publishing history, 5, 33
death trips, 28, 93–94
debt peonage, 171
decontextualization of events, 174–75
de Escandón, José, 146–47
Defoe, Daniel, *Moll Flanders*, 107
de Hinojosa, Juan José, 146–48
de la Cruz, Art, 68–69
Del Monte, 186
Dembro, Walt, 178–79
Democratic Party, 184, 188, 189
de Quevedo Villegas, Francisco, *La vida del buscón,* 107
descriptions of physical characteristics, 27
"los desposeídos" (CONDADO) (Hinojosa), 118
dialogues, 37, 40
dietary ethnocentrism, 176
diglossia, 3
Disneyland, 85

"The Dispossessed" (KLAIL) (Hinojosa), 118
domestication, 204(pt. 1)n2
Doña Margarita/Doña Modesta, 18
Donovan, Culley, 191
Dorough-Johnson, Elaine, 110, 122, 176
Dorson, Sam, 66, 69, 71
Doyle, Susan, 61–62, 79
Dr. Perlman, 59
Duke dos Santos, María I., and Patricia de la Fuente, "The Elliptic Female Presence as Unifying Force in the Novels of Rolando Hinojosa," 43–44, 130
duo serial texts
  AMIGOS/FRIENDS, 43, 48, 51–56
  CONDADO/KLAIL, 15–18
  ESTAMPAS/VALLEY, 9–10, 15
  literary criticism of, 35–36
  RAFA/RAFE, 33–36
  Spanish-English usage in, 34–35, 51–52, 54–55, 89

Echevarría, Esteban, 16, 138–43
  death of, 27, 141–43
  as the Valley's collective memory, xv, 11–12, 26–28, 94, 103–4, 192
editorial negligence, 57, 59, 207–8 (ch. 13)n5
education, 26, 123–24, 131, 188
  interracial, 118–21
  segregated, 175–78
Ejército Liberador México Texano, 165–67
Elder, Gus (Dutch), 40–41, 65
"The Elliptic Female Presence as Unifying Force in the Novels of Rolando Hinojosa" (Duke dos Santos and la Fuente), 43–44, 130
empathy, 90
Encyclopedia of American History (Morris), 58
endurance, 13, 101
English-Spanish binary, 1–3, 126, 189
  in Chicano literature, 206–7(Ch. 9)n1
  usage in duo texts, 34–35, 51–52, 54–55, 89
  vs. English only, 58

Enlightenment, 82–83
entailment, 150, 156
epic heroes, 25
epistolary novels, 2–3, 29–30, 33, 35
Escobar, Ira, 45–46
　as monolingual, 53, 189
　as a political puppet, 30, 128–29, 184, 187
Escobar, Rebecca (Becky), 43, 45–46, 130, 133
　See also Malacara, Rebecca (Becky)
essentialism, 82
ESTAMPAS. *See Estampas del Valle*
estampas, 8–13, 18, 25, 40
Estampas del Valle (ESTAMPAS) (Hinojosa), 7–8, 176, 186
　Bruce-Novoa's topological reading of, 97, 99–100
　duo text with VALLEY, 9–10, 15, 83
　"Los Leguizamón," 8, 154–55, 163
　"Los revolucionarios," 109
　publishing history, 5–7, 87
　thematic study by Dorough-Johnson, 110–11
Estampas del Valle y otras obras (ESTAMPAS) (Hinojosa), 5
Estebanillo de Gonzalez, 107
ethnic conflicts, 154
ethnic identity, xi, 118–19, 158, 192
　and acculturation, 189
　in a bicultural society, 53–54, 123
　independence from, 70–71
　in a multicultural society, 89–90, 94
"Ethnicity and the Post-Modern Arts of Memory" (Fisher), 208(ch. 16)n2
ethnocentrism, 56
　dietary, 176
exclusion, advocated by the formerly excluded, 189

fairness, xv, 114
farm society, 142–43, 149–50, 169–74
　irrigation farming, 163–65
　race relations, 169–73
Faulkner, William, 12
　The Sound and the Fury, xv, 91, 101–3, 105, 209(ch. 20)n1
　The Unvanquished, 69

"Faulknerian Elements in Rolando Hinojosa's *The Valley*" (Busby), 101
fiction as accurate as reality, xvi, 34, 198
　real-life interactions, 86–88, 104
　real-life models, 56, 70
Fiedler, Leslie, 84, 88
Fielding, Henry, *Tom Jones*, 107
Firing Line, 189–90
first impressions, treacherousness of, 68
Fischer Gutiérrez, Rufino, 114–15, 129, 166
Fisher, Michael M. J., "Ethnicity and the Post-Modern Arts of Memory," 208(ch. 16)n2
Flora (city), 111
foreignization, 204(pt. 1)n2
foster parents, 117
FRIENDS. *See Becky and Her Friends*
fronterizos, 34, 70

gachupines, 159
Galindo, P., 11–12, 26–27, 30
　awareness of his fictional condition, 197–98
　biography of, xv, 195–96
　on Esteban Echevarría's death, 140–41
　as Hinojosa's alter ego, 34, 103–4, 191
　with the last word, 201
　in metafictional territory, xvi, 87, 198
　origin of, 209(pt. 4)n1
Gallardo Gómez, Blanca, 192
Gavira, Leocadio, 181
gender, 88–89
　as identity, 82
　roles, 49, 53–54
"Gender and the Sense of Place in the Writings of Gloria Anzaldúa and Rolando Hinojosa" (Karrer), 46, 49
genealogies, 46, 98, 109, 122
　of illustrious men, 25
Generaciones y semblanzas (CONDADO) (Hinojosa)
　publishing history, 5, 11–12
　Rosaura Sánchez's translation of, 11
　See also El condado de Belken: Klail City
generic experimentation, 40, 78, 83–84, 102–5, 198
　See also specific genres

GGL (Good Government League), 162
GI Bill, 29, 123–24
Gil Blas de Santillane (Lesage), 107
Goetsch, Paul, *Mündliches Wissen in neuzeitlicher Literatur*, 93
Gómez, José Antonio, 66, 69, 192
Gómez, Juan Carlos, 69, 192
Gómez Solís, Felipe Segundo, 69, 192
Gómez Solís, Lisandro (alias *Juan José Olivares*), 65, 69, 191
Gonzalez-Berry, Erlinda, 79, 149
Good Government League (GGL), 162
Goodman, John, 159, 168
Guerrero, Conce, 18, 27
Guzmán, Manuel, 21
Guzmán de Alfarache (Alemán), 107

Habermas, Jürgen, 82–83
hacienda society, 150–60
　race relations, 153–54
　transition to ranch society, 139, 142–43, 149–50, 152–54, 160
Hauer, Peter, 66–67, 70–71
Hernández, Guillermo E., *Chicano Satire: A Study in Literary Culture*, 77–78, 103
Hernández, Paula, 59
Hernández, Rodolfo, 59
Hernández, Rudy, 59, 165–66
heroes, 25, 107
Hidalgo, Texas, 173
Hidalgo County Rebellion, 1928, 162
high culture vs. low culture, 81, 84–85
Hinojosa, Juan José, 146–48
Hinojosa, Romeo, 56, 87, 207(ch. 12)n4
Hinojosa-Smith, Rolando R., 203(Intro.)n1
　agenda as a storyteller, 88, 168, 197
　age of, 39–40
　appearances as Romeo Hinojosa, 56, 87, 207(ch. 12)n4
　family history, 77, 145–48
　Hinojosa's alter ego, 34, 103–4, 191
　on literary experimentation, 2, 53, 83–84, 102
　See also specific works
historical figures, 25

history, Anglo-centric
　revision of, xv, 62, 91, 145–46, 149–54, 168
　See also South Texas history
Holland, Martin, 159
homosexuality, 128
hooks, bell, 90
horse culture. *See* hacienda society
Huffington, Ariana, 189–90
Huyssen, Andreas
　After the Great Divide: Modernism, Mass Culture, Postmodernism, 208(ch. 16)n3
　"Mapping the Postmodern," 84
hygiene-germ theory, 176
hyperreality, 85

identity, 108
　as gender, 82
　as race, 82
　See also ethnic identity
illusion vs. reality, 81, 85–88
Imás, Tomás, 19–20, 112, 123
　bitten by a rattlesnake, 115–16
immobilization of workers, 180–82
information networks, 124–25, 129–30
insurrections, 151–52, 161–62
integrated society, 48, 149–50, 182–85, 182–93
intermarriages, 152, 158–59, 189
"Interview with Rolando Hinojosa" (Bruce-Novoa), 102
irredentist movement, 161, 165–68
irrigation farming, 163–65

Jehu (son of Jehosh'aphat, King of Israel), 24, 135–36
journals, 57–58, 78–79, 191
judicial system, Anglo, 7
justice, xv, 114

k, lacking in Spanish language, 126
Kanellos, Nikolas, 52
Karrer, Wolfgang, 23, 203n3
　"Gender and the Sense of Place in the Writings of Gloria Anzaldúa and Rolando Hinojosa," 46, 49

KBC clan. *See* Klail-Blanchard-Cooke (KBC) clan
Keefe-Ugalde, Sharon, 30–31
King, Henrietta, 126
King, Richard, 126, 153
2 Kings
   9:19, 23, 135
   10:28, 135
   10:34, 136
KLAIL. *See Klail City*
Klail, Rufus T., xii, 132
Klail, Rufus T., V. Junior (Junior), 126
Klail-Blanchard-Cooke (KBC) clan, xii, 30, 158
   KBC Ranch modeled on the King Ranch, 125–26
   political lineup, 128–29
Klail City, xii
Klail City (KLAIL) (Hinojosa), 19–22, 118–21, 140, 177–78, 180–81
   "A Classy Reunion: The Homecoming," 21, 210n11
   "The Dispossessed," 118
   duo text with CONDADO, 15–22, 83
   publishing history, 6, 11, 15, 204(ch. 3)n1, 204(ch. 3)n4
   "The Searchers," 180–81
Klail City Death Trip Series (KCDTS) (Hinojosa), xi–xvi, 1–4, 26, 103–5, 180
   aesthetic concept of, 197
   charted topological paradigms, 191–93
   as a continuous and integrated novelistic project, 73–74, 91
   postmodernist reading of, 82
   publishing history, 4–6
   reassembling and repositioning episodes, 10
   as revisionist history, 145–46
   themes/motifs carried across the series, 8, 23, 57, 99, 117
Klail City First National Bank, 30, 125, 127–31
Klail City y sus alrededores (CONDADO) (Hinojosa). *See El condado de Belken: Klail City; Generaciones y semblanzas*
Kleberg, Robert J., 126
Koch, Ed, 190

Korean Love Songs/Korea Liebes Lieder (SONGS) (Hinojosa), 57–58
   publishing history, 5–6, 23, 205 (ch. 5)n1
Korean War, 23–24, 29, 37–38, 57–60

labor relations, 170–72, 180–82
land loss, charted topological paradigm, 157
land ownership, 129, 151, 155–57, 210–11n15
   entailed land titles, 150, 156
   land grants, 147–48, 151, 163
language of Indians, 20
Lazarillo de Tormes, 8, 107
League of United Latin American Citizens (LULAC), 173
Leal, Luís, 108–9
Lee, Joyce Glover, *Rolando Hinojosa and the American Dream*, 201
legal documents, 7, 40
"Los Leguizamón" (ESTAMPAS) (Hinojosa), 8, 154–55, 163
Leguizamón, Alejandro, 69, 155
Leguizamón, Antonia, 158
Leguizamón, Javier, 118
Leguizamón family, xii, 8, 47, 129, 154–55
   intermarriages, 158
Lesage, Alain René, *Gil Blas de Santillane*, 107
Lesy, Michael, *Wisconsin Death Trip*, 9
libraries, banishment from, 119
Libro de los Claros Varones de Castilla (Pulgar), 25, 205(ch. 6)n1
"The Limits of Cultural Studies" (Saldívar), 78–79, 196
Limón, José, 198
linguistic behavior, true-to-life, 2–3, 53
literary awards
   Premio Casa de las Américas, 11, 22
   Premio Quinto Sol, 7, 87
literary history
   Chicano, 95–100
   classical *pícaros*, 107–8, 120–21
   Spanish, 11, 25, 28, 41, 84
literary theory, 74, 86
literary traditions, transition from oral traditions, 77, 91, 93–94, 154, 198

Literature and the Delinquent (Parker), 113–14
loan translations, 211n2
loyalty, xv, 114, 152, 163, 187, 199
Lucero, Damián, 21
Luke 17:10, 62–63
LULAC (League of United Latin American Citizens), 173
Lyotard, Jean-François, 82, 88

machismo, 118
Macías, Rosendo, 179
Macías Rosales, Otila, 159, 189
Madrid, Enrique, 34
Malacara, Andrés, 48, 55–56, 122
Malacara, Jehú, 26–27, 29–30, 103–5, 186
   age, incongruities regarding, 39–40, 109, 209(ch. 21)n1
   birth, xiii
   childhood, 8, 10–11, 13, 107–18, 175
   education, 26, 118–21, 123–24, 131, 175–76
   employment, 26, 118
      career at Klail City First National Bank, 21, 30, 38, 40, 127–31
      as a teacher, 21, 124
   engagement to Olivia San Esteban, 131–32
   family tree, 97–98
   marriage to *Becky Escobar,* 46, 133–35
   military service, 123
   as a moral delinquent, xv, 114, 118
   name
      pronunciation of first name, 206 (ch. 7)n1
      surname, 122–23
   parallels with the biblical Jehu, 24, 135–36
   as a *pícaro,* 18–19, 110–18, 120–21
   Rosaura Sánchez's comments on, 23, 29, 122
Malacara, Rebecca (Becky)
   Rosaura Sánchez's comments on, 48–49
   See also Escobar, Rebecca (Becky)
Malacara, Roque, 97–98, 109, 121–22
Manzano, Abel, 38, 163–64, 166, 168

"Mapping the Postmodern" (Huyssen), 84
Markham, Charles, 155
Márquez, Antonio C., 43
Martín Rodríguez, Manuel M., 9, 41, 44–45, 51–52, 145
McKinlow, David, 40
Mejía, Jaime Armin, 35–36, 51–52, 59, 126, 210nn13–14
mestizaje, 158
metafictional space, xvi, 34, 198
   real-life interactions, 86–88, 104
   real-life models, 56, 70
Mexican-Anglo communities, 46, 48, 149–50
   political kinships, 159–60
   race relations, xvi, 12, 35, 37–38, 89–90, 132
      farm society, 169–73
      hacienda society, 153–54
      ranch society, 160–61
Mexicans, xi, 63, 70–71, 149
   acculturation, 189
   assimilation, 29, 189
   defending rights and privileges of Anglos, 188
   sellout Mexicans, xii, 8, 124–25, 187
   stereotyping, 211n19
migrant harvest workers, 17–18, 172, 180–81
migration, 180
militarization of the border, 66–68, 71, 185, 199, 212n10
minorities in the U. S. Army, 60–61, 188
Mi querido Rafa (RAFA) (Hinojosa), 130, 201
   duo text with RAFE, 33–36
   publishing history, 5, 29
Miss Bunn, 175–76
Miss Moy, 175–76
mixed-code, 3, 17, 29
   narration, 36
   translation, 33–34
modernism, xiv
   and postmodernism, 81–84
Moll Flanders (Defoe), 107
monoculturalism, 34
monolingualism, 34
monologues, 11, 16, 26–28, 55, 140–42
Monroy, Emilia, 18

Montejano, David, *Anglos and Mexicans in the Making of Texas: 1963–1986*, 125–26, 143, 149–50, 188
  Incorporation (1836–1900), 138–39, 150–54
  Integration (1940–1986), 182–85
  Reconstruction (1900–1920), 160–63
  Segregation (1920–1940), 169–73
Morales, Tiburón, 66
moral imperatives, 83
Morris, Richard B., *Encyclopedia of American History*, 58
la mujer nueva, 43–45, 48, 51, 88–89, 133
multiculturalism, 89–90, 94
Mündliches Wissen in neuzeitlicher Literature (Goetsch), 93
mystery genre, 39–41, 65–66, 84

Naranjo brothers, 163, 166
narration techniques, xiii
  anecdotes, 27
  conversations, overheard, 13, 17
  legal documents, 7, 40
  monologues, 11, 16, 26–28, 55, 140–42
  narrative poems, 23
  narrative portraits, 8–13, 18, 25, 40
  reportage style, 7, 30, 37–38, 46, 83
narrators
  as androgynous listeners, 46–47, 53–55, 88–89, 196–97, 208(ch. 17)n3
  first person, 23
  omniscient, 37
  as protagonists, xv, 26, 42, 73, 103–5
  relating a common story from different viewpoints, 91, 103–4
  switching of, 119
Nashe, Thomas, *The Unfortunate Traveller*, 107
National Farm Workers Association, 183
Nepomuceno Seguín, Juan, x–xii
Nericcio, William Anthony, 61–62
newspaper clippings, imaginary, 7, 83
nicknames, 109–10
Norris, Christopher, 208(ch. 17)n2
nostalgia, xv, 141
novels in verse, 23
Nuevo Santander, 146–47

Olivares, Juan José (alias of *Lisandro Gómez Solís*), 65, 69, 191
"On the Use of Chronicle, Biography, and Sketch in Rolando Hinojosa's *Generaciones y semblanzas*" (Calderón), xiii
"Oral Culture and Print Culture" (Broyles), 15–16
oral history of South Texas, xvi, 191
  personified, 26, 28
oral traditions, xiv, 28, 41
  in Chicano culture, 99–100, 133–34, 191–93
  readers' participation in oral rituals, 100, 134, 197–98
  transition to literary traditions, 77, 91, 93–94, 154, 198
  verbal improvisation, 112–13
orphaning, 110, 116–17
otherness, 82, 88–90
"Our Southwest: An Interview with Rolando Hinojosa" (Saldívar), 45

Paredes, Américo, 198
  With His Pistol in His Hand, 137, 139, 168
Paredes, Irene, 44–45, 132
Parker, Alexander, *Literature and the Delinquent*, 113–14
El Partido Raza Unida, 183–84
Partners in Crime: A Rafe Buenrostro Mystery (PARTNERS) (Hinojosa), 33, 39–42, 191–92
  plot development, 40–41, 84
  publishing history, 5
PASSO, 183
paternal love charted topological paradigm, 116–18
Patterson, O. E., 158
peace, reconstruction of, 70–72
"*pega poco, pero pega lindo,*" 201, 209(pt. 4)n1
Peláez, Víctor, 111, 121–22
Peñalosa, Agustín, 21
Peñalosa, Fernando, *Chicano Sociolinguistics*, 3
Peñaloza, Bob, 124
Peralta twins, 211n16

Pérez de Guzmán, Fernán, 11, 25, 205(ch. 6)n1
Perkins, Arnold (Noddy), 30, 70, 89, 127, 129–31, 189
Perkins, Sammie Jo, 54, 56, 87, 127, 130
Phillips, Gwen, 68
photojournalism, 10
physical descriptions, 27
picaresque journeys, xv, 12, 107–8
pícaros, 18–19, 107–8, 110–18, 120–21
Pike, Johnny, 178–79
El Plan de San Diego, 161
Plato, *Republic*, 58
plots
  open ended, 108
  uniting KCDTS books, 26
poems, 23
point of view, 53, 101
POLICEMAN. See *Ask a Policeman: A Rafe Buenrostro Mystery*
political agendas, 185
politics, 28, 129–31, 162–63, 184–89
  KBC political lineup, 128–29
  political kinships, 159–60
polyglossia, 3
"Por esas cosas que pasan" (Hinojosa), 5, 7–8, 47, 186
portraits, 8–13, 18, 25, 40
postmodernism, xiv, 75, 81–90
  appearance of in Hinojosa's work, 54, 78–79, 81
  Hinojosa's work labeled as, 62, 74, 76
  and modernism, 81–84
postmodernity, 75
"The Precession of Simulacra" (Baudrillard), 85–88
Premio Casa de las Américas literary award, 11, 22
Premio Quinto Sol literary award, 7, 87
"La Prensa. A Lifelong Influence of Hispanics in Texas" (Hinojosa), 209(pt. 4)n1
Pulgar, Hernando del, *Libro de los Claros Varones de Castilla*, 25, 205(ch. 6)n1
Pumarejo, Leo, 176
Purdy, Tom, 17

El Quieto. See Buenrostro, Jesús (El Quieto)
Quinto Sol, 7, 87

race, 128, 189
  as identity, 82
race relations, Anglo-Mexican, xvi, 12, 35, 37–38, 89–90, 132
  farm society, 169–73
  hacienda society, 153–54
  ranch society, 160–61
racial discrimination
  in education, 118–19, 176–78
  in politics, 162–63
racism, 55, 61, 183
RAFA. See *Mi querido Rafa*
RAFE. See *Dear Rafe*
Ramírez, Lucy, 176
ranch society, 142–43, 149–50, 161–69, 173
  race relations, 160–61
rattlesnakes, 115–16
la raza pendeja, 124
readers
  bilingual, 3
  collaboration with narrators and characters, 86–87, 119–20
  efforts required of, xvi, 10
  monolingual, 3
  participation in oral rituals, 100, 134, 197–98
  participation in the quest, 52, 68, 125, 157, 165–66
reality of fiction, xvi, 34, 198
  real-life interactions, 86–88, 104
  real-life models, 56, 70
reality vs. illusion, 81, 85–88
recasts, 2–4, 33–35, 52–53, 55, 89
  Hinojosa's comments on, 56, 83–84
  original/rendition differences, 109–10
  process, 15–22
reform of electoral structures, 188
renditions. See recasts
reportage style, 30, 37–38, 46
Republic (Plato), 58
Republican Party, 184, 188
revenge, 66, 68–72

"Review of *Claros varones de Belken/Fair Gentlemen of Belken County*" (Bruce-Novoa), 148–49, 154
"Los revolucionarios" (ESTAMPAS) (Hinojosa), 109
Ridings, Marcia, 68
Rincón-Buenrostro, Agnes, 192
Rites and Witnesses (RITES) (Hinojosa), 37–38, 57–58, 84–85, 163–64, 168–69, 176–79
  plot development, 127–29
  publishing history, 5
Rivera, Tomás, *. . . y no se lo tragó la tierra*, 18, 97, 211–12n6
Rolando Hinojosa and the American Dream (Lee), 201
"Rolando Hinojosa's Klail City Death Trip: A Critical Introduction" (Saldívar), xiii, 78
Romano, Octavio, 198
  living in Belken County, 87
Rudin, Ernst, 206–7(ch. 9)n1
Ruíz, Sonny, 59

Salazar, Epigmenio, 21
Saldívar, José David
  Border Matters: Remapping American Cultural Studies, 75, 148, 185, 189, 192
  "Chicano Border Narratives as Cultural Critique," 38
  "The Limits of Cultural Studies," 78–79, 196
  "Our Southwest: An Interview with Rolando Hinojosa," 45
  "Rolando Hinojosa's Klail City Death Trip: A Critical Introduction," xiii, 78
Salinas, Eduardo, 69
Sánchez, Mario L., *A Shared Experience*, 146–48
Sánchez, Rosaura, 174–75, 185
  on *Becky Malacara*, 48–49
  on *Jehú Malacara*, 23, 29, 121–22
  on *Rafa Buenrostro*, 122
  translation of *Generaciones y semblanzas*, 11
San Esteban, Martín, 44
San Esteban, Olivia, 44, 130–32
Sartre, Jean Paul, 102
schools
  interracial, 118–21
  segregated, 175–78
Script Oralia, 91
scripts for screenplays, 37, 40
script writers, third-rate vs. second-rate, 56, 87
"The Searchers" (CONDADO) (Hinojosa), 17–18
"The Searchers" (KLAIL) (Hinojosa), 180–81
secrets, keeping of, 134
segregation, 119, 149–50, 161–62, 169
  of cities, 170–71, 175, 178
  rationale of, 172–73
  rules of contact with Anglos, 178
  in schools, 175–78
self-translations, 2–4, 33–35, 52–53, 55, 89
  Hinojosa's comments on, 56, 83–84
  original/rendition differences, 109–10
  process, 15–22
sellout Mexicans, xii, 8, 124–25, 187
sense of place, 12, 46, 99, 101
"The Sense of Place" (Hinojosa), 1–2, 83
SERVANTS. See *The Useless Servants*
A Shared Experience (Sánchez), 146–48
sheriffs, 40
short stories, 27
Simulacres et simulations (Baudrillard), 85
slave-labor, 171
soap operas, 37, 84–85
social classes, 29, 161
social commentary, 41–42
SONGS. See *Korean Love Songs/Korea Liebes Lieder*
The Sound and the Fury (Faulkner), xv, 91, 101–3, 105, 209(ch. 20)n1
South Texas history, 30, 182–93
  as Buenrostro family history., 145, 148–51, 154–56
  oral history, xvi, 26, 28, 191
  See also Anglo-centric history; farm society; hacienda society; ranch society
space, fooling around with, 102
spanglés, 36
Spanish-English binary, 1–3, 126, 189
  in Chicano literature, 206–7(Ch. 9)n1
  usage in duo texts, 34–35, 51–52, 54–55, 89

vs. English only, 58
Spanish heritage of Mexicans, 158–60
Spanish language
　lack of letter *k*, 126
　literary criticism of English-language works, 41–42
　shift away from, 29, 37
　suppression, 28
sponsorships *(compadrazgos)*, 152
St. Louis, Brownsville, and Mexico Railway, 160
Steiner, George, "Topologies of Culture," 96
stereotyping of Mexicans, 211n19
storytelling style of Jehú, 114
stream-of-consciousness style, 102, 141–42
Streng, R. L., 48, 54
Strickland, Barbara, "Crossing Literary Borders," 46–47
subjugation, 151–52, 161–62
surnames, 121–23, 142
synthesis of tradition and new order
　charted topological paradigm, 166

Taboada, Antonio Prieto, "El caso de las pistas culturales in *Partners in Crime*," 41–42, 79
Tamez, Ernesto, 7–8, 47–48, 186, 204(ch.1)n3
Tapia, Braulio, 47, 97–98, 108–9
Tapia Vilches, Matilde, 98
telenovelas, 37
Terry, Roger (Morse Terry), 128–29
Texas Anglos, 70–71
"Texas Border Literature" (Calderón), 25, 79, 148
Texas Farm Placement Service, 172, 181
Texas Mexicans, xi, 63, 70–71, 149
　defending rights and privileges of Anglos, 188
Texas Rangers, 38, 40, 161, 167–68
"The Tex-Mex Border" (Conniff), 34
textual variation, 207–8(ch. 13)n4, 208(ch. 14)n1
　See also duo serial texts
"They were unarmed," 69
This Migrant Earth (Hinojosa), 211–12n6

Tienda de Cuervo, José, 147
time, fooling around with, 102
Timmens, Ben, 127–28
Timmens, Edith, 55, 127–28
Tom Jones (Fielding), 107
topography, 96
"The Topological Space of Chicano Literature" (Bruce-Novoa), xiv, 91, 95–100, 157, 165, 210n7
"Topologies of Culture" (Steiner), 96
"Toyota of thought," 75, 78
translations
　of Bible passages, 2
　loan translations, 211n2
　of mixed-code, 33–34
　side-by-side, 26
truth, quest for, 84–85, 195–201
typology, 96

U.S. Army and minorities, 60–61, 188
under erasure, 210n7
The Unfortunate Traveller (Nashe), 107
The Unvanquished (Faulkner), 69
urban-industrial society, 149–50, 182–93
The Useless Servants (SERVANTS) (Hinojosa), 24, 57–61, 62–63, 159, 165–66
　publishing history, 6, 57

vagrancy laws, 171–72
Valencia, Florencio (Chip), 66, 71, 190
The Valley (VALLEY) (Hinojosa), 4, 110, 116, 155, 175–76, 178
　duo text with ESTAMPAS, 9–10, 15, 83
　publishing history, 5, 7, 9
VARONES. *See Claros Varones de Belken: Fair Gentlemen of Belken County*
vengeance. *See* revenge
verbal improvisation, 112–13
Verser, Rebecca Ruth, 169, 176–77, 189
La vida del buscón (de Quevedo Villegas), 107
Vidaurri, Enriqueta, 129
Vielma, Angela, 44–45
Vielma, José (Pepe, Joey), 28, 38, 44, 58–59, 63
Vilches, Jehú, 97–98, 109
Vilches, Timo, 119

Vilches Malacara, Teresa, 98, 122
Villalón, Charlie, 28, 58–59, 63
violence, 68–69
Vizcarra, Vicente, 178–79
von Grimmelshausen, Hans Jakob Christoffel, *Der abentheuerliche Simplicissimus Teutsch*, 107

warrior ethic, 69
wars, 23–24, 29, 37–38, 57–60, 151–52
Watergate, 85–86
Watling, Thelma Ann, 179
Webb, Walter Prescott, 38, 145–46
Weber, David J., 146, 151, 158
white supremacy, 38, 169, 211n19
Wisconsin Death Trip (Lesy), 9
With His Pistol in His Hand (Paredes), 137, 139, 168

women
　marginalization of, 49
　nontraditional, 43–45, 48, 51, 88–89, 132–33
"WORD TO THE WISE (GUY)" (Hinojosa), 88
workers
　exploitation of, 171
　immobilization of, 180–82
World War II, 182

. . . y no se lo tragó la tierra (Rivera), 18, 97, 211–12n6

Zamudio, Pedro, 19, 111–12, 209n5
Zaragoza, Práxedes, 65
Zok brothers, 54